The Far Reaches of Empire

CAMPAIGNS & COMMANDERS

GREGORY J. W. URWIN, SERIES EDITOR

CAMPAIGNS AND COMMANDERS

The Far Reaches of Empire

War in Nova Scotia, 1710–1760

John Grenier

University of Oklahoma Press : Norman

ALSO BY JOHN GRENIER

The First Way of War: American War Making on the Frontier, 1607–1814 (New York, 2005)

Library of Congress Cataloging-in-Publication Data

Grenier, John, 1967–
The far reaches of empire : war in Nova Scotia, 1710–1760 / John Grenier.
p. cm. — (Campaigns & commanders series ; v. 16)
Includes bibliographical references and index.
ISBN 978-0-8061-3876-3 (hardcover : alk. paper)
1. Nova Scotia—History, Military—18th century. 2. Nova Scotia—History—1713–1763. 3. Nova Scotia—Ethnic relations—History—18th century. 4. New Englanders—Nova Scotia—History—18th century. 5. British Americans—Nova Scotia—History—18th century. 6. Frontier and pioneer life—Nova Scotia. 7. Imperialism—History—18th century. 8. Great Britain—Colonies—America—History—18th century. I. Title.
F1038.G79 2008
971.6′01—dc22

2007028592

The Far Reaches of Empire: War in Nova Scotia, 1710–1760 is Volume 16 in the Campaigns & Commanders series.

The paper in this book meets the guidelines for permanence and durability of the Committee on Production Guidelines for Book Longevity of the Council on Library Resources, Inc. ∞

1 2 3 4 5 6 7 8 9 10

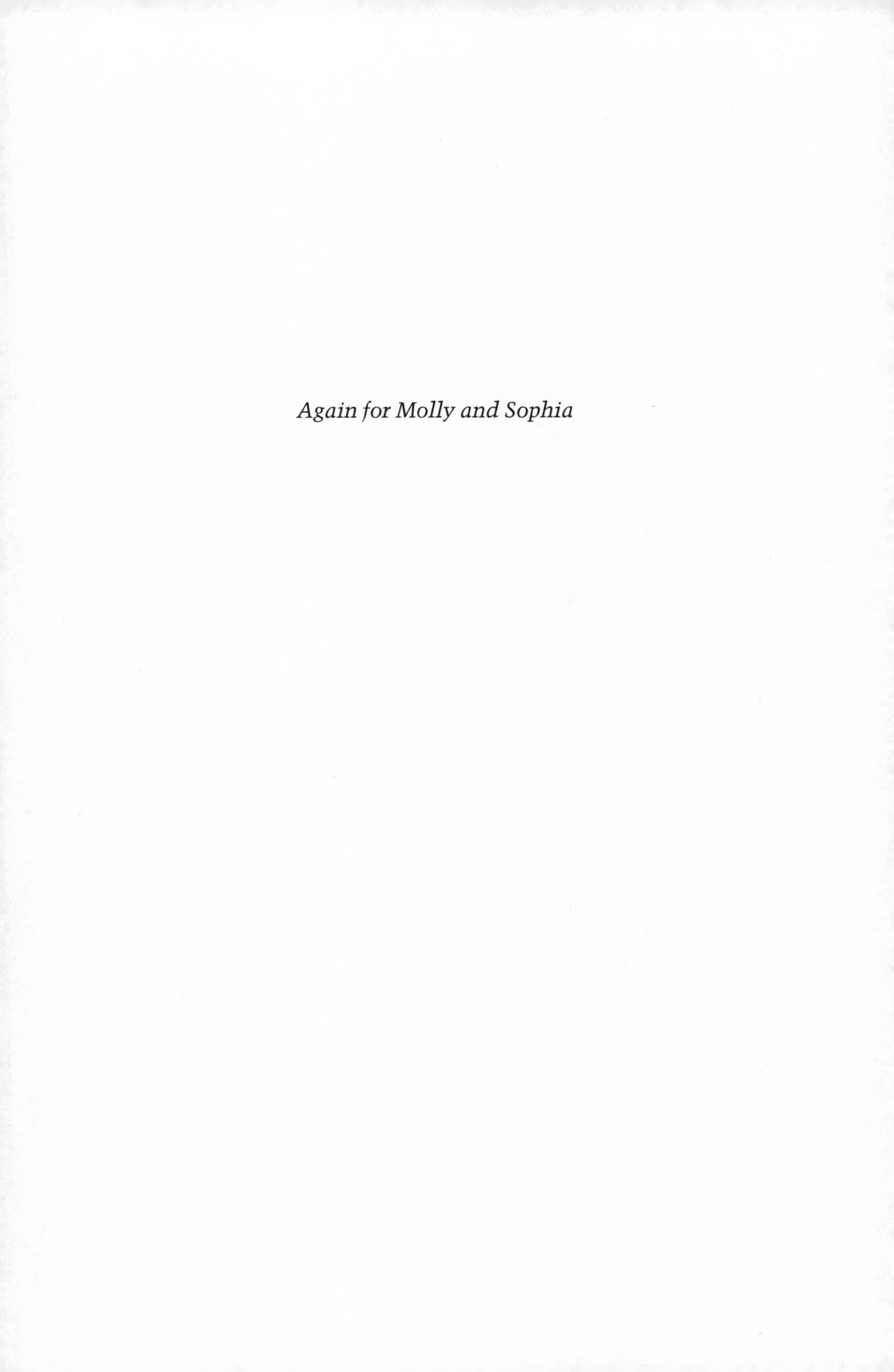

Again for Molly and Sophia

The rulers of Great Britain have, for more than a century past, amused the people with the imagination that they possessed a great empire on the west side of the Atlantic. The empire, however, has hitherto existed in imagination only.

Adam Smith, *The Wealth of Nations,* 1776

Contents

Illustrations

Figures

Maps

PREFACE

I began this book by asking how eighteenth-century Anglo-Americans built their empire on the frontiers of North America. My previous work on American war making suggested that Nova Scotia's military history, which early Americanists generally overlook except for the Acadian diaspora, helped define Americans' military heritage. I wondered how Anglo-American "imperialism" in Nova Scotia fit into the larger themes of the early history of what became the United States. I wondered whether Nova Scotia was exceptional to the story of an American empire, whether it was a component part of that story, or whether it offered a path not chosen. In a sense, then, this book became my effort to use Nova Scotia, at least its history, for American purposes.

This book focuses on Anglo-Americans' fifty-year struggle to establish effective dominion over the peoples of the Nova Scotia frontier. It argues that Anglo-Americans took nearly half a century to bring Nova Scotia fully into the fold of the First British Empire. In the fifty years of war in that far reach of the empire, Anglo-Americans initially relied on coercion to establish dominion over Nova Scotia. The initial failure of those policies, attributable to inherent Anglo-American weaknesses in Nova Scotia, forced British occupiers to adopt more conciliatory and accommodating policies toward the colony's native peoples, both Acadians and Indians. The breakdown of accommodation in the middle of the eighteenth century, precipitated by the geopolitical realities of empire as well as local antipathies, led Anglo-Americans to reassess their methods for ruling Nova Scotia. In the end, operating from a newfound position of strength, Britons and Yankees returned to coercion and waged a brutally efficient counterinsurgency that crushed all remnants of Acadian, Indian, and French resistance in Nova Scotia. In the final analysis, this book illuminates the primacy of war in the establishment of the British Empire in northeastern North America.

Delineating the names of places in Nova Scotia's eighteenth-century history can lead to no end of confusion. For my purposes, "Acadia" generally is present-day New Brunswick and northeastern Maine. "Nova Scotia" is what we know today as peninsular Nova Scotia, and therefore distinct from Cape Breton Island, which the French called Île Royale. Following the removal of the Acadians in the late 1750s (if not before, in some cases), Anglo-Americans changed the names of many locales in Nova Scotia. I have tried where possible to use the names for a place that its possessors would have used. For example, I use "Port Royal" for the period when the French occupied it and "Annapolis Royal" after 1710, when it became a British town. In many cases, I have placed the modern name in parentheses following the first mention of the eighteenth-century French or Indian name—for instance, "Beaubassin (Amherst)"—to help clarify the landscape. Three specific areas need further explanation. Minas Basin, known as Bassin-des-Mines to the French, contained the Acadian villages of Grand Pré—also known as Les Mines (Horton)—Pisiquid (Windsor), Cobequid (Truro), and Rivière-aux-Canards (Canning). Anglo-Americans often used the blanket name "Minas" rather than refer to an individual village. "Chignecto" refers to the region of the Isthmus of Chignecto, which included the main settlement of Beaubassin (Amherst). The final area included the settlements in present-day New Brunswick: Chipoudy (Shepody), Petitcodiac (Hillsborough), Memramcook (Dorchester), and Tantamare (Sackville).

Names for participants offer many choices as well. "Anglo-Americans" refers to British and American members of the First British Empire. When specifically referring to officials, soldiers, or settlers who were not native-born Americans, I use "Britons" as the noun and "British" as the adjective. For British subjects either born in or permanent immigrants to New England, I employ "Yankee," "New Englander," and "American." "Acadians" were the French-speaking Roman Catholic progeny of the first French men and women who settled the Maritimes in the early seventeenth century. In the mid-eighteenth century, some Acadians were the products of French-Indian unions.[1] Thus, "Acadians" generally refers to what today we know as whites. If contemporaries specifically identified an individual as having both Indian and Acadian blood, I describe that person as a métis. I utilize "French" to describe the Jesuit and Franciscan-Recollet priests who ministered to the Acadians, Indians, and métis, as well as the officials and military men who ran France's colonial possession in northeastern North America, which included, at various times, Acadia, Île Royale, and New France (Canada). The French did not refer to the Acadians as "Acadians" until the early eighteenth century. Prior to the British occupation in 1710, the Acadians were grouped together with "Frenchmen and Frenchwomen." For the names of French individuals, I use the standard established in the *Dictionary of Canadian Biography* and cite the full name at first mention, but after that, I refer to them by the name by which their contemporaries would have known them. For immigrants to and native-born inhabitants of New France, I depend upon "Canadians."

Names that Europeans used for the Indians of the colonial Maritimes and Northeast were inconsistent. The French governor of Île Royale noted in 1703 that there were three different "nations" of Indians in Acadia, which then encompassed much of present-day northeastern Maine, New Brunswick, and Nova Scotia: these were "the Canibas, the Malicites and the Micmacs."[2] Each group spoke a different although related language. The Canibas were the Abenakis of Maine. Among the Maine Abenakis were groups identified by the dialect they spoke and the immediate area in which they lived: the Androscoggins, Kennebecs, Penobscots, and Passamquoddies. The Abenakis who lived in present-day New Hampshire and Vermont, the "western" Abenakis, had only minimal influence on the course of events in Nova Scotia. The Malicites, or Maliseets (Wolastokwiyik), inhabited the rivière Saint-Jean (Saint John River, or in Maliseet, Wulstukw) drainage basin, where they intermingled with their Passamquoddy cousins. The Micmacs, or Mi'kmaq, lived on peninsular Nova Scotia, on Cape Breton Island, and in large portions of New Brunswick, with the borders of their hunting areas touching those of the Maliseets.[3] A fourth group that often appears in the documents is the Abenquis d'Acadie. Because the Abenakis, Maliseets, and Mi'kmaq were loosely joined in the Wabenaki Confederacy—a creation of the late seventeenth century among Abenakis, Maliseets, and Mi'kmaq to oppose both the Iroquois League and Anglo-Americans—some French officials included the Maliseets as part of the Passamquoddies. Thus, the Abenquis d'Acadie were the Maliseets. A fifth grouping of Indians with importance for Nova Scotia history was the *sauvages domiciliés,* or the "settled Indians" of the towns along the Saint Lawrence River. They included the Hurons of Lorette outside Quebec, the Abenakis at Bécancour across the Saint Lawrence from Trois-Rivières and those at Odanak on rivière Saint François, and the various settlements of Iroquoian (Houdenasaunee) peoples and their cohabitants.[4] The Saint Lawrence Valley mission Indians, particularly the Abenakis of Bécancour and Odanak, offered important support to Nova Scotia's Indians in the latter's struggle to resist Anglo-Americans. One last note on the Indian peoples is necessary. I use "Mi'kmaw" as an adjective; "Mi'kmaq," the noun form, is both singular and plural; and "Mi'kma'ki" is the Mi'kmaq name for the Mi'kmaq homelands.

All translations from French to English are mine, and I accept responsibility for any errors. All dates are based on the Gregorian (New Style) as opposed to the Julian (Old Style) calendar unless otherwise specified.

Acknowledgments

I have incurred many debts while writing this book. While I am quite grateful to all my colleagues and friends who helped with this project, several individuals deserve special mention. Fred Anderson remained my role model and the historian whom I most respect. I am most grateful to him for both his mentorship and his friendship. Mike Neiberg is a fine historian and friend, and I could not have completed this book in a timely manner without his support and encouragement. Art Worrall and John Roche graciously agreed to read drafts of this work, and I am indebted to both of them for their thoughtful suggestions and criticisms. Although he and I have never met face-to-face, Professor John Reid offered encouragement and profound insight through e-mails. I appreciate his willingness to keep me on the straight and narrow on the finer points of Canadian and Maritime history. My thanks also go out to all the individuals at the University of Oklahoma Press, especially Charles Rankin, Gregory Urwin, and the anonymous readers of the manuscript version of this book. An exceptional student in my seminar on colonial American warfare at the United States Air Force Academy—Katherine Mack (*née* Hippely)—helped me refine my thinking about colonial military history into a more accessible form. She generally kept me from spiraling into abstractions, as I am wont to do. My niece, Danielle Grenier, drew the maps for this book.

I received generous support from several organizations, particularly the National Archives of Canada and the Massachusetts Historical Society (MHS). I especially want to thank the MHS for awarding me its Colonial Wars of Massachusetts Fellowship for 2002. My wife, Molly, and my daughter, Sophia, unfailingly supported me as I wrote this book. I hope they will accept this finished product as some small compensation for all our missed times together.

The Far Reaches of Empire

INTRODUCTION

This study examines how Anglo-Americans conquered Nova Scotia for the First British Empire.[1] For fifty years, from 1710 to 1760, Anglo-Americans struggled to establish effective dominion on that distant frontier of the empire.[2] Besides the officials and armies of Old and New France, Anglo-American colonizers confronted and fought Acadians, Maliseets, Mi'kmaq, and Roman Catholic priests for control of Nova Scotia. However, most historians, with the few notable exceptions mentioned below, have made the conquest of Nova Scotia little more than an afterthought in the larger British-French competition for empire in eastern North America. Indeed, Nova Scotia has been viewed as a mere stepping-stone toward the conquest of Canada in the Second Hundred Years' War (1689–1783), as some historians have termed the British-French conflict for North America that stretched from the start of King William's War to the end of the American War of Independence.

Yet the series of wars and quasi-wars that wracked the Nova Scotia frontier supported, and at times supplanted, the better-known imperial struggle between France and Great Britain. Indeed, only after successfully countering Acadian resistance movements, fighting the Abenakis, Maliseets, and Mi'kmaq in two separate wars, twice confronting the armies of France, and waging a counterinsurgency against Acadian and Mi'kmaq guerrillas were Anglo-Americans able to bring Nova Scotia fully into the First British Empire.

The Far Reaches of Empire details Anglo-Americans' half-century struggle to establish dominion in Nova Scotia. It examines the contest for Nova Scotia primarily from the perspective of the Anglo-Americans who found themselves on one of the First British Empire's distant frontiers.[3] Several strands combined to shape Anglo-Americans' actions in Nova Scotia; the same elements influenced this book's narrative. First, there were (and within the narrative, are) the Anglo-Americans' relations with Acadians, Indians, and French. A second theme centered on Abenaki, Maliseet, and Mi'kmaw actions in shaping Nova Scotia's history. A third focus was the machinations of French officials, military officers, and Catholic priests who intrigued to use both the Acadians and the Indians against the British.

This book offers an alternative way—that of military history—of understanding the conflict of cultures and peoples in the colonial Northeast. It sheds light on the varied means, those both adopted and abandoned, of Anglo-American conquest. Moreover, in the traditional narrative of European-Indian relations in the Maritimes, Abenakis, Maliseets, and Mi'kmaq generally are little more than pawns of French colonial officials, Roman Catholic missionaries, or their Acadian neighbors. But in stressing Indian agency and how the actions of Indians vis-à-vis Anglo-Americans resulted from internal motivations and aspirations, this study helps explain the larger theme of American Indian opposition and accommodation to imperialism. Of course, any study of eighteenth-century Nova Scotia must address the *grand dérangement* (great tragic times) of the 1750s, when Anglo-Americans attempted to "ethnically cleanse" Nova Scotia of Acadians.

The Far Reaches of Empire strives to show that the Acadians were more than helpless victims in the events that befell them.[4] It explains why and how some Anglo-Americans reached the conclusion that the only effective way to solve the "Acadian problem" was to remove them. This book describes how both individual actions and the larger forces of history influenced the decision to proscribe the Acadians. *The Far Reaches of Empire* thus points to the adaptive and brutal means that Anglo-Americans employed to establish dominion on one of colonial America's marchlands, and in that way I hope to provide insight into the complex and often danger-fraught process of empire building.[5]

Several problems face the American historian who wishes to put Nova Scotia history in context with the development of the eighteenth-century British Empire and the colonies that became the United States. First, the events that transpired in eighteenth-century Nova Scotia generally are thought of as Canadian history. Although some historians have termed Nova Scotia the fourteenth colony in recognition that it should be studied in concert with the mainland British possessions, and there is a growing attempt to examine all the North American colonies as part of a larger empire, there still remains far to go in this attempt. Second, historians normally focus on the landmarks of Nova Scotia history, such as the British occupation in 1710, the expulsion of the Acadians in 1755, and the arrival of the Loyalists during and after the American War of Independence. Last, Nova Scotia as the backcountry or one of colonial America's frontiers has yet to attract the detailed attention of practitioners of the "new frontier history."[6]

Nevertheless, there is a well-developed, albeit incomplete, historiography that helps frame Anglo-Americans' fifty years' war on the Nova Scotia frontier. The nineteenth and early twentieth centuries saw several multivolume narrative histories of Nova Scotia, of which Beamish Murdoch's three-volume work is the best. Other historians—such as W. A. Calnek, who wrote about Annapolis Royal—produced more-specialized studies that focused on specific locales. John Bartlet Brebner led the way in putting Nova Scotia's history in the context of a larger eighteenth-century colonial and imperial world. He saw New Englanders' *Drang Nach Osten*—impulse to the East—as a near-constant impetus for Yankee involvement on the Nova Scotia frontier. His primary critic, George Rawlyk, countered that New Englanders only intermittently were interested in Nova Scotia. Either way, through the period covered in this book, some, perhaps many, saw Acadia, and later Nova Scotia, as an area for the expansion of New England society, culture, and institutions. The imperial historians who followed, meanwhile, were most interested in how Great Britain administered from afar its colony in Nova Scotia; Robert MacFarlane's work on the interrelation of the "Indian problem" with the struggle of France and Great Britain for empire in North America is an outstanding model of the "older" imperial historiography.[7]

Historians and Acadian nationalist authors have taken the Acadians as their subject and with the 250th anniversary of the Acadian removal in 2005 presented several studies focused on the important decade of the 1750s. Most recently, John Mack Faragher has offered *A Great and Noble Scheme.* Although this is an engrossing piece of scholarship, Faragher overstates his case; his focus on the grand dérangement "as an early example of ethnic cleansing" carries too much present-day emotional weight and in turn overshadows much of the accommodation that Acadians and Anglo-Americans reached. Naomi E. S. Griffiths remains the premier scholar of the Acadians, and her magnum opus (*From Migrant to Acadian*) on the growth of Acadian society and identity is the natural starting place for any study that touches on Acadian history. Other fine scholars likewise have focused on the Acadians. Carl Brasseaux has looked in depth at their expulsion from the Maritimes. Examining the history of the Acadians without the horrendous events of 1755 looming on the horizon has long been difficult. The Acadians may appear as freedom fighters for the French in the Second Hundred Years' War, but more often they have been portrayed by historians as victims. In 1932, for example, one historian parochially judged the grand dérangement as the greatest tragedy in the history of America and one of the most abominable affronts in the annals of humanity.[8]

In the 1960s, the first of two major trends developed that reshaped views of eighteenth-century Nova Scotia. First, Elizabeth Hutton examined the fate of the Mi'kmaq and the social depths to which they fell after Great Britain won the Seven Years' War (1754–63). On the heels of her study came an explosion in Mi'kmaw social histories. Leslie F. S. Upton established himself as the dean of Mi'kmaw studies with his focus on French-Mi'kmaw relations. Upton's intellectual heirs have carried forth his work. Olive Patricia Dickason has been especially productive in explaining the dynamics of French-Indian relations in the Maritimes, as well as Mi'kmaw methods of overtly resisting Anglo-American domination. William Wicken made a fine contribution to the literature with a Mi'kmaw ethnohistory. All saw particularly close (at times, almost symbiotic) relations between Mi'kmaq and Acadians. Scholars have pointed out the ways in which Mi'kmaw-Acadian relations similarly were inseparable from Mi'kmaw dealings with French colonial officials. The Mi'kmaq thus have large roles in the many works that address the grand dérangement.[9] Nonetheless, the intense focus on the Mi'kmaq led to a problem that has yet to be remedied completely. Scholars have overlooked the Maliseets in favor of the Mi'kmaq, or more generally grouped the former with the Mi'kmaq until the two peoples become indistinguishable. Thus, Michaud Ghislain's question "Mais qui sont les Malécites?" (But who are the Maliseets?) remains as current today as it was in the eighteenth century.[10] One positive step toward explaining the varied motivations and thereby the differences within American Indian communities in Maine and Nova Scotia is Emerson Baker and John Reid's recent article on Indian power in the region.[11]

In the second major development, historians returned to the areas of study that would have seemed quite familiar to the imperial historians. Rather than examining Nova Scotia from London's perspective, however, they embraced the new Indian and imperial histories. In that context, Kenneth Morrison's study on the diplomacy and attempts at consensus building within the Wabenaki Confederacy was a first step in giving diplomatic and political agency to the native peoples of the Maritimes. John McNeill examined how French colonial officials managed inter- and intra-imperial trade from the perspective of Île Royale, as opposed to Paris. Stephen Patterson elucidated the importance of British military operations against the Mi'kmaq during King George's War (1744–48) and the Seven Years' War from local and regional perspectives, as opposed to strictly imperial terms. Mark Robison examined the interactions among New Englanders, Frenchmen, and Mi'kmaq and placed them on a developing trajectory from local through regional to imperial conflicts. Geoffrey Plank has made an important contribution by examining the ways in which Britons, Frenchmen, Acadians, Mi'kmaq, and Yankees interrelated in Nova Scotia. He added identity studies to previous approaches and pointed to the social and cultural mosaic that made up Nova Scotia in the middle of the eighteenth century. He admirably delineated the metamorphosing boundaries of "nationality" in the Maritimes, and his argument that "the inhabitants of Nova Scotia need to be studied together" is well placed. Most of the leading historians of eighteenth-century Nova Scotia contributed to *The "Conquest" of Acadia.* That volume superbly examines the implications of the British imperialism in Nova Scotia but generally carries the story through only the first couple of decades of British rule. The editor of *The "Conquest" of Acadia* notes that "the truth is that there is no single valid narrative, and to pretend to construct one would do violence to complexities that were characteristic not only of Mi'kma'ki-Wulstukwik/Acadia/Nova Scotia but also (with local variations) of early modern North America as a whole."[12]

Thus, despite the efforts of the many skilled historians who have taken Nova Scotia as their topic, one still wants for an interpretative narrative of Nova Scotia's military history across the entirety of the eighteenth century.[13] Historians of imperialism and the frontier often write about conquest and hegemony without considering military history at more than a superficial level. The fighting, killing, and suffering that came with building—for the Acadians and Indians, opposing and then being expelled from or accommodated into—an empire becomes lost in theory and abstraction. The details of campaigns, battles, and skirmishes won and lost, however, are precisely what most profoundly affected the lives, and often brought about the deaths, of all in early Nova Scotia. *The Far Reaches of Empire* offers a military history that delves into the minutiae of war.

John Shy warns that "we can exaggerate the frequency and intensity of colonial American military experience. Most American colonists, most of the time, lived in peace, and even in wartime daily life went on more or less untroubled by events on the frontier or at sea."[14] Such, however, was not the case in Nova Scotia, which, after all, was the frontier. Nova Scotia, from an Anglo-American perspective, remained an unsettled marchland, infested with potentially hostile Acadians, Indians, and Frenchmen. There is no exaggeration in the contention that war, or the threat of war, often troubled the daily lives of the colony's inhabitants.

Anglo-Americans' fifty years' war with the Acadians, Indians, and French on the Nova Scotia frontier occurred in six stages, each of which is the focus of a chapter in this book. The study of *petite guerre*—the eighteenth-century term that encompasses the elements of war making known today as irregular warfare, unconventional warfare, low-intensity conflict, and counterinsurgency—requires that scholars approach military history from different and new perspectives. Thus, students of eighteenth-century North American military history may recognize much, but not all, of the chronology outlined in this book.

The first three stages of the fifty years' war constitute the first half of this book's narrative. Chapter 1 discusses Nova Scotia during the first decade (1710–22) of Anglo-American occupation. It focuses on Acadian resistance to putative British rule in Nova Scotia and how that resistance motivated and spilled over into a Yankee-French conflict over Canso, the main staging ground for the fishing fleets of the western North Atlantic. Chapter 2 examines the importance on the Nova Scotia frontier of the Wabenaki Confederacy's war with New England (also known as Dummer's War, Lovewell's War, or Father Râle's War of 1722–27). That conflict rapidly took on regional and imperial importance in Nova Scotia. In the Maliseet-Mi'kmaw War of 1722–26, Anglo-Americans deflected the Indians' first concerted challenge to their authority in Nova Scotia. The key to the Anglo-American victory was their willingness, albeit motivated by weakness, to negotiate with the Maliseets and Mi'kmaq. The third chapter addresses how, in the wake of the Maliseet-Mi'kmaw War, Anglo-Americans looked to solve their "Acadian problem," namely, the Acadians' refusal to subscribe an oath to the British monarchy and continued external (French and Catholic priests') interference in Acadian-British relations. During the Thirty Years' Peace that lasted from the signing of the Treaty of Utrecht in 1713 to the outbreak of King George's War in 1744, the Anglo-American colonizers of Nova Scotia were left to their own devices in bringing the Acadians into the empire. By 1744, the Acadians had gotten the better of Anglo-Americans, and the former had just lived through their golden age. The decision to proscribe them in 1755 thus stood as a radical change of course for the British. Through the golden age, Anglo-Americans compromised with and accommodated the Acadians. Anglo-Americans, Indians, and Acadians all inhabited a middle ground in Nova Scotia.[15] But in the middle of the eighteenth century, events in both the Old and the New World foisted profound changes on all who lived on the Nova Scotia frontier.

The second half of the book centers on the years of the Anglo-French imperial struggle in North America in the 1740s and 1750s. Open warfare between France and Britain returned to Nova Scotia in King George's War. Chapter 4 addresses the course of the Anglo-

Americans' war against the French, Indians, and Acadians inside Nova Scotia. New England's campaign against Louisbourg in 1745 often overshadows the scale and scope of the fighting in Nova Scotia between 1744 and 1748. Yet King George's War set the stage for the hard-fought and obscure conflict called Father Le Loutre's War, covered in chapter 5.[16] Father Le Loutre's War saw invigorated attempts by Anglo-Americans to consolidate their hold on Nova Scotia, as well as continued Mi'kmaw resistance to their rule. Although Father Le Loutre's War was primarily an Anglo-American–Indian affair, it ended in 1755 with Anglo-Americans expelling the Acadians. By that point, the Seven Years' War had begun. Most scholars consider the Acadian proscription as the first act of that war. It marks the denouement of Father Le Loutre's War. Chapter 6 addresses the guerrilla war of 1755–60, rather than the Seven Years' War per se, that erupted as a consequence of Father Le Loutre's War. The guerrilla war that ran concurrently with the Seven Years' War was one of the eighteenth century's most notable guerrilla conflicts, and the Anglo-American response stands as one of the most successful instances of what today one would call counterinsurgency.

The epilogue attempts to give the Anglo-Americans' fifty years' war on the Nova Scotia frontier greater historical relevancy. After 1760, Nova Scotia took a path different from that of the rest of the mainland British North American colonies. By the end of the fifty years' war, Nova Scotia had become the most British of Great Britain's mainland colonies in North America. The troubled half century in Nova Scotia's history thus offers a striking case study of the mentality of imperialism in action. Beyond showing that conquest could involve a several decades–long process that incorporated periods of both war and peace, it also suggests the central importance of individuals with personal goals and aspirations—usually to extract the best possible bargain in difficult situations—who find themselves on the far reaches of empire.

1

The First Decade of British Rule, 1710–1722

In the autumn of 1710, Anglo-Americans celebrated their capture of Port Royal, Acadia, with a day of thanksgiving. Since the mid-seventeenth century, both Old and New England had eyed Acadia with a mixture of uneasiness and acquisitiveness. A prosperous French colony on New England's northeastern flank presented both a military and an economic threat. From Acadia, and Port Royal in particular, France could launch privateers to devastate New England's merchant marine fleet, supply the American Indians who threatened the Maine frontier, provide a refuge for the French fishing fleet that plied the North Atlantic banks, and potentially provision Canada from the thriving granary and growing settlements of the Annapolis, Minas, and Chignecto basins. Acadia also offered the possibility of profits and untold riches in the growing Atlantic-wide economy.[1]

New England's previous record of action against Acadia reflected poorly on the Yankees' military acumen. Although Major Robert Sedgwick and his band of New Englanders occupied Port Royal from 1654 to 1670, during the interregnum the Acadians went on with their lives with little disruption from Boston. Following the withdrawal of the New England occupiers, the Acadians expanded their settlements along Baie Françoise (Bay of Fundy) to the Minas Basin and along the banks of the Pisiquid River, as well as to Beaubassin on the Isthmus of Chignecto.[2] During King William's War (1689–97), Acadia offered a tempting target for New England privateers. In May 1690, William Phips's army of New England militia spent twelve days sacking Port Royal before returning to Boston to prepare for their botched attack on Quebec.[3] The Acadians rebuilt their homes, and through the rest of the war (while the Maine frontier suffered under the blows of Abenakis, Maliseets, and Mi'kmaq), New Englanders bemoaned their fate and, short of Major Benjamin Church's sacking of Beaubassin in 1696, virtually ignored Acadia.[4] With the renewal of war between England and France in Queen Anne's War (1701–14), New Englanders again resolved to conquer Acadia. Still, only raids—Church and his rangers sacked Grand Pré in the Minas Basin in 1704, and companies of raiders under Colonels John March and Francis Wainwright twice unsuccessfully besieged Port Royal in 1707—defined the English war effort for the first half decade of the conflict.[5] Finally, in 1710, Colonel Francis Nicholson's Anglo-American army moved against Acadia, besieged the French garrison at Port Royal, and "conquered" the colony for Queen Anne. The British finally held Annapolis Royal, Fort Anne, and Nova Scotia, their new names for the former French possessions.[6] One wonders, however, whether even during the celebrations occasioned by the conquest of Annapolis Royal, some Anglo-Americans felt a sinking feeling about the obstacles that they faced to reap the benefits of their new conquest.[7] Indians, Frenchmen, and Acadians still stood between them and the untapped wealth of Nova Scotia's forests and fisheries.

Nova Scotia was the first French territory that the British Empire seized and held in the New World. Prior to 1710, groups of English adventurers had only raided, sacked, and temporarily occupied France's colonial possessions. All the territory that the English conquered in the Americas thus far had come at the expense of Indians, the Spanish (Jamaica in 1655), or the Dutch (New Netherlands, or New York, in 1664).[8]

Nova Scotia thus became a test for British imperialism. The overarching question centered on how the British Empire would impose dominion over a large and potentially unfriendly European population (Acadians) supported by a foreign government (France) and allied with American Indians (Mi'kmaq, Maliseets, and Abenakis). Because

Acadia and the colonial Northeast.

Indian populations generally were small and dispersed, the British did not need to impose day-to-day dominion over them. The Acadians, however, would require much closer control. Complicating matters, because the empire and centralized British state had yet to coalesce fully in 1710, those assigned the task of bringing the Nova Scotia frontier into the fold of the empire found that they had a paucity of useful models to which to turn. The mainland colonies such as Virginia and Massachusetts were not military conquests, but rather plantation or settler communities.[9] Whereas the English—and after the 1707 Act of Union, the British—naturally looked to their experiences in Ireland, early eighteenth-century Anglo-Americans would find little of use there. Englishmen had grappled with the management of Ireland since the twelfth century with only marginal effectiveness. Ireland thus had become a place occupied, not governed.[10] Moreover, Nova Scotia and Ireland differed in another important aspect. The Irish generally stood alone in dealing with the English, while in Nova Scotia a hostile power intent on complicating the task of Anglo-American conquest remained on the borders. French settlements, and Indian missions, remained across the Bay of Fundy in present-day New Brunswick, on the Isthmus of Chignecto, on Île Royale (Cape Breton Island), and on Île Saint-Jean (Prince Edward Island), ready to do mischief at the first opportunity. The "Black Legend" of abuse, rapine, and plunder in Latin America ruled out adopting the Spanish model of empire. Even models from antiquity—to which most eighteenth-century British thinkers looked for inspiration and guidance—seemed only to offer partial answers. The British could rule Nova Scotia in the ancient Greek method, as an autonomous colony that they would settle with surplus populations from the British Isles. In that scenario, they would have to do something such as enslave or make tributary people of the Acadians, Mi'kmaq, and Maliseets. Or the British could treat Nova Scotia as the Romans would have, in which their army overawed local populations and kept them in continual subjugation.[11]

Moreover, little specific help, either materially or in terms of useful advice, was coming from the mainland colonies, particularly in the area of dealing with the Indians. Indeed, the most distinctive characteristic of the English colonies in North America (what historians Fred Anderson and Andrew Cayton have called the "Anomalous English Empire") was the reluctance to build military alliances with native groups.[12] If the natives were not to be friends, then they would have to be something else. In the end, Anglo-Americans simply blundered blindly from one crisis to the next as they tried to find the proper mix of force and accommodation with the peoples they supposedly had conquered in Nova Scotia.

In nearly ten years of false starts and confusion, the Acadians resisted, the French interfered, and, at the end of the decade, the Maliseets and Mi'kmaq remained aloof and oftentimes openly hostile. The first decade of Anglo-American rule in Nova Scotia thus points to the difficulties that British colonizers faced in staking out the empire in the Maritimes. Nonetheless, the years between 1710 and 1722 became the nursery for the ideas and practices that defined Nova Scotia's eighteenth-century history.

THE "CONQUEST" OF ACADIA

Anglo-Americans' miscalculation of the problems they faced in Nova Scotia is understandable. A wave of self-congratulatory enthusiasm clouded their assessment. In the autumn of 1710, New Englanders had joined with Englishmen such as Nicholson, had put aside the disappointment of the stillborn 1707 and 1709 land invasions of Canada, and had shown that they possessed at least the basics of military competency. Against a force over five times the size of his, and in a dilapidated fort that had not been resupplied in three years, Daniel d'Auger de Subercase, the French commandant at Port Royal, proved unable to resist the Anglo-Americans for long and surrendered on October 2.[13]

Anglo-Americans occupied the fort with all the pomp and ceremony of having captured one of the great fortresses of Europe. Nicholson allowed the French garrison to march out under arms with their colors flying and drums beating, important points of honor for eighteenth-century officers. He agreed to transport the garrison to France and granted the French officers permission to take their personal possessions with them. Although they had resisted the Anglo-American forces for only a week, under the rules of the eighteenth-century's *siège en forme,* both Nicholson and Subercase agreed that the French had comported themselves bravely and deserved the full honors of war.[14]

The respective commanders' actions occurred in context of Europe's emerging "age of limited warfare." Both Nicholson and Subercase fought for their respective monarchs and their personal aggrandizement. As soldiers who served fundamentally conservative monarchies, they had no interest in radically upsetting the status quo or unleashing inimical forces that might undermine their monarch's authority. For them, and for most European officials involved, the transfer of power in Nova Scotia was akin to a geopolitical chess match. European concerns shaped their thinking, and they gave relatively little thought to the local implications of their actions. If the Treaty of Ryswick, which had ended the previous Anglo-French war in a return to the status quo antebellum, was any indication, Nova Scotia stood a good chance of reverting to France once the fighting in Europe ended.[15]

Local concerns, however, quickly came to dominate affairs in Nova Scotia. The Acadians, Mi'kmaq, and Maliseets cared little for the evolving imperial balance of power between France and Great Britain. The conquest of their homes threatened to radically upset the order and patterns of their lives. They therefore waited and warily watched to see what their new overlords would require of them.

The Acadians surely found Nicholson's first pronouncements on October 2, 1710, troublesome. While allowing the Acadians within an approximate three-mile "cannon-shot" radius of Fort Anne—the area called the *banlieu* (neighborhood)—to remain in possession of their homes, farms, and other property, Nicholson demanded that within two years they take an oath of allegiance to Queen Anne.[16]

The English commonly demanded oaths of allegiance to the monarchy. With the near-constant threat from Jacobites—those who hoped to see the Catholic and Scottish Stuarts who had fled during the Glorious Revolution of 1688–89 returned to the throne—facing the English/British state until the final suppression of the Highland clans in 1746, the rulers of Britain demanded to know exactly who it could consider loyal and whose fidelity was questionable.[17] In the British Isles, the great majority of Protestants took oaths of allegiance; most Catholics, a minority everywhere but Ireland, were ignored because they were not technically considered subjects and because of the assumption that their faith made them not to be trusted. Thus, the Protestant dissenters who refused to subscribe on religious grounds were an easily identifiable minority. The problem, of course, was that the Acadians of Nova Scotia were overwhelmingly Catholic. Because of the absence of a large, established, and powerful pro-English party such as the Anglo-Irish Protestants who ruled over Ireland for England, the prospects of dividing and conquering the Acadians proved more challenging than in the Emerald Isle.

At the same time, the post-1710 British administration differed considerably from previous periods when Anglo-Americans had occupied Acadia. Nicholson directed that the Acadians and Indians were to avoid seizing or molesting any British subjects in or off the coasts of Nova Scotia. In effect, he stated that he did not trust the locals and expected problems from them. He then ordered that they were to break all ties of commerce and trade with Canada. Henceforth, Annapolis Royal would serve as the only entrepôt for trade in the colony, one of course that Nicholson and his cronies would control. It was Nicholson's final aside, however, that surely most troubled the Acadians and Indians, when they learned that they would "answer to the contrary att their highest perrill" should they refuse to comply with his orders.[18]

If the Acadians and Indians had known of it, Nicholson's message to the governor-general of New France, Philippe de Rigaud, marquis de Vaudreuil, would have concerned them even more. Nicholson saw the Acadians as hostages for the French and Indians' future good behavior and warned Vaudreuil that all the inhabitants of the colony "are left absolutely prisoners at discretion." The Acadians, he threatened, would pay in blood for any further French hostilities on the New England and New York frontiers. Moreover, should Vaudreuil not immediately release the Anglo-American captives that the Indians or French held, including Eunice Williams (who had been kidnapped from Deerfield, Massachusetts, in 1704), Vaudreuil "must expect that the like number of the Chiefe inhabitants of this country shall in the same manner be made slaves amongst our Indians."[19] Presumably, by "our Indians," Nicholson meant either the pro-British Mohawks of distant New York or perhaps the "praying Indians" of New England. In either case, the threats did not bode well for the Acadians.

Fortunately for the Acadians, Nicholson did not have the means to make real his threats. With his work in the colony done and his name made as the conqueror of Acadia, Nicholson departed for England and left his lieutenant governor, Colonel Samuel Vetch (who would later engage him in an acrimonious blame game over the handling of postconquest Nova Scotia) to manage the British occupation. With the British lacking an overall plan on what to do with Nova Scotia, it was up to Vetch to work out the specifics of Anglo-American governance in the new colony.

Vetch, an inveterate schemer, struggled with what to do with the Acadians.[20] His predilection was to expel them. In his 1708 "Canada Survey'd," which he wrote to draw patronage and support for a campaign against New France that he would lead, Vetch called for the deportation of the locals. He proposed moving the Acadians to the West Indian sugar islands and replacing them with Protestant settlers. Vetch's plan was vague but certainly grandiose. Where, for example, would the English find Protestant settlers willing to emigrate, and how soon could they get to North America?[21] It took the British over four decades to muster the resources and the will to send large numbers of Protestant settlers from Europe to Nova Scotia; only then did deportation become practical.

Meanwhile, Vetch oversaw a disaster waiting to happen. The conquerors, more so than the Acadians, faced expulsion from the Nova Scotia frontier. The only secure British position in Nova Scotia was Fort Anne, and it stood in such gross disrepair that Vetch had to order his troops on onerous fatigue duty to cut the four thousand spars of timber that his engineers needed to reinforce the palisades.[22] Facing a potentially hostile population of nearly 2,000 Acadians and perhaps 4,000 Mi'kmaq, Maliseets, Abenakis, while still at war with France, Vetch had only 500 troops on hand, of whom 250 were Yankee militiamen. Although the heads of the fifty-seven banlieu families—those who lived directly under the British guns and no doubt could see the financial advantages to be had in supplying the garrison with food and stores—took Nicholson's oath of allegiance, Vetch's hands were tied in dealing with the other Acadians—those of the *haute rivière* (upriver from Annapolis Royal), Minas, and Chignecto.[23] He had received no instructions from London on whether to offer the Acadians who resided outside the banlieu an oath of allegiance, and he could not do so without direct orders. Had he given the outlying Acadians the oath and they had taken it, and the Crown then decided to deport them or in some other way use them as leverage against the French in peace talks, it would have reflected most poorly on Vetch. "This uncertainty of their circumstances," Vetch wrote in January 1711, "keeps them [the Acadians] still in a ferment, and makes them hinder the Indians altogeither from comming in and keeps them at warr with us, to that degree that they have severall times threatened to dispossess us of the fort before spring."[24]

Little new direction was forthcoming. Part of the failure of the home government to send detailed instructions to Vetch may have resided in the confusion of metropolitan politics. A Whig government had planned the invasion of 1710. That ministry had looked favorably on the idea of deporting the Acadians. The Tory government that replaced it amended the Nova Scotia plan to include offering the Acadians under British control property rights in return for oaths of allegiance.[25]

Vetch could do little against the Mi'kmaw and Maliseet warriors who continued to threaten his small garrison. The French and Indians had him penned within Annapolis Royal. Sending his troops from the fort to battle woodland Indians in the hinterland of the colony would only tempt fate by dangerously exposing his only stronghold in the colony. At the same time, French privateers still prowled the coast. Until the home government sent reinforcements of troops as well as an armed frigate with which he could control Nova Scotia's bays and rivers, Vetch wrote, he would remain unable to protect the fishing fleet from the French or maneuver throughout the colony and reduce the outlying Acadian and Indian settlements.[26]

By the spring of 1711, whatever inroads Anglo-Americans had made with the families of the banlieu over the previous winter were in danger of disintegrating. The outlying Acadians and Mi'kmaq continued "in a great ferment and uneasiness" and had threatened banlieu Acadians who had taken Nicholson's oath of allegiance. When several banlieu residents went into the forest to cut firewood for the fort and procure provisions, Mi'kmaq pillaged and robbed them. The Mi'kmaq had strong support in their disagreement with the banlieu Acadians on the question of accommodating the Anglo-Americans in their midst; priests (most notably Antoine Gaulin, the vicar-general in Acadia) assured the Acadians and Indians that the French would soon retake Nova Scotia. Besides threatening the banlieu Acadians with "Ecclesiasticall vengeance for their subjection to Hereticks," they encouraged Mi'kmaq to threaten and bully anyone who openly sided with or aided the British. Throughout the summer, Indian war parties skulked about the environs of Fort Anne, which intimidated both Anglo-Americans and would-be friendly Acadians.[27]

Catholic priests soon emerged as a significant problem for Vetch. In addition to the dozens of troops that he lost to sickness over the course of the winter, 116 of his men had deserted. Vetch learned that several of the deserters were "Irish Papists," whom Recollet Justinien Durand, the parish priest at Annapolis Royal, had prevailed upon to

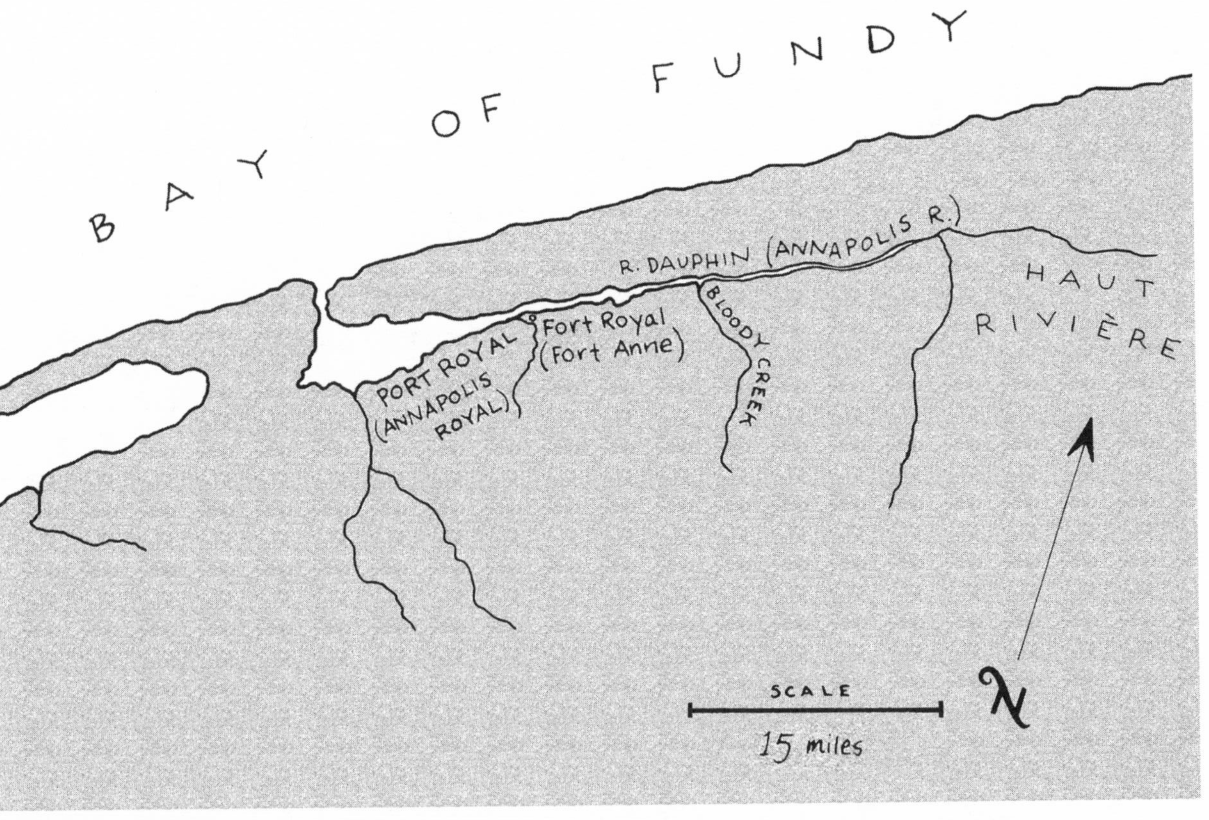

The Annapolis basin.

flee to Canada. Vetch arrested Father Durand and had him transported to Boston, but that did little to alleviate the possibility that a dangerous fifth column resided among his own troops.[28]

Vetch realized that while he could do little against the outlying Acadians—he still had received no instructions as to whether he should treat them as enemies, neutrals, or friends—he must do something against the Indians. He therefore requested that authorities in New York raise one hundred Mohawks for service in Nova Scotia. The New England Indians that had accompanied the invasion force as scouts and guides had returned to their homes.[29] New York had amiable relations with the Mohawks because of the Covenant Chain, the system of treaties between the English and factions of the Iroquois begun a generation earlier. Given his experiences as a merchant at Albany, Vetch believed that the pro-English Mohawks would join him despite their professed neutrality in the Anglo-French conflict. Not coincidentally, the Mohawks would be under the command of his brother-in-law, Major John Livingston, who was said "to be more at home with the Indians than with his fellow colonials." Vetch figured that the Mohawks would cost little more to equip and pay than the soldiers who had already died or deserted; what was more important, they could meet the Indians on their own terms outside the fort. "It is impossible for us to prevent the sckulking partys which so plague us but by a party of Indians who are equal to them in the woods," he wrote.[30]

The Mohawks could not arrive in Nova Scotia soon enough for Vetch. In early June 1711, his command suffered a major loss at the hands of the Indians. Major Francis Forbes, the fort's chief engineer, had informed Vetch that the construction crews were running short of lumber. Most of the banlieu Acadians had taken to avoiding the British for fear of Mi'kmaw reprisals. Vetch therefore directed Forbes to take sixty men from the garrison to collect timber and show the Acadians that they had little to fear from the Indians. While passing through a narrows a short distance from the fort, the soldiers were ambushed by Maliseets and Abenakis. Vetch described the troops as being unable to see the ambushers; as for the troops, "thronged in the boats[,] they were such a mark as could not be missed." The Indians killed Major Forbes, Major William Elliott, and sixteen others; they wounded a captain, an ensign, and nine privates and noncommissioned officers. Only one of the wounded avoided capture. The

Indians offered their prisoners to Vetch for £150. Powerless to do otherwise, and knowing that a forced march covering the hundreds of miles to Quebec (where the Indians would take the captives to sell to Vaudreuil) would surely kill them, Vetch agreed to pay. He offered only £5 for a private, £20 for the ensign, and £50 for the captain. In the end, he shelled out £70 worth of blankets as ransom for the eight privates; the Indians had rushed the two officers to Vaudreuil, from whom they could expect a greater payoff.[31]

Any banlieu Acadian who cared to notice would have seen who was truly in control of Nova Scotia. Because of the battle at what came to be called Bloody Creek, they refused to help the British. As a result of the skirmish, as well as the blockade of Fort Anne by Bernard-Anselme d'Abbdie de Saint-Castin at the head of an Abenaki-Maliseet war party and some Acadians, the garrison became "so intirely blockt up by the Indians that wee cannot gett one stick of wood to burn." The troops remained "weak and sickly" while Irish Catholic marines continued to desert to the French. Rumors then began circulating among the Acadians and the garrison that a French naval squadron and 1,600 troops and Indians were en route to lay siege to Fort Anne to liberate the Acadians. Although Vetch personally discounted the threat, he learned that two French ships had landed at Baie Verte (Port Elgin) and provisioned the Mi'kmaq with food, guns, and ammunition.[32] Although Saint-Castin had to abandon the blockade when New England troops sacked his home near present-day Bangor, Maine, the British standing in Nova Scotia remained shaky through the summer.

In August, disaster struck the British when Admiral Sir Hovenden Walker's armada of fourteen warships and thirty-one transports, carrying 5,300 troops (including many of the duke of Marlborough's battle-hardened veterans from the campaigns in western Germany and Flanders), foundered at the mouth of the Saint Lawrence River. Walker had planned to sail up the Saint Lawrence and reduce Quebec, while a provincial land force would advance up Lake Champlain and take Quebec from the west. Instead, the land army never materialized, and—more important for the Anglo-Americans in Nova Scotia—nine of Walker's ships sank and 742 men and women were lost in treacherous currents and fog off Île-aux-Oeufs (Egg Island). The tiny garrison in Nova Scotia, for the immediate future, would have to live under the threat posed by New France.

After just one year of occupation, the British colonization of Nova Scotia was in tatters. From Boston, where he had traveled to marshal support for the failing colony, Vetch reported that Nova Scotia indeed had fallen into dire straits. Everything seemed to be going wrong. Besides having his men cut the spars needed to reinforce the palisades, Vetch also had them labor at harvesting and hewing twenty prime masts for the ships of the Royal Navy. A major draw of Nova Scotia for the British was its abundant forests that could supply the Royal Navy with high-end building materials. Yet nothing would come of the garrison's labors; after the troops hid the masts in what was assumed to be a safe place, Mi'kmaw warriors found them and torched them in a gigantic bonfire. Frustration over losing the masts further convinced Vetch that the garrison was prisoner in its own fort. "Whereas now not having one person in all the country our friends," Vetch wrote, "wee never know of the enimys approach until they have done some mischief."[33]

The ever-scheming Vetch, however, did not give up on the colony and the potential for his personal gain. Instead, he rushed off a flurry of letters and reports detailing his plan to make the British enterprise a success. The primary imperative, as Vetch saw it, was to deal with the Acadians. If the Acadians fell into line, so then, the assumption went, would the Indians. Thus, beginning in the fall of 1711, controlling the Acadians became the focus of Vetch's and thus Anglo-American efforts in Nova Scotia.

Short of conquering Canada, Vetch again argued, nothing would strengthen the British hold over Nova Scotia more than settling it with loyal subjects. He recommended that the Board of Trade petition the Crown to give free transportation, tools, and a year's supplies to any Protestants from Britain and Ireland who desired to settle in the colony. Vetch was no longer interested in deporting the Acadians. Instead, he would overwhelm them with settlers more amenable to British colonization and use Acadian labor to further his interests. With loyal settlers on hand, as opposed to just sickly and exhausted soldiers, he could muster them into a militia that would allow the soldiers to concentrate on their main responsibility, dealing with the French and Indians. The farmers would eliminate the need for the colony to receive its subsistence from New England, and if the Crown agreed to send four hundred or five hundred Protestant families with two clergymen to Nova Scotia, Vetch believed he could reduce the influence of the priests among the Acadians and Indians. As a typical eighteenth-century British Protestant, Vetch believed that most Catholics were only waiting for the opportunity to convert to Protestantism and abandon the "bigoted" traditions of Roman Catholicism.[34] At its most basic level, Vetch proposed to fundamentally change the culture of Nova Scotia. He believed that Great Britain could bring its notions of religion and governance to a part of the world that held, in many respects, antithetical beliefs.

While knowing nothing of the Board of Trade's opinion of his latest recommendations, Vetch, in January 1712, could take some satisfaction that he would finally have an adequate military force to deal with the Acadians and Indians. Major Livingston's company of Mohawks had arrived in Boston and was awaiting transportation to Annapolis Royal. The company consisted of only fifty-eight officers and men, however, not the hundred he had requested.

Vetch recognized the Mohawks as vital to his plan for the colony. They fit nicely into his preference to intimidate the Acadians rather than find a middle ground with them. He recommended that the War Office pay the Mohawks as if they were part of the regular British military establishment and refund Livingston the substantial out-of-pocket expenses he had incurred in forming the company, thereby making the Indians a permanent presence within the occupying garrison. Vetch also recommended that the War Office form the garrison at Annapolis Royal into a regular regiment and incorporate the Mohawks as a company within the regiment, one that would receive full military pay and allowances.[35] Naturally, his brother-in-law would receive a regular commission as a company commander, perhaps even one as a field-grade officer. The regiment might even become "Vetch's Foot."[36]

Regardless of Vetch's machinations, the Mohawks immediately proved themselves of immense value. After disembarking in February, the Mohawks secured positions about a quarter mile from the main town and constructed several blockhouses—one of which came to be known as Mohawk Fort[37]—and began patrolling the banlieu. The Acadians must have found their presence disconcerting. In short order, the banlieu inhabitants took a stance that was, if not more cooperative, at least passive toward the British. By June, Vetch could report that the garrison was "perfectly healthy" and had made significant progress in repairing Fort Anne.[38]

Vetch judged the Mohawks "worth four times their number of Brittish troops." Besides bullying the banlieu Acadians, they "struck a terrour into" the Mi'kmaq and Maliseets, leading Vetch to predict that "but in a little time they will either wholly banish our troublesome Indians, or oblidge them to submit." Even the intelligence of a plot by Father Antoine Gaulin and the Mi'kmaq to seize Fort Anne in June did not overly concern him. His Mohawks were of "verry great use" and would be more than up to any task the hostile Indians could present.[39] Matters, after a pained year and a half of false starts, seemed to be falling in place for the British. Then the best news possible arrived: France and Great Britain had agreed to peace. In April 1713, the warring European powers had signed a bundle of treaties at Utrecht in the Netherlands.[40]

Post-Utrecht Nova Scotia and the British Empire

The Peace of Utrecht was a watershed event for the British state and the larger British Empire.[41] Despite having won an empire at the peace table, Britons had yet to fully resolve whether they would even have an overseas empire. Powerful interests in London, most notably Robert Walpole's Whigs, preferred "economy" to empire building, while the Hanoverians, who would take the throne in 1714, preferred British foreign policy focus on the Continent.[42] An example of the confusion that defined British foreign policy in 1714 was the lobbying by King George I to dispatch a British fleet to the Baltic. George hoped to precipitate a war between Great Britain and Sweden (embroiled in the Great Northern War with Russia, Poland, Prussia, and Denmark) that he could use to Hanover's gain.[43] Nevertheless, within the empire-building lobby, there remained the question as to which kind of empire Britons should pursue—one of territorial colonization (like the Spanish) or one of oceanic commerce (like the Dutch).

As the first major multilateral treaty in which Great Britain, France, and Spain attempted to formalize the territorial and trade boundaries of their respective Atlantic empires, Utrecht proved effective political salve. France and Britain had fought to a draw in Europe, and the army's campaigns had emptied the British treasury. While the Hanoverians saw the end of the war as an abandonment of Britain's continental allies, they would not back away from taking the spoils of war. British negotiators therefore demanded all the lands of Acadia, not just Port Royal.[44] As a result, both the advocates for a commercial empire and those of a territorial empire got what they wanted. Those favoring an empire of trade rejoiced in Spain's acquiescence to the *asiento*—the concession that allowed British slavers to sell 4,800 Africans a year in the Spanish Empire but also fueled the British public's infatuation with ridiculous get-rich-quick schemes such as the South Sea Bubble that nearly wrecked the economy[45]—as well as the acquisitions of Gibraltar and Minorca. In addition to acquiring the riches of the Nova Scotia fisheries and forests, advocates for an empire of colonization could claim victory in the annexation of Nova Scotia, Hudson Bay, and Newfoundland. In a case of not being able to decide which of two delightful desserts to have, the British chose both. In the end, the possibility that Great Britain might return Port Royal to France at the peace negotiations had proved ephemeral. Although peace treaties often saw conquests sacrificed like pawns on a chessboard, in the early stages of the imperial game, Nova Scotia (née Acadia) was a powerful rook that the British potentially could use to sweep aside its opponents' mercantile interests and colonial possessions in northeastern North America.

At the same time, the abandonment of Port Royal also fit nicely into France's evolving North American policy. In the mid-1690s, the French decided to focus their efforts in Canada on the fur trade and a core of settlements in the Saint Lawrence Valley. Outlying settler communities such as Port Royal had become little more than drains on the treasury. The cash-strapped French state—Louis XIV had devoted most of France's monetary and human resources to conducting his wars of *Gloire*—could spend little on Acadia. Abandoning Port Royal caused little concern for the Ministry of Marine, which preferred to secure the lines of trade and communication with the native allies of New France in the *pays d'en haut* (the Upper Great Lakes region), the Illinois country, and Louisiana. The French thus constructed a string of small military outposts in the northwest such as Detroit (1701) and Michilimackinac (1715). All that greater Acadia needed to provide was a post to serve as a haven for French privateers and protect the Saint Lawrence River, the lifeline to Old France along which the valuable goods that fueled the fur trade traveled.[46]

Of course, the French did not completely ignore the Acadians in their new policy. Part and parcel of their strategy was the determination of officials in New France to harass the British in Nova Scotia. It did not require a master of Machiavellian stratagems to see that the Acadians and Indians offered an ideal foil with which to deny the Anglo-Americans the fruits of their conquest. During the Thirty Years' Peace that followed the war, New France's leaders regularly attempted to use Acadians and Indians to make life as difficult as possible for the British, short of actions that might lead to another major European war.

The Acadians, however, were more than pawns of the French. Although since 1670 Port Royal had been a jurisdiction of New France and its governor reported to the governor-general in Quebec, for the most part the Acadians lived with little assistance or interference from either Old or New France. The Acadians had many motivations—separate though not mutually exclusive from the grand-imperial designs emanating from Quebec or Paris—for watching both the British and the French closely. They were in a precarious but potentially fortuitous position. If the British would guarantee their property and religion, why should they not join their empire? When the Treaty of Utrecht promised "the free exercise of their Religion according to the usage of the Church of *Rome* as far as the laws of *Great Britain* do allow the same" and when, in June 1713, Queen Anne gave them title to their lands for those "willing to continue our subjects," there was little reason to oppose British rule.[47] Of course, the inclination of the Acadians, based on cultural and social preference, probably was to stay committed to and allied with the French. But the British essentially offered them everything they had had under the French, and recent experience had shown them that they could not count on France's armies to defend their homes. Thus, to suggest that the Acadians were united in a *grande famille acadienne* in opposition to the Anglo-Americans would be a gross overstatement. Trade with *les Bostonians* was lucrative; many *entrepreneurs-commerçants* had developed close financial ties with the Yankees, and the pool of potential "collaborators" was deep, especially in the banlieu where the Anglo-Americans seemed firmly entrenched. Despite a petition to Vaudreuil in which they restated their "zeal to serve the King of France" and the church, the Acadians wisely were reluctant to profess public allegiance to either the British or the French monarchy.[48] They saw themselves as Acadians first and Frenchmen (and Frenchwomen) second.

The Acadians had lived for generations outside the firm grasp of the French state and had developed a unique Acadian identity in which they essentially considered themselves neutrals. As early as the 1690s, they had staked out a position of neutrality among the Indians, Anglo-Americans, and French. In 1692, when Joseph Robinau de Villebon, commandant of Acadia, tried to impose French control over the colony in the aftermath of Phips's occupation of Port Royal, the Acadians refused to take up arms on behalf of the French, although they agreed not to interfere with French privateers. The Acadians' refusal to fight for the French had two long-term consequences. First, an Acadian militia never materialized (unlike in the British colonies, where the militia tradition was robust).[49] Second, and of far greater import, the Acadians who lived on the distant frontier had little regard for the finer points of the meaning of "subject" and "citizen" that their putative European masters found so useful. For most western Europeans until the era of the American Revolution, sovereignty was indivisible and sacrosanct.[50] Subjects obeyed; so did citizens, although they could in limited circumstances negotiate the terms of their allegiance to a ruler. In contrast, the Acadians believed—rightly as events proved—that they possessed the right to negotiate the parameters of their membership in whichever community or empire they joined. Most striking in their negotiations with both Anglo-Americans and the French were their consistent refusals to consent to any demands that they found unacceptable. Indeed, the Acadians never negotiated in full faith—they never honestly considered offering either the British or the French a real quid pro quo.

Nevertheless, with Nova Scotia won at the bargaining table, the British could have taken a light-handed approach with their new subjects. Queen Anne implied that she wanted the Acadians to be included in the empire, but whether they were to be subjects or citizens with the full panoply of rights remained murky. The queen's lack of explicit instructions, however, was not insurmountable. The English grudgingly had taken to tolerating—though continuing to discriminate against—both Catholics and Protestant dissenters (non-Anglican Protestants such as Presbyterians, Quakers, Baptists, and Methodists). Indeed, dissenter populations became the pools from which the English populated their colonies in the New World. The absorption into the empire of the Roman Catholic Acadians, and for that matter the Indians, therefore did not present too radical a departure from contemporary practice. Although government officials and the Anglican hierarchy discriminated against them by not allowing them to hold office and in some cases own property, by the early eighteenth century the nonconformist and Catholic churches at least were no longer being driven underground and their members no longer risked being killed. As the eighteenth century progressed, the Whig governments in Britain increasingly tolerated the dissenters, especially when compared to the Tories in the later stages of Queen Anne's reign.[51] But according to Griffiths, "the particular combination of the specific language and religious beliefs of the Acadians with the political geography of the colony was about to demand flexibility of mind and vision from its new administrators."[52]

On-scene British officials distrusted the Acadians and therefore were reluctant to embrace them fully. They saw Acadian behavior, such as remaining aloof from the garrison and continuing to trade with the French, as "insolent." That insolence soon led to questions of Acadian loyalty. For the officers of the occupying army, the surest way to guarantee more than just Acadian obedience was to extract an oath of allegiance from them.

There is certainly irony to be found in Anglo-Americans choosing to take the hard line with the Acadians on the loyalty issue. If they had believed their own rhetoric that most Catholics would convert to Protestantism, they had nothing to gain in forcing the Acadians to declare their allegiance in the immediate post-Utrecht years. If their assumptions had been correct, both Acadians and the Indians, in the fullness of time, voluntarily would have abandoned Roman Catholicism, converted to Protestantism, and incorporated themselves into the empire, where they would be "good" subjects. The insistence that the Acadians make a public declaration of their loyalty was a sleeping dog that the British should have let lie.

Anglo-Americans in Fort Anne needed the Acadians more than the Acadians needed them. All the rhetoric about loyalty and Protestantism was just that. British colonizers were far more interested in economic profit or glory than in ideology or religion. Utrecht's provision that gave the Acadians liberty to "remove themselves within a year to any other place, as they shall think fit, together with all their movable effects" threatened to turn Nova Scotia into a wasteland.[53] Further complicating matters, the French (with the acquiescence of British authorities abiding by the spirit of the peace treaty) had sent Captains Louis Denys de La Ronde and Jacques d'Espiet de Pensens to

Nova Scotia to offer a year's rations to any Acadian who wanted to leave the colony.[54] A mass exodus of the Acadians, however, threatened disaster. Without them, the colony would be "intirely destitute of inhabitants." If they emigrated and took their movable livestock (five thousand head of cattle and untold numbers of sheep, hogs, and horses), they would "strip that country and reduce it to its primitive state." Vetch estimated that the freight costs alone to resupply the colony with livestock and draft animals from New England would exceed forty thousand pounds. The option of converting Annapolis Royal into a trade factory like those along the coast of Africa was similarly impractical. Because some Acadians had intermarried with the Maliseets and Mi'kmaq and shared the same Catholic faith and some "Indians" were métis, Vetch correctly predicted that the departure of the Acadians also would mean the loss of the valuable trade in furs from beavers, otters, and martens, of which the Indians were the primary suppliers; the Indians could just as easily trade on Île Royale or Île Saint-Jean. Most important, should the Acadians emigrate—or worse yet, be forcibly removed—they would make Île Royale "at once the most powerfull Colony the French have in America, and of all the greatest danger and damage to all the British Colonys as well as the universal trade of Great Britain."[55] Complicating matters, the French were hard at work building trade outposts and settlements at Port Toulouse (Saint Peters) and Louisbourg on Île Royale and at Port-La-Joie (Charlottetown) on Île Saint-Jean.[56]

The British thus had to find a way to win over the Acadians and convince them to remain in the colony. One positive step was found in the disbanding of the Mohawk company. With the war over, the British no longer needed their services, and the Acadians were glad to see them leave. The Mohawks had taken to pillaging the Acadians' property, while at the same time the regulars who garrisoned Annapolis Royal must have found the "savage" Mohawks' presence disconcerting.[57]

Yet after that small gesture of goodwill, the British in Nova Scotia pressed the oath issue in 1715. Their instance on demanding the oath at that particular time, however, is understandable. Queen Anne, who had held the crown via a direct Stuart hereditary line, had died. With the threat of Jacobitism overshadowing the accession of the Hanoverians, a public statement of allegiance to the new monarch from all within the empire became imperative. Thus, Lieutenant

Governor Thomas Caulfield, a relatively young army officer who was Vetch's replacement, took the initiative and administered an oath to the officers and men of the garrison, before he had even received instructions from Britain to do so. Caulfield then sent emissaries to the Acadian and Indian villages to demand that they "be faithful to take true allegiance to his Majesty King George." Although by taking the oath they were assured of the right to remain in Nova Scotia, nothing specific on their property, Catholicism, or neutrality was mentioned.[58]

Most of the Acadians refused to subscribe. Only thirty-six banlieu Acadians, all members of the Allain and Gourday families who had traded for years with the Yankees, took the oath. Among the inhabitants of the Minas Basin who even bothered to meet with the British envoys, all proclaimed that they had chosen the previous summer to leave for Île Royale, though they promised to do nothing "contrary to the service of King George." The Acadians of Beaubassin, which sat on the Isthmus of Chignecto and thus off peninsular Nova Scotia, reported that they would wait to learn whether France actually had transferred their land to Great Britain. While the Treaty of Utrecht had ceded Acadia, the question of whether Acadia encompassed more than the peninsula of Nova Scotia remained open. The Indians of the rivière Saint-Jean valley likewise informed Caulfield that they would wait for Vaudreuil's instructions before they took any oath. Adding insult to injury, when the British emissaries asked why they had not brought their furs to Annapolis Royal to trade, they retorted that "the high prices of goods there, and the low prices given for their effects, had compelled them to take them elsewhere." The Maliseets were more forthright. Father Pierre de la Chasse translated their message as stating that they "do not proclaim any foreign King in my country; Port Royal is too far away." All told, only 118 people—a few banlieu residents and one small band of Maliseets—made public pronouncements affirming their loyalty to Great Britain.[59]

Caulfield could do little but stew in his own anger and not enforce even symbolic control over the Acadians. No reinforcements were forthcoming, so the Acadians and Indians could do as they wanted and suffer no repercussions. Although the Board of Trade had detailed Colonel Richard Philipps's Regiment of Foot—later known as the Fortieth after the numbering of regiments became standard in the mid-eighteenth century—for service in Nova Scotia, that was a paper change only. The regiment would be manned from the four independent companies (those that were not attached to a regiment) that had remained at Annapolis Royal and the four at Placentia (Plaisance), Newfoundland, following Queen Anne's War. For the men of the newly formed regiment, nothing had changed. They found themselves on the far reaches of the empire, their fort was again falling in upon itself, they lacked significant stores of materiel, and their weapons were in gross disrepair.[60]

Indeed, the regiment proved little more than a passive bystander in the management of Nova Scotia. In July, a party of Cape Sable Mi'kmaq seized several New England fishing boats and took the crews hostage. They demanded a ransom of thirty pounds. Caulfield, Great Britain's lieutenant governor for Nova Scotia and supposedly the most powerful man in the colony, had little choice but to pay.[61] It was hardly the high point of his career.

The answer to British problems with the Acadians and Indians resided in negotiation and trade. The Acadians, after all, were loath to leave their homes and start anew on Île Royale, which Caulfield at the time had not unfairly judged as little more than "a rock covered over with moss."[62] Several Acadian families in fact had emigrated to Île Royale and Île Saint-Jean following the conquest in 1710, only to return to Nova Scotia. Acadian families had labored for over a century to claim much of their land from the ocean by building an extensive network of dykes and sloughs in the tidal marshes of the Annapolis Valley and Minas Basin. They had made Nova Scotia one of the most productive agricultural regions north of the Caribbean. The banlieu alone produced nearly 10,000 bushels of grain a year, while Minas Basin produced another 20,000. At the same time, the Indians would have preferred trade, which "differed from war in every way."[63] Indians used trade to create mutual obligations and alliances; peoples who traded with one another generally did not fight and kill each other, unless competition grew too intense or one side attempted to manipulate trade without the other. It therefore was a positive sign when the Maliseets at Father Jean-Baptiste Loyard's mission in the valley of rivière Saint-Jean requested that Caulfield send two British merchants with a hearty supply of trade goods to encourage an Anglo-Maliseet trade in furs. On top of that, New England fishermen caught over 100,000 quintals (each quintal is a hundredweight, or 112 pounds) of fish on the North Atlantic banks, which fueled much of

Massachusetts' participation in an Atlantic-wide economy.[64] There were large sums of money to be made in Nova Scotia, if only Anglo-Americans, Acadians, and Indians could find a cooperative middle ground. In fact, no one, except perhaps the men of Fort Anne's garrison, was in a hurry to leave Nova Scotia. Perhaps if the British had exercised patience, matters would have fallen into place more to their liking.

John Doucett's Administration

Caulfield died in 1717, and with Colonel Richard Philipps—the colony's governor—still in England, Captain John Doucett, a son of Huguenot expatriates who had settled in Britain, took over as lieutenant governor. Nova Scotia had slipped into something akin to a "garrison government," in which military officers in the colonies (most notably Ireland) for all intents and purposes ran the empire as best they could with little supervision from London.[65] The alternative would have entailed any of the many government organizations that had a stake in Nova Scotia—the Board of Trade, the secretary of state of the Southern Department's office, the War Office, the Admiralty, or the Board of Customs that regulated colonial commerce—to send civilian appointees to manage and direct affairs in Nova Scotia. A fundamental flaw in that scenario, beyond the fact that there was no single office that could send forth administrators, was the reality that most civilian appointees to the colonies received commissions as a political reward. Usually, they possessed no special competence or training for handling problems of governance or administration. Their primary task, like that of all political appointees both then and now, centered on not angering their political masters.[66] Thus it fell to the professional soldier, John Doucett, to solve problems for which his experiences had not prepared him.

Doucett naturally had aspirations for advancement. He decided that allowing the Acadians and Indians to continue to flout British authority by ignoring the oath would be the ruin of both his career and the empire in Nova Scotia. He therefore determined to bend the recalcitrant Acadians to his will. In late 1717, he summoned the banlieu Acadians and ordered them to subscribe to a new oath: "Wee the french Inhabitants . . . doe declare and most solemnly swear before God to own him [King George] as our Sovereign King and to obey him as his true and Lawfull subjects."[67] Doucett was forthright in announcing that he would truck no opposition. He reminded the Acadians "how dangerous it was to triffle with so great a monarch," and he henceforth forbade anyone who was not a subject of the king—as he saw it, anyone who had not taken the oath—to fish or trade in Nova Scotia. Acadians who previously had taken the oath had little choice but to subscribe to the new oath.[68]

Yet the Acadians who had refused the first oaths also refused Doucett's. Experience had shown them that the British were paper tigers and could do little to compel them to take the oath. Some of them informed Doucett that it was their intention to leave the colony for the other side of the Bay of Fundy.[69] The Acadians of Minas, distant from the banlieu and therefore with little to fear from the garrison at Fort Anne, proved particularly recalcitrant. They first wrote that bad weather and roads had prevented them from assembling as a community. When they finally attained a quorum, they openly refused to take the oath. Their reasons, they wrote, were threefold: first, Doucett's oath did not guarantee them the free practice of their religion that previously had been promised to them; second, if they signed the oath, they would expose themselves "to the rage and fury of the Indians," and third, their ancestors had not been required to take such oaths.[70] While the first point rang true, and the second was debatable (not that the British would have known this, since they rarely left Fort Anne and were uninformed about Acadian-Indian relations), the third frustrated Doucett. True, when the Yankees had occupied Port Royal between 1654 and 1670, they had allowed the Acadians to remain "unmolested" in their homes and faith.[71] But much had changed since the mid-seventeenth century. Whereas Yankee traders had demanded only minimal allegiance, the new empire could not be as permissive. The Acadians twice had flouted British authority in refusing Nicholson's and Caulfield's oaths. Doucett decided not to become the third official they snubbed.

Doucett suspected that the Acadians were playing semantic games with him. He dismissed their threat to leave the colony as an idle one, observing that "this has been their declaration every winter for five or six years past."[72] At the same time, he viewed them as duplicitous in their dealings with the Indians and considered their claim of fearing the Indians a shibboleth. From the little he had seen of Acadian-Indian interactions, the former had little to fear. "If an

Indian is att any time insolent in their houses," from what Doucett had observed in Annapolis Royal, the Acadians "not only turn them out, but beat them very severely."[73] As far as their not being required to take an oath, there was really little he could do short of debating the Acadians on the colony's history over the previous seventy years.

Doucett's hands were tied against ratcheting up the pressure on the Acadians. Any direct moves against their economic well-being would be akin to cutting off his nose to spite his face. Since the conquest in 1710, small numbers of Yankee "carpetbaggers" had settled at Annapolis Royal. From their *faubourg*—their suburb—the Yankees engaged in a brisk trade with the Acadians, a trade that almost never met the basic requirements of British mercantilist policies. Yankee smugglers certainly would not let the imperatives of imperial policy put a dent in their profit margins. The Acadians and their bedfellows in the faubourg looked for a silver lining in the oath-controversy cloud. If they would be forced to take the oath, they might as well gain something out of it. They therefore proposed to Doucett that they would subscribe if he formally offered them neutral status. "We are," the Acadians told Doucett, "ready to take an oath not to take up arms against France or England."[74] Doucett flatly refused to negotiate. He was, after all, an officer in the British Army and, more important, lieutenant governor of Nova Scotia. His future in the army as well as his pride could not permit him to allow a handful of "Frenchmen" to dictate the policies of the British Empire.

Yet Doucett knew that in rejecting neutrality for the Acadians, he might drive them into the arms of the French in Canada and on Île Royale. He therefore demanded that Vaudreuil issue a public statement that the Acadians were at "free liberty" to become British subjects. In a letter to the recently appointed French governor at Louisbourg, Joseph de Monbeton de Saint-Ovide de Brouillan, Doucett wrote that he expected Saint-Ovide to order Frenchmen to desist in establishing fishing flakes (racks) upon which the fishermen cured their catch on the shores of Nova Scotia.[75] He then turned toward the priest at Minas, Father Félix Pain. The lieutenant governor commended Pain for acting "very prudently in leaving the people to themselves in temporal affairs."[76] It was clear that Captain Doucett expected Pain to tend only to his flock's spiritual needs and leave worldly matters to the British.

If he could not hit the Acadians in their pocketbooks, perhaps he could make life difficult for them spiritually. Doucett, in the anti-Papist tradition of the Huguenots who, Voltaire noted, remembered the persecution of the families that followed the revocation of the Edict of Nantes "as the most violent the Church sustained in the primitive ages of Christianity,"[77] viewed the Catholic priests as the main cause of Acadian intransigence. From his perspective, they "were continually doeing all in their power to prevent an English settlement in this Country."[78] Naomi E. S. Griffiths reminds her readers that "the unity of the Catholic Church has almost always been more apparent to those outside its realm than to those within" and that the Acadians "did not consider the priests a people who could not be contradicted"; moreover, "the immense political importance given to the priests by officials at Annapolis Royal, and by a number of later historians, has obscured the reality of Acadian Catholic life." She adds that "in assessing the extent to which Acadian opinion was moulded by their clergy, it is well to bear in mind that the priests were few in number and not all of one mind, and that, during their sojourn in the colony, they sometimes changed their attitude to[ward] the British and/or French authorities. There were never more than five priests, at any one time, working within the colony and usually only three or four."[79] Doucett nonetheless schemed to drive them from Nova Scotia or at least wean the Acadians from their influence.

An opportunity presented itself to Doucett in the spring of 1717. He learned that the priests in Minas had spread rumors that they had received news from France that Nova Scotia would soon be in the French monarchy's hands. Supposedly, the Jacobite Pretender—the exiled James VIII of Scotland, James III of England—was to land in England at the head of a ten-thousand-man French army and reclaim the British crown. In the settlement that would follow, James would return all of Acadia to the king of France.

But Doucett knew that during the winter of 1715–16, George I's government had suppressed the Jacobites' uprising across England and Scotland. On September 6, 1715, the earl of Mar proclaimed James king of Scotland, England, Ireland, and France (which was insulting to his French allies). Mar assembled nearly ten thousand Scottish rebels and marched to Sheriffmuir. There, he met the army of King George I, under the earl of Argyll. Although neither side could claim victory in the engagement, Mar withdrew to Perth. James landed at Peterhead in December to find that Mar's army had disintegrated. On February 4, 1716, with Argyll closing in on them, James and Mar sailed for France. The Hanoverians subsequently attempted to stamp out all remnants of Jacobitism in England and Scotland. They executed many of the ringleaders, transported the rank and file as convict laborers to the West Indies and as indentured servants to the southern colonies, and abolished nineteen Scottish peerages.

Doucett therefore saw events in Great Britain as an opportunity to "convince these people [the Acadians] that their priests are fallible."[80] Few things, moreover, would demonstrate better to the Acadians that they were firmly under British control than a statement from the French on Île Royale or in Canada stating that fact. Doucett therefore encouraged the Board of Trade, with the Crowns of Great Britain and France supposedly at peace and the French possibly looking to soothe British anger over the latter's support of the recent uprising, to extract a guarantee from French officials in Europe that they would "suppress and severely punish" anyone (i.e., priests) who instigated trouble in Nova Scotia.[81]

Doucett also planned to undercut the missionaries' influence with the Mi'kmaq and Maliseets. Since his assumption of the lieutenant governor's post, the Indians had beset him with demands for the annual gifts that they previously had received from the French. With the British entrenched in Annapolis Royal, the Indians astutely understood that they occupied a position from which to extract presents from both the French and the British. "Presents," Olive P. Dickason has observed, "were essential in Amerindian diplomacy, in which they had designated roles; metaphorically, they could, for example, dry tears, open doors of foreign countries, appease anger, ask for fair value in trade, or bring the dead back to life."[82] The Indians thus informed Doucett that if the British "expected them to continue our friend's, they expected presents yearly from H.M., as they allway's receiv'd when this country was in the hands of the French King."[83] Doucett took a cynical view of the Indians' acquisitiveness for European clothing, guns, and brandy. He saw a potential wedge to drive between them and their French missionaries. "There is no mean's better then presents to gain them to our interest, and keep them from goeing to Cape Breton and Canada," he wrote. He discounted the Indians' commitment to their priests and Catholicism (and was proved correct, at least for the Maliseets) in observing that "the Indian's would be sway'd more by the beneffitts they receive in this world, then trust to all benefits their priests can tell them, they will receive in the next."[84]

Colonel Philipps, still in London, aggressively lobbied the Board of Trade to send Doucett a hearty shipment of trade goods. Philipps planned to secure Nova Scotia by overwhelming the Acadians and Indians with British settlers and trade. He first recommended that the British consolidate their holdings in the Maritimes by withdrawing the small garrison from Newfoundland. Not only was the fort at Placentia continually in disrepair and a money pit, but the presence of another British "colony" in the Maritimes, no matter how small and isolated, drew New England trade from Nova Scotia. Concerning the Acadians, Philipps advised that although they deserved to "be treated in the manner they deserve for so undutiful a behavior," until large numbers of British inhabitants were settled in the colony, the British should tread lightly on the oath issue.[85] Of greater and more immediate importance remained the Indians. The Board of Trade needed to fund annual presents for the Indians that would both engage them in the British interest and secure the fur trade. An additional helpful action would be found in establishing a boundary commission with the French to formally delineate the borders of Nova Scotia. At the same time, Philipps wrote, the British had to extend their military presence in the colony, which would include building a fort under the direct supervision of a qualified engineer at Canso (on the northeastern tip of Nova Scotia). Last, Philipps requested that the Admiralty dedicate a frigate as a station ship for Nova Scotia to protect Anglo-American fishermen and aid in communications and trading ventures across the colony.

The Board of Trade's failure to act decisively points to the gulf, even at that early stage in the empire's development, that separated the officials in London from the military officers tasked with running the colonies. With a swipe of its pen, the Board of Trade could have dedicated the resources that Doucett and Philipps needed, particularly the trade goods for the Indians. Instead, the board saw "no great necessity of sending them till Col. Philipps should have been settled some time in Governmt. there." Only after repeated pleas, which they called "being informed on numerous occasions" that presents were a vital necessity, did the members of the Board of Trade authorize that "some cloathing and utensils of small value, should be sent with Col. Philipps, to be distributed to the Chiefs of the Indians."[86]

While the Board of Trade concerned itself over what in the end amounted to perhaps a couple hundred pounds sterling worth of trade goods, the French stepped into the void. Philipps noted that the French "spare no pains and take the proper methods to estrange" the Indians from the British.[87] Each spring and fall, they sent a ship laden with wine, brandy, linen, and other trade goods from Île Royale. Inexpensive French products flooded the markets for both furs and Indian loyalty. In return for their largesse, the French received not only the friendship of the Indians but also the Acadians' cattle and grain that should have gone toward feeding the garrison at Annapolis Royal. Of course, earlier British pronouncements had made the French-Acadian-Indian trade illegal. The Acadians, Maliseets, and Mi'kmaq simply ignored the law, and the British were in no position to enforce it. Indeed, the French had the "sole trade with the Indians," with the latter completely ignoring British merchants. In November 1718, Doucett reported that he had seen only two Indians at Annapolis Royal since the previous spring.[88] He finally begged the Board of Trade to correct the problem: "I humbly offer my opinion that, if your Lordships can't find some method to send presents to the Indians, they will be intirely estranged to us, and be allways ready to obstruct us in any undertaking for the good of this Colony and H.M. subjects, and I think there can be nothing done better than weaning the Indians from the interest of the French."[89]

Despite the nadir to which Anglo-Indian trade and thus relations had fallen, there remained a small glimmer of hope that some Indians could be won to the British side. The Maliseets, who resided distant from the French on Île Royale and much closer to Annapolis Royal, were willing at least to talk with the British. Although the Maliseets probably hoped to trade with both the French and the Yankees, the British had to see any communication between themselves and the Indians as a positive sign. The Indians informed Doucett that they would meet with him in the spring of 1719 to fix "the prices of commoditys, and establish a commerce betwixt the English and them."[90]

Over the same time period, however, British relations with the Acadians continued to deteriorate because of French interference. Although in January 1717, France and Great Britain nominally had joined forces in a treaty first known as the Triple Alliance and then the Quadruple Alliance to oppose Spanish ambitions in France and Italy,[91] Anglo-French amity did not necessarily transfer to Nova Scotia. In 1718, Vaudreuil began instigating the Acadians to trouble the British. He did not suggest that they take arms against the British but instead proposed that they leave the colony. Although he publicly advised them to decide among themselves if they wished to remain in Nova Scotia, in secret correspondence that the British intercepted, he wrote otherwise. Commenting on how war and British occupation must have been hard to endure, Vaudreuil coyly reminded Louis Allain—one of the banlieu Acadians who had taken the oath—that the rivière Saint-Jean area fell under French jurisdiction. He promised support and land for any Acadian who migrated there. If the banlieu Acadians wished to leave, Vaudreuil told them all they had to do was reach Father Loyard at his mission, where the governor-general had authorized him to grant "habitation to those who shall ask for them."[92]

With Vaudreuil backing their play, the Acadians became openly derisive toward the British. The patience of Doucett, already irked by the oath controversy, quickly wore thin. He overreacted and jailed an Acadian for openly suggesting that the French soon would reclaim Annapolis Royal. The Acadian's arrest violated the very principles that supposedly differentiated the British from the "despotic" French. British subjects, and others who lived on British occupied lands, were entitled to the safeguards of habeas corpus, to include trial by jury. Yet Doucett arrested the Acadian and locked him in jail for expressing his opinion—by this point in time, an opinion Doucett clearly found most irritating. His observation that Great Britain's "neglect of this place so long" had resulted in "not one inhabitant" believing that a British government would function in Nova Scotia was telling in at least two ways.[93] The abeyance of the traditional rights of Englishmen in Nova Scotia not only reinforced the Acadians' belief that the British were little more than oppressive occupiers but also suggests that Doucett and others believed they were dealing with foreigners bereft of the rights of citizens in good standing.

Crisis over Canso

At the same time the Acadians were proving difficult, Doucett faced a crisis at Canso. The peninsula and chain of small islands off the tip of northeastern Nova Scotia provided an ideal staging area for a fishing fleet on the North Atlantic banks, as well as the most convenient place to process catches. Article XII of the Treaty of Utrecht had left the status of Canso and the small islands between Nova Scotia and Île Royale unclear. In the treaty, the French had ceded Acadia, which they interpreted to mean only peninsular Nova Scotia, in return for a guarantee that they would retain possession of the islands in the Gulf of Saint Lawrence and at the mouth of what they called the Canada (Saint Lawrence) River.[94] Yet, for both British and French fishermen, Canso was the real prize. The French therefore speciously treated Canso as one of the Gulf of Saint Lawrence islands. They went as far as to christen the Gut of Canso, the passage between Nova Scotia and Île Royale, the "Little River of Canada." As a ploy to claim Canso for the French crown, Doucett wryly noted, they "may as well claim Guernsey or Jersey, if they will call the Channell of England the River to Canada."[95]

By 1718, a New World confrontation over Canso had been brewing for two years.[96] In August 1716, the Royal Navy's station ship at Boston, the *Rose* under Lieutenant Benjamin Young, sailed to Canso to assess the state of French encroachments on the islands. Massachusetts had the most to lose if Canso fell into French hands, and Lieutenant Governor Joseph Dudley was concerned when Young reported back that there were many Frenchmen and Acadians using the islands. Dudley then directed Young to submit a petition to the French governor at Île Royale, Phillipe Pastour de Costebelle, stating that the French had no right to fish from Canso. After receiving the warning from Massachusetts, Costebelle assured Young that "he would order the French away from fishing there." The *Rose* then made its way to the Gulf of Canso, where thirty French fishing crews were hard at work. Young seized the French vessels and sent the fishermen to Île Royale.[97] Despite Young's effort, French fishermen took 15,000 quintals of fish from Canso in 1716. In 1717 they caught another 20,000, and in 1718 they increased their catch to 25,000 quintals.[98]

In the spring of 1718, Governor Saint-Ovide, Costebelle's recent replacement, reasserted the French claim to Canso. The newly appointed governor seemed eager to assert his authority. The Ministry of Marine had directed him in his assumption-of-command instructions to foster the loyalty of the Acadians and the Indians but maintain strict secrecy to hide France's hand in interfering with British rule in Nova Scotia. "Your steps in this regard should be taken very cautiously," advised Jean Frédéric Phelypeaux, comte de Maurepas, the minister of marine.[99] But with the British colony in Nova Scotia thoroughly isolated and appearing to be on its deathbed, the opportunity to move on Canso seemed right. The previous year, Bernard LaSonde, a banlieu Acadian who had fled to Île Royale and established himself as a fisherman with a camp at Canso, had threatened some Yankees that "if the French did not, the English shd. never fish there more."[100] In May, two New England fishermen reported that both Saint-Ovide and LaSonde had appeared and publicly forbade the English from fishing at Canso. Several days later, Mi'kmaq fell upon the New Englanders and destroyed their fishing flakes and buildings. The Mi'kmaq told the fishermen that they were under orders from Saint-Ovide and that the New Englanders must never return to Canso. In the meantime, nearly three hundred French fishermen seized the islands and occupied "the best places to make their fish."[101] Among Saint-Ovide's instructions was a prohibition of any trade with the English.[102]

Massachusetts governor Samuel Shute responded forcefully. Shute, who found himself at odds with the Massachusetts Assembly over the prerogatives of his office and badly in need of allies in the Bay Colony, could not afford to stand by with the indispensable New England cod fishery threatened. He sent Captain Cyprian Southack (Sondricq in the French records), an experienced pilot in the Maritimes who had helped transport the New England force to Port Royal in 1710 and whose map of the east coast of New England was the first to be engraved in copper and distributed in the colonies, and the *Squirrel,* commanded by Captain Thomas Smart (Lissart to the French), to present the New Englanders' case to Saint-Ovide. The *Squirrel* arrived at Canso on September 6; there it found a ship flying the French colors, a brigantine (the *Catherine*), a sloop (the *Abigail*), and thirty shallops—the small open sailboats used for fishing.[103] Five days later, Southack and Smart had their conference with Saint-Ovide at Louisbourg. They reminded him that per Article XII of the Treaty of Utrecht, France gave Great Britain all of Nova Scotia "with its ancient boundaries," which included all the islands to Cape Saint Lawrence east of Cape Breton Island. Moreover, the treaty directed that all French inhabitants "shall hereafter be excluded from all kind of fishing in the said seas, bays and other places on the coast of Nova Scotia."[104]

Saint-Ovide listened patiently and then dismissed Smart and Southack without giving them the slightest satisfaction to their demands. The *Squirrel* set sail for Canso two days later, leaving (as Saint-Ovide said) "with a thousand protestations of amity and assurances of a good and perfect union."[105]

Whatever the state of relations between the envoys and Governor Saint-Ovide upon their leaving each other's company, on September 18, Smart "began like a fury" to destroy the French fishery at Canso.[106] Even the New England fishermen who had returned to Canso found his enthusiasm for his task excessive; George Vaughan observed that "all things was peaceable & quiet, the French and English fishing with all friendship and love, and the Indians thô numerous very ready to do all friendly Offices, but I fear they are now exasperated."[107] Smart seized the French ship, the brigantine, the sloop, four thousand quintals of fish, and none other than LaSonde. A week later, he returned the ship to its captain (because he did not have the means to sail it to Boston) but kept the brigantine and sloop and transported LaSonde as a prisoner. The assessed value of his prizes amounted to over two thousand pounds.[108]

Naturally, Saint-Ovide did not take the British attack on the French fishermen lying down. He first wrote to Governor Philipps, not Shute, and claimed that he had a different copy of the Treaty of Utrecht than Captains Smart and Southack, noting that on different versions "the points of the compass are not equall." Saint-Ovide wrote that he did not "think it convenient for private subjects who ought to be no more than the interpreters of the orders of the Kings their masters to decide points so nice."[109] Unable to abandon his monarch's claims to Canso—and probably not inclined to do so anyway—Saint-Ovide then sought to split the British counsel and offered Shute a disingenuous compromise, especially considering that the French had to travel only from Île Royale to fish at Canso while the New Englanders came all the way from Massachusetts. Until they had "a perfect decision from our Courts," he would withdraw the French inhabitants from Canso, provided the British evacuated their people.[110] He then seized a New England brigantine and sloop as reprisal for Smart's actions.[111]

Both the Board of Trade and the French Ministry of Marine preferred caution. The British and French governments cared less for the developments in Nova Scotia than maintaining their peace and balance of power in Europe. In 1719, "in order to cultivate a good understanding between the two crowns," the Board of Trade recommended that the British consider offering restitution for the French ships.[112] Saint-Ovide, based on instructions he received from Paris, determined to let the British make good that offer and spent 1719 watching to see how events would unfold.[113]

In the summer of 1720, after it had become clear that little or no restitution would be forthcoming from Great Britain, Saint-Ovide acted. Despite giving Philipps empty assurances that he had counseled the Mi'kmaq to hold fast at peace with the British, he in fact schemed with the Indians to attack the New Englanders at Canso. On August 8, sixty Mi'kmaq surprised the Yankee fishermen on the shore of Canso. With the aid of the Acadians from the fishing settlement of Petit Degrats, whose livelihood was tied to the fishery, they killed two New Englanders and drove the rest into the sea, where another man drowned in the panic and confusion. The Mi'kmaw and Acadian fishermen took over eighteen thousand pounds' worth of fish and equipment. When on the next day the Yankees reported the previous night's events to Saint-Ovide, the governor "made light of it and answer'd if any french men were taken in the fact they should make satisfaction, but as for the Indians he had nothing to do with them."[114]

The New Englanders at Canso responded as best they could. Thomas Richards, a captain of one of the New England schooners, fitted out two smaller vessels and pursued the killers and thieves. Richards's party quickly caught up with them and seized two Mi'kmaq and fifteen Frenchmen. Upon interrogating the Indians, they "confessed they were incouraged and had orders to robb us from the Governor of Cape Breton."[115] When Richards questioned the Acadians, they too confirmed that "they did as their captains commanded them" and stated that French officers had supplied the Indians with guns and ammunition and, after the raid, received the stolen fish.[116]

The prisoners justified their raid as avenging the "wrong the French had suffered from Capt. Smart."[117] Indeed, the attack on the Anglo-American fishery had less to do with the escalating French efforts to harass the British and more to do with Smart's raid two years earlier. Nonetheless, Governor Philipps did not see the struggle through local lenses. From London, the Acadians and French appeared to be united in a grand conspiracy. "Nothing is so evident," he wrote, "as that our French [Acadian] inhabitants, and the neighboring French Governments are equally secrett enemys to the Brittish . . . and that the savages are the tooles in their hands, with which they work the mischeifs which they themselves dare not appear in."[118]

Regardless of France's culpability in precipitating the crisis at Canso, British authority in Nova Scotia was in tatters. Indeed, the British rule in Nova Scotia had seen a string of failures—so many, in fact, that the accuracy of calling Nova Scotia a colony at all was questionable. A lack of commitment by London had plagued on-scene administrators. Yet the home government did not deserve all the blame. The military leaders in the colony had unnecessarily antagonized the Acadians by forcing the oath issue. Only handfuls of the Acadians had taken the oath of allegiance, and those who had done so had repeatedly proven that they could not be trusted. Although the period had passed during which the Treaty of Utrecht had authorized the Acadians to leave the colony with their property, many Acadians threatened emigration (and thus the economic ruin of the colony) at any British request for support. The overwhelming majority of Indians, meanwhile, refused to acknowledge British rule or, for that matter, even trade with them. Without trade, there was no hope of a lasting peace with the Indians. Meanwhile, the French and priests interfered in Nova Scotia, as did the Yankees. At the end of the first decade-plus years of British rule, when the crisis over Canso erupted, Doucett could do little more than watch Shute and Massachusetts engage the French. Neither coercion nor accommodation had resulted in any British success in Nova Scotia. Indeed, Nova Scotia remained a far distant frontier where Acadians, Mi'kmaq, Maliseets, Frenchmen, and even Yankees went about their lives as if the British Empire were a figment of the imagination.

2

The Maliseet-Mi'kmaw War, 1722–1726

On January 3, 1720, Colonel Philipps wrote to the Board of Trade informing them that he had finally arrived at his posting in the colonies. It would have been more accurate to say that he had reached New England. Philipps related that he had sailed into Boston harbor in October but had to spend five weeks waiting for the ship to be fitted out that was to take him to Nova Scotia. Upon finally departing for Annapolis Royal, however, severe winter weather forced a landing at Casco Bay, Maine. With the dangerous sailing season in the Bay of Fundy upon him, Philipps felt compelled to return to winter in Boston "not by choice but necessity."[1]

Philipps's lack of enthusiasm to risk life and limb to reach Annapolis Royal is understandable. Nothing of significance had changed in the colony in a decade, and Nova Scotia remained an unwelcoming posting for the governor. He observed that the same issues awaited him that had plagued earlier governors—uncooperative Acadians, French interference from Quebec and Île Royale, aloof Indians, and a paucity of both presents and troops with which to govern the colony effectively.[2] No wonder that despite his protestations to the contrary, he preferred to winter in the relative comforts of New England.

As he sat in Boston, Philipps probably did not suspect that his colony was about to enter a period of profound change. As would become the pattern in Nova Scotia, war dramatically altered the nature of Anglo-American–Acadian–Indian–French relations. In the early 1720s, the Maliseet-Mi'kmaw War catalyzed the changes. Obscure wars on the ends of empire (now called "small wars"[3] or "low-intensity conflicts") generally are difficult events to understand, as both participants and historians often have trouble discerning when they begin, their train of events, and when they end. The Maliseet-Mi'kmaw War of 1722–26, this chapter's subject, proves no different. The Maliseets and Mi'kmaq were opportunists, and when their Eastern Abenaki allies found themselves embroiled with Yankees in a war on the Maine frontier—the conflict alternately known in American military history as Father Râle's War, Lovewell's War, or Dummer's War—they moved against the British in Nova Scotia. Although in terms of battles and casualties for both sides, the Indian war did not become as large a conflict in Nova Scotia as in Maine, the British nevertheless needed nearly four years to quash it. Engaged more in subversion than in overt armed conflict—the hallmarks of low-intensity conflict—Maliseets and Mi'kmaq, with the clandestine encouragement of the French, threatened to break Great Britain's fragile hold on Nova Scotia.

The Maliseet-Mi'kmaw War set the Indians on the path to their eventual undoing. The Indians accomplished little more than forcing the British hand in Nova Scotia. The four years between 1722 and 1726, when the British saw the greatest threat of Indian attacks, compelled them to focus on securing Nova Scotia. As a result, they abandoned juggling Acadian, French, and Indian issues and skillfully employed both the carrot and the stick to overawe the Maliseets and Mi'kmaq. While it would be a substantial reach to suggest that after 1726 Anglo-Americans had completely solved their "Indian problem" in Nova Scotia, it is fair to say that they had made significant progress toward eliminating unified Indian opposition to their rule. If prior to the Maliseet-Mi'kmaw War Anglo-Americans had faced an Acadian-Indian-French triad of challenges, in confronting the Maliseets and Mi'kmaq, they significantly weakened the Indian leg of that triad. Their actions during the Maliseet-Mi'kmaw War illuminate how force and compromise engendered negotiation at this early stage of the empire's development.

Anglo-French Competition for Indian Friendship

The Board of Trade made it clear to Philipps that it expected him to make Nova Scotia produce profits to fill its and the empire's bank accounts. His first order of business centered on keeping a watchful eye on the French and avoiding provoking them into hostilities. So as to not antagonize them, the Board of Trade directed him to invite the Acadians "in the most friendly manner" to take an oath of allegiance. Because the time had expired during which they were allowed by the Treaty of Utrecht to leave the province with their possessions, Philipps was to make sure that if any Acadians chose to emigrate, they would abandon their property and (what was equally important) not damage it. He also was to bar any non-British subjects from fishing off Canso. Despite the recognized need to encourage Protestant settlers to go to Nova Scotia, however, Philipps was not to make any large grants of land until surveyors, who would arrive later, had set aside reservations for the Royal Navy's timbers. He could make smaller grants of land at an annual rent of one shilling or three pounds of hemp for fifty acres. On the subject of to whom he would give those grants, the board said nothing. At the same time, instead of providing the trade goods for which so many Indians and administrators had clamored, the Board of Trade instead directed Philipps to encourage intermarriage between Anglo-Americans and Indians. Indians and métis held the key to the fur trade; the board assumed that marriage between British men and Indian women would foster relationships that in time would replace the fur-trade alliance among the Acadians, Indians, and métis. Thus, any Anglo-American who married an Indian would receive a gift of ten pounds and fifty acres of land free of quit rents—the small annual fee in lieu of services that proprietors were allowed to collect—for twenty years. Perhaps the only two tangible positives that the Board of Trade issued in its instruction to Colonel Philipps were the authorization to pull back from Placentia, Newfoundland, with orders to leave only a fifty-man garrison there and permission to convene a council of twelve members at Annapolis Royal to aid his governance.[4]

Philipps, when he finally made his way to Nova Scotia from Boston in the spring of 1720, thus had a full plate. His task would require deft handling, compromise, patience, and aid from the metropolis. Yet it quickly became clear that only minimal help would be coming from the Board of Trade. One of the board's first acts upon hearing of Philipps's tardy arrival in Nova Scotia was to chastise him, in the oblique language of bureaucrats, for taking so long to reach his posting. It also directed that Philipps, with no reinforcements of troops or additional outlays of money forthcoming, build a small fort at Minas to keep watch over the Acadians. On the questions of how he was to pay for that fort, or with what troops he was to garrison it, the board remained silent. Still, not all was doom and gloom. The board reported that it had heard the Admiralty had authorized a sloop for service in Nova Scotia.[5]

Philipps only thinly concealed his frustration with the board, his position in Nova Scotia, the Acadians, and even the New Englanders in his first major report on the state of the colony. In noting that "there are not frequent opportunities of correspondence"—who can blame him for not taking the initiative to keep the Board of Trade well informed when all it seemed to do was criticize his actions and levy more requirements on him?—Philipps laid out a litany of complaints that should have spurred the board to action.[6] The Acadians again refused to take the oath. Philipps believed that they would become good subjects if the British gave them "proper encouragement," although he did not say what that was, to wean them from the Catholic priests. The French continued "makeing use of all stratagems to draw them to their party" and called a council on Île Royale in which they warned the Acadians "that the promise made them of injoying their religion is but a chimera" and they would be "reduced to the same state with H.M. Popish subjects in Ireland." Harkening back to earlier officers who had reported that a mass Acadian exodus would win the British nothing, Philipps noted that even if the Acadians left, the Indians would prevent Anglo-American settlers from occupying the vacated lands. All the talk of trying to influence the Acadians, however, was moot. Philipps knew that he was "shut up within" Annapolis Royal and that the Acadians of Minas and Chignecto "know very well they are out of my power." He reported that he could do little with the Indians because of his "want of the presents which I have expected." Despite his apprehension to summon the Indians without having gifts to give them, he nonetheless felt required to do so because the French "have so well made their advantage of our neglect of this countery." The clandestine trade with Île Royale continued, meanwhile. New Englanders, who price-gouged the garrison, monopolized the little trade that did reach Annapolis Royal. They, in Philipps's estimation, took eighty thousand to one hundred thousand quintals of fish and upwards of ten thousand pounds' worth of furs from Nova Scotia each year. In return, they inflated the prices that they charged the garrison 400 to 500 percent, "without paying the least dutty or import towards the support of this Government."[7]

None of the issues in Philipps's litany of complaints demanded greater attention than the Gordian knot of Indian affairs. Starting in the spring of the previous year (1719), the French had made a concerted effort to drive a wedge between the Indians and the British. Upon hearing that the Maliseets of Father Jean-Baptiste Loyard's rivière Saint-Jean mission had agreed to meet Doucett at Annapolis Royal to fix the prices of trade goods and to establish the borders of their territories with the English, the French saw the Indians slipping away from them. They therefore proposed to establish a commission between the two Crowns that would fix the French-English boundaries along Baie Françoise (Bay of Fundy). The French hoped to bring the Indians under their protection by ensuring that the Catholic missions sat on French lands; any British dealings with the Indians that resided on French territory, as a result, would have to go through the governor-general at Quebec.[8]

The Maliseets and Mi'kmaq watched the French and British dealings closely. They knew that their Abenaki cousins in Maine were in the midst of a border dispute with the colonial government of Massachusetts. Since the Treaty of Portsmouth in 1713, which had ended the Yankee-Abenaki portion of Queen Anne's War (in this context known as the Third Anglo-Abenaki War) and paralleled the treaty of Utrecht, the northeastern boundary of Massachusetts had remained undefined. At Portsmouth, the Abenakis (but not the Maliseets and Mi'kmaq) supposedly accepted their status as British subjects. With the transfer of Acadia to the British, the French saw upholding the Abenakis' remaining territory rights as a way of constructing a *cordon sanitaire* between New England and New France.[9]

Some Abenakis (particularly the Kennebec River valley band), meanwhile, seemed eager to renounce the Treaty of Portsmouth. In the fall of 1719, Sébastien Râle, the resident Jesuit at Norridgewock, at the confluence of the Kennebec and Sandy rivers, sent six of his mission's leading Indians to Quebec to confer with Governor-General Vaudreuil on how best to oppose New England's encroach-

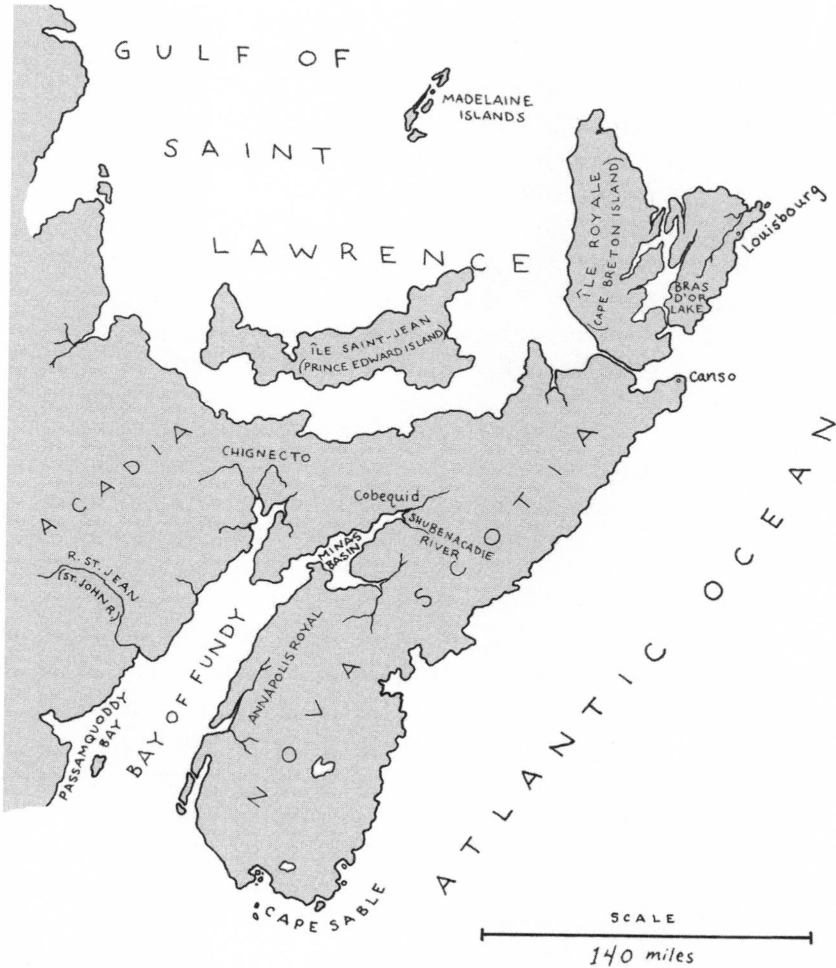

Area of operations in the Maliseet-Mi'kmaw War.

ments into Maine. Governor Shute, the Indians told Vaudreuil, had blustered that he intended to send five hundred settlers to the base of the Kennebec River to establish a fort. Although the provisions of the 1713 treaty allowed the British to build a fort there, Shute's actions reeked of provocation. Vaudreuil assured the Abenakis that Shute hoped only to intimidate them and told them that New France would support them if they chose to fight. Soon after the Indians had departed for Father Râle's mission, Vaudreuil rushed off a letter to the

Ministry of Marine in which he predicted that war was imminent between Massachusetts and the Abenakis.[10]

The French could call on support from Abenakis other than Kennebecs as well. Over the previous two generations, many Abenakis had left the Maine frontier for the Catholic missions at Saint-François (Odanak) and Bécancour (Wôlinak).[11] Odanak sat on the site of the village that the Abenakis called Arsikantegouk and had been established in the 1670s. Following King Philip's War in 1675–76, it became a refuge for Abenakis who fled New England. In 1701 Jesuit fathers relocated their mission of Saint François de Sales near the rivière Chaudière to Odanak, which among the English took the new name Saint Francis. Four years later, as Odanak swelled with Abenaki refugees from the Third Anglo-Abenaki War, many Abenakis moved to the mission at Wôlinak, which became Bécancour. Still, those sauvages domiciliés could do less to protect New France's border with New England than the Indian villages on the frontier could do.

The Abenakis who remained on the frontier thus became the focus of a French initiative to win their closer friendship. It was a difficult row to hoe. In Queen Anne's War and its immediate aftermath, the Abenakis had gained an awareness of the perils of an alliance with the French. Like the Iroquois of New York who had found that they had little to gain and much to lose in serving as a European power's proxies, some Abenakis had come to insist on neutrality in the Anglo-French conflict. Abenaki unity fractured and splintered further after the war when some Indians from the Lower Kennebec Valley settled at Reverend Joseph Baxter's Protestant mission at Arrowsic Island. The Penobscots, further removed from the direct and immediate threat of New England encroachments on their lands, meanwhile, were wary of antagonizing the British.[12]

Vaudreuil and the Ministry of Marine turned to the priests to help New France secure the loyalty of the Indians of Maine. In June 1720, the ministry authorized two thousand pounds to build churches at Father Râle's mission at Norridgewock, as well as Father Loyard's mission among the Maliseets at Médoctec (near the confluence of the Eel and Saint John rivers near present-day Meductic, New Brunswick). By funding the construction of those churches, the French strengthened the buffers against British advances from the south (New England) and east (Nova Scotia) and bracketed the wavering

Penobscots with pro-French Indians. Likewise, besides constructing missions for the Maine Indians, the ministry added two thousand pounds for presents for the Indians in the three Catholic missions in Acadia and Nova Scotia—Father Loyard's, Father Antoine Gaulin's at Antigonish (established in 1715 at the mouth of Baye d'Artigoniche, or George Bay), and Father Félix Pain's at Minas. As an immediate acknowledgment of their efforts, Vaudreuil told the Indians that Louis XV offered his "special approval" for the consistency they had shown in withstanding British efforts to expand settlements on the frontier.[13]

Vaudreuil also hoped to use the influence of the larger Wabenaki Confederacy—the informal union of Abenakis, Maliseets, and Mi'kmaq—as leverage. He endeavored to convince each of the members of the confederacy that in allying with the French, they were in fact helping themselves. While the Maliseets and Mi'kmaq probably would have been inclined to help their Abenaki compatriots, as rational actors on the diplomatic stage in the Northeast, they might need further inducements to help the French. The greatest benefit that Vaudreuil could offer them was to stand steadfast in claiming that Acadia, which in its entirety the French had ceded to the British at Utrecht, encompassed only peninsular Nova Scotia.[14] Because the French made no direct claims to Indian hunting areas and preferred trade rather than settlement, present-day New Brunswick was therefore de facto Maliseet and Mi'kmaw land. For the Maliseets who had told Philipps that they would never accept British rule over them, Vaudreuil's promise to hold the British border at peninsular Nova Scotia at least offered nominal independence.

Vaudreuil's support for the Indians emboldened them. In the fall of 1720, Mi'kmaq sent Philipps a terse note that shaped Anglo-Indian relations in Nova Scotia for the immediate half decade and in some ways through the final British conquest of 1760. Philipps had noted that the French "insinuating" with the Indians had been "very prejudicial" to the Crown's interest in Nova Scotia and therefore had called a meeting with the rivière Saint-Jean Maliseets to "undeceive them" from the French.[15] Of course, with few presents to give the Indians, he could have expected to accomplish little. Still, the Indians' response must have been shocking. Writing from Minas Basin, and clearly under the influence of their missionaries if their choice of words is any indication, the Indians responded that "they believe that

God had given them this land [Nova Scotia]" and they would oppose the British efforts to reduce them to "servitude."[16]

The Indians' open disdain for the British would have made sense to Philipps if he had been privy to the continued workings of the French officials in Quebec, at the missions, and in France. The French quickly finished construction of the churches at Norridgewock and Médoctec and congratulated themselves on how the new structures were certain to "attach" the Indians to their cause. Vaudreuil also took care to give the Indian leaders a tangible memento of his and Louis XV's gratitude for their fidelity; he cast and distributed thirty "fine medals" to the leading Indians of the missions. All the while, Father Râle continued to rail against the British and encouraged the Indians to stand up for their rights. He continually "excited" his flock at Norridgewock not to "suffer the English to extend themselves on their [the Abenakis'] lands." Of course, Father Râle worked with the tacit approval of both Vaudreuil and the Ministry of Marine. The king, as late as June of 1721, was so pleased to hear of Râle's efforts that he made special notice to thank the priest and the Indians for their "continual harassment" of Anglo-American settlers on the Maine frontier.[17]

In the summer of 1721, with no resolution in sight to the fundamental issues that separated the Abenakis from the New Englanders, tensions continued to escalate on the Maine frontier. Governor Shute complained to Vaudreuil that the Indians had taken to treating the British settlers in Maine in an "insolent manner." He also hoped—he used the French verb *souhaiter* (to hope) rather than *exiger* (to demand)—that Vaudreuil would recall Father Râle. Shute's request probably elicited little more than a wry smile from Vaudreuil. Most important, Shute hoped that if the Abenakis approached Vaudreuil, he would encourage them to live in peace with New England.[18] Perhaps that too produced a smile from the crafty governor-general.

While the news of the Anglo-American standoff with the French and Indians on the Maine frontier swirled around him, Philipps reported from Nova Scotia that affairs in his province had remained quiet. Canso was calm, probably because the frigate *Seahorse* was riding on station there. The ongoing exchange of messages in Boston between Massachusetts and the Abenakis offered a small ray of hope. But upon learning that several Maliseets had traveled to Boston to observe the talks, Philipps dismissed their skills as peacemakers—

their sojourn was in his estimation "no more than a drunken inspiration"—and presciently observed that "if a rupture ensues, we shall not long be quiet here."[19]

War engulfed the Maine frontier in 1722 after Shute chose to launch a punitive expedition against Norridgewock. Two years earlier, Massachusetts, at its wits' end with Father Râle, had placed a hundred-pound bounty (which eventually rose to two hundred pounds) on his head rather than try to buy off the Indians with presents and gifts.[20] In March 1722, the Massachusetts Assembly funded three hundred rangers to find Râle and transport him to Boston for trial. When the rolls of those who were supposed to arrest Râle did not fill as quickly as hoped, the legislature provided added incentives—first sixty-pound and then hundred-pound bounties on Abenaki scalps—for rangers to take the field.[21] In the winter of 1721–22, several parties set out to abduct Râle at Norridgewock and collect Abenaki scalps, but all returned empty-handed. Finally, a group under Colonel Thomas Westbrook reached the mission just behind an Abenaki scout who warned Râle of the New Englanders' advance. Râle fled the mission with the church's chalice and crucifix in hand, just ahead of his pursuers. Frustrated in their mission to kidnap Râle, the rangers plundered the church and Râle's cabin and posted a note on the chapel door stating that they would return to kill the priest.[22]

Abenakis retaliated by sacking the Yankee settlement at Merrymeeting Bay near the mouth of the Kennebec River. Shute then declared them in rebellion—by his logic they were British subjects per the 1713 Treaty of Portsmouth and subsequent agreements made in 1717 and 1719. He proclaimed that "the said *Eastern* Indians, with the Confederates, [were] to be [treated as] Robbers, Traitors and Enemies to his Majesty King George."[23] As the Wabenaki Confederacy and the Kahnawakes from the Catholic Mohawk mission opposite Montreal prepared to rain a firestorm on the northern New England frontier, Vaudreuil undoubtedly congratulated himself on having another excellent opportunity to contain the British fall into his lap.

While the New Englanders aggressively pursued an offensive war against the Abenakis, Philipps proceeded slowly and cautiously. He met the Saint-Jean Maliseets and gave them the few presents he had on hand.[24] Believing that he had won their favor, and understanding that the most likely target of any Indian attack would be the fishery at Canso, he focused his attention there. He led most of his regiment to reinforce the small force under Lieutenant Colonel Lawrence Armstrong, who had been at Canso since the troubles of the summer of 1720. Doucett remained at Annapolis Royal, where he was to put Fort Anne on an improved defensive footing.[25] The British would wait for the Indians' next move.

War Clouds Spread over Nova Scotia

The Maliseets across the Bay of Fundy proved either unimpressed with or ungrateful for Philipps's gifts. They first robbed James Blinn's sloop *Ipswich* as it rode in Passamquoddy Bay. Another party captured Joseph Bissell's sloop *Dove.* Acadians, who clearly saw at least the dangers of antagonizing the British, if not their shared economic ties with the Yankees, saved Bissell and his crew's lives by hurrying them into the woods to protect them from the Indians. The Maliseets sailed the *Dove* to the fort on Saint George's River, where they attacked the garrison of New England militiamen under Colonel Westbrook. They took seven prisoners. Another group of Maliseets commandeered George Lynham's sloop *Prosperity* and sailed it to Minas, where the Acadians proved more than happy to purchase the goods the Indians were offering at reduced prices—at, according to Doucett, "bon marché." When William Winniett, a Huguenot officer of the occupying army who took an active role on the Nova Scotia Council, had the poor timing to arrive at Chignecto from Annapolis Royal to trade with the Acadians just as hostilities were commencing, the Indians—whether they were Maliseets, Mi'kmaq, or a combination of both remains unclear—seized his ship and goods as well. More ominously, the Maliseets who had seized the *Prosperity* used it to transport 45 warriors up the bay to join with 120 Mi'kmaq from Shubenacadie and Cape Sable in preparation to march against Annapolis Royal.[26]

The news of the Maliseet attacks on the trading vessels convinced Doucett that he faced an imminent Indian attack. He ordered twenty-two Mi'kmaw men, women, and children in Annapolis Royal arrested and held hostage. Flushed with that small success—one that greatly influenced the course of the war—Doucett spoiled for a fight. He determined to make a show of force to the Acadians and Indians; when several of the garrison's oxen wandered off and the Acadians reported that they could not retrieve them for fear of an Indian attack,

Doucette marched a company from the fort to round up the wayward animals. While the sortie to gather the oxen may have seemed like a minor detail, Doucett rightly judged it vitally important in demonstrating to the Indians that the British were "not such close prisoner's as they thought wee were."[27]

While the majority of Indians were pro-French or at least anti-British, the Acadians remained firmly committed to neutrality. Yet Doucett, after his dealings with the Acadians on the oath controversy, did not trust them. He fretted that the priests would convince the banlieu and outlying Acadians to join the French and Indians. In fact, he placed the blame for the entire crisis that was developing squarely upon the French; he thought the attacks on the traders were little more than French moves to control all the trade in the colony outside Annapolis Royal. He learned from some of the Indians' captives who had managed to escape from Minas that they had seen French traders from Île Royale supplying the Indians with trade goods. Despite all their pronouncements that they feared the Indians, the Acadians would seize the first opportunity, Doucett believed, to take arms against the British, all the while laying "their rebellion on them [the Indians]."[28]

As events unfolded in the summer of 1722, Doucett became more distrustful of the French. Winniett arrived from Minas in July carrying both Indian demands for ransom and a letter from Father Antoine Gaulin. The demand for ransom was expected, but the letter from the priest was more than Doucett could take. All his experiences with Gaulin—whom he scorned as "a half Indian, and a zealous bigot, with a capacity to follow the tenets of the Romish faith"[29]—had been difficult. Gaulin had been implicated in a failed plot to attack Annapolis Royal soon after the British occupation in 1710. His relations with the British had deteriorated since then. Although the priest was supposed to have presented himself to the council in Annapolis Royal, the "old" man—he was fifty-five in 1722 but remained "indefatigable in his traveling through the woods from place to place"[30]—ignored the British and went about his missionary activities as if British requirements were nothing more than a shout in a hurricane. The few times that Father Gaulin had consented even to acknowledge the Anglo-Americans' presence in the province, he had taken to lecturing them. Just the previous March, for example, he had informed Doucett that he was establishing a mission near the confluence of the Shubenacadie and Stenuak rivers. It was his highest duty, Gaulin wrote, to minister to "these savages, who recognise no master" and implied that it was simply too bad if the British did not want him to expand the missionary complex.[31] Doucett naturally saw the new mission as part of a French master plan to hem the British into Annapolis Royal. Castigating Gaulin on the grounds that his letter was "verrie late" in "requesting" permission to build the mission, Doucett called him to task. His openly disrespectful letter and failure to appear before Governor Philipps, Doucett said, "contradict[ed] the great zeal" that the missionary supposedly expressed for "public tranquility."[32]

When he received Gaulin's latest letter, Doucett was predisposed to find acrimony in it. He did not have to read too deeply. Gaulin protested that his Mi'kmaw flock had no hand in seizing the ships. Doucett judged that claim an outright lie; he knew that some of the plunder taken from the Anglo-American ships adorned the chapel in which Gaulin held mass for the Mi'kmaq. More important, when Winniett had asked Gaulin to intervene with the Mi'kmaq on his behalf, Gaulin chose not to and "replied that he was very sorry for my [Winniett's] misfortune, but was no way concerned with the savages," who were their own masters.[33]

Doucett's sole solace, and Gaulin's main concern, was that he still held twenty-two Mi'kmaw hostages. Gaulin could propagandize all he wanted, but the fact remained that Doucett occupied a strong position from which to influence Mi'kmaw behavior. Gaulin again addressed Doucett. Telling the lieutenant governor that Doucett's uncivil tone was the reason he had not responded to earlier letters, Gaulin related that the Mi'kmaq hoped Doucett would release the prisoners "whom you hold unjustly, since they have had no part in what has occurred." Should Doucett refuse, the Mi'kmaq threatened that they "would find means to take four of your people for every one of theirs." Gaulin then closed with assurances, which by this point surely seemed empty, that the Indians at his mission only desired peace, which in a closing jab he noted Doucett had been the "first to break."[34]

Doucett would not give up the Mi'kmaw hostages. They seemed Nova Scotia's only protection from a general Indian uprising while the Maine frontier had suffered "in a great Consternation and sum places in great Confusion" under the repeated blows of Indian raiders.[35] The war in fact was going badly for Massachusetts, and the possibility that warfare with the Indians might spill into Nova Scotia was very real.

Massachusetts proved unable to bring the Abenakis to submission. Despite the best efforts of its negotiators and the promise of a thousand-pound gift, the Iroquois League (as well as New York) remained on the sidelines to watch events unfold. It thus was up to volunteer companies of Yankee rangers to defend the frontier.[36] In the end, they could do little to stop the Indians who fell on the frontier settlements and put them to the torch. Even the larger garrisons sprinkled across the Maine and New Hampshire frontiers were not immune from attack. In August, five hundred to six hundred Indians laid siege to the blockhouse on the Saint George River—the easternmost New England outpost in Maine—for twelve days. Most ominously for the Anglo-Americans in Nova Scotia, the Indians communicated with the settlers through an unnamed French "fryar"—later identified as Father Étienne Lauverjat, who resided among the Penobscots and thereby implicating them in the war—who several times asked the garrison to surrender under a flag of truce and offered a prisoner exchange. After it became clear that they could not breach the fort's walls, and the garrison refused to negotiate with them, the besiegers withdrew. Still, they killed five Anglo-Americans. In September, Wabenaki Confederacy Indians and sauvages domicilés systematically laid waste to virtually all the Anglo-American settlements in the Lower Kennebec Valley.[37]

The only bright spot that Doucett could take from news of the Indian activities in Maine was that they remained there, and not in Nova Scotia. Of course, reports that a priest (Father Lauverjat) had been with the war party that laid siege to the Saint George River blockhouse concerned him: the as-yet-unidentified priest could just as easily convince the Indians to turn their attention on Annapolis Royal. A force of five hundred or six hundred Indians, with most of Philipps's regiment at Canso, might overwhelm the small garrison at Fort Anne. Yet for the time being, the Mi'kmaw captives proved an effective deterrent against a Maliseet-Mi'kmaw attack.

Anglo-American Engagement

Affairs in Nova Scotia soon took a turn in the Anglo-Americans' favor. Mi'kmaw "pirates" had seized several wayward shallops off the coast of Canso. Colonel Philipps, spurred to action, commissioned fishing captains John Elliot and John Robinson to use their schooners to patrol the waterways for Mi'kmaw raiders and, if possible, rescue the fishermen. Philipps also attached officers and men from the regiment to the ships and gave the New England volunteers arms, ammunition, and supplies. The Yankee volunteers under Elliot and a party of "marines" commanded by Ensign John Bradstreet attacked a schooner crewed by thirty-nine Indians. In the ensuing melee, Bradstreet led a boarding party that overwhelmed the Indians with hand grenades and disciplined fire. Rather than stand against the better-armed soldiers, most of the Indians jumped overboard, whereupon the soldiers systematically shot those who could not escape. Those who retreated to the ship's hold "were tore to pieces by Shells." The short engagement proved a one-sided affair: the Anglo-Americans had only one killed and several wounded (including Captain Elliot); only five Indians escaped with their lives, and all of them had been wounded. Captain Elliot retuned to Canso with fifteen rescued Yankee fishermen and six hundred quintals of fish. He also carried with him the heads of two Mi'kmaq whom the marines had killed, which Philipps placed on spikes as a grim warning to the Indians.[38]

The Yankee fishermen and Bradstreet's marines drove the Mi'kmaq from Canso. Captain Robinson and his men killed three Indians. Of course, there was concern that the Mi'kmaq might retaliate and kill the New England fishermen they still held, but Robinson "warned them to use them [the hostages] well" because Doucett held the captives at Annapolis Royal. Bradstreet's marines engaged the Mi'kmaq a second time. Although he was unable to kill any of them, he managed to reclaim three more fishing vessels. James Blinn negotiated a prisoner exchange between the Mi'kmaq and the Yankees at Canso and won the release of twenty-four fishermen. Soon after the exchange, Blinn kidnapped another three or four Indians at Cape Sable. Not to be left out, Captain Southack decided that he would raid Father Gaulin's mission at Antigonish. Finding six Mi'kmaq in canoes in the Gut of Canso, Southack killed one of them and took the other five as captives. Considering his design well met, he abandoned the advance on Antigonish and returned to Canso.[39] All told, the hostages at Annapolis Royal as well as the Anglo-American successes at Canso allowed the British to breathe more easily in the fall and winter of 1722.

With the colony then seeming secure, Philipps left Nova Scotia for London in the autumn of 1722; Armstrong, taking advantage of his commander's absence, followed suit. Although some might question the propriety of the governor's leaving his posting at such a crucial juncture, Doucett had proven himself a very capable officer and leader. Armstrong's departure, however, was inexcusable, especially because he spent the next several years arguing with Philipps and ingratiating himself into the duke of Newcastle's political/patronage machine. Still, with the two officers in London bombarding the Board of Trade with letters, requests, complaints, and other details, the board seemed to take a renewed interest in the colony.

The Board of Trade acknowledged Philipps's concern that he could do little to bring Nova Scotia under a firmer grasp with the regiment so thinly spread across the province. The only remedy, the board admitted, would be to "send a greater force for the protection of the Province."[40] Near the same time, it also considered taking a harder line toward the Acadians. Up to this point, while not entirely trusting the Acadians, the board had directed Philipps not to antagonize them. But in 1722, the board placed the blame for the Indian troubles squarely on the Acadians and their priests. "The French inhabitants remaining in Nova Scotia," one letter stated, "and the French missionaries who travel up and down the country are very industrious in instigating the Indian Natives to insult and plunder H.M. subjects." Perhaps, the board wondered, the Acadians "who have refus'd to take any oath of allegiance to H.M. may be compell'd to evacuate the Province."[41] For this first time since the initial days of the occupation, the British had broached the subject of forcing the Acadians to leave Nova Scotia. Of course, that would have been an unmitigated disaster, as Vetch and others had warned. Nonetheless, Anglo-American attitudes toward the Acadians were beginning to take their later shape.

Meanwhile, Massachusetts experienced little more than frustration in trying to strike at the Indians in early 1723. In February, Captain Johnson Harmon took 120 men on snowshoes and with twenty days' provisions to march up the Androscoggin River to destroy Abenaki villages but quickly found that the river ice was "wholly broke up & ye Designed march frustreat."[42] Harmon then divided his men into several parties and set them about the Maine wilderness looking for Indians to kill. They found none. Westbrook and his ranger company patrolled the coast between the outlet of the Kennebec River and Mount Desert Island (Île des Monts Déserts), where they found nothing "save Wigwams." Westbrook's company later pushed up the Penobscot River and burned Father Lauverjat's residence. The New Englanders were certainly disappointed, but perhaps also relieved, when they found the village abandoned.[43] The Indians had disappeared from the frontier.

Nova Scotia remained similarly calm through most of 1723, with only minor skirmishes disrupting the tranquility. In July, for instance, Mi'kmaq killed five fishermen at Canso.[44] Still, the Maliseets and Mi'kmaq generally acted as if they were content with aiding their allies in Maine. If the Abenakis' primary objective had been to halt the Anglo-American advance on the Maine frontier, the skirmishes in which they had received Maliseet and Mi'kmaw support had accomplished just that and pointed to a reinvigorated Wabenaki Confederacy. Few settlers dared to tread east of Casco Bay, and in Nova Scotia, the British remained bottled up in Annapolis Royal and at Canso.

The British wisely took advantage of the lull to build and improve their fortifications. Colonel Philipps funded the construction of a twelve-gun blockhouse at Canso, from which Bradstreet and his command stood watch over the fishery. With the necessity of improving Fort Anne for an attack, Doucett ordered Captain Paul Mascarene to make haste in improving the ramparts—a third of which had fallen—and preparing a detailed account of the ordnance stores in the armory. Mascarene's laborers worked quickly and efficiently, and it soon became clear that the Indians would not be able to breach the walls of the fort without cannon. When by early autumn no Indians had shown themselves outside Annapolis Royal, Mascarene extended the fort's main defenses. He ordered the old guardhouses outside the fort demolished and replaced with sturdy blockhouses that could serve as skirmishing positions.[45] If the Indians somehow managed to get their hands on some artillery, the new blockhouses would prevent them from getting close enough to the fort proper to do serious damage.

Indeed, as 1723 progressed and melded into 1724, observers on both sides of the Atlantic could see that the Indian troubles of the previous year had been a minor inconvenience and had not evolved into a general Indian uprising in Nova Scotia. Philipps nonetheless continued to lobby the Board of Trade. His investment in time appeared to have paid dividends when the board agreed to send settlers to Nova Scotia. The first thirteen years of the colony's history had seen it primarily occupied by the soldiers of the British garrison at Fort Anne, a few Yankee carpetbaggers from the faubourg, and the fishermen who worked at Canso on a seasonal basis. The Board of Trade welcomed Major Charles Davidson's scheme to settle four hundred families near Chebucto Bay on the eastern coast of the colony.[46] Philipps welcomed the news. He believed that from a fort at Canso, and with a reinforcement of manpower, he could control the Gut of Canso and interdict the French trade between Île Royale and Baie Verte and Chignecto. Any trade from Louisbourg would have to go the long way around Cape Breton Island rather than run under the eyes and guns of the British position at Canso. He then proposed building a fort on the Isthmus of Chignecto that would cut off all Acadian-Indian-French trade and commerce between New France and Nova Scotia.[47] With the Acadians and Indians deprived of French trade goods, they would have to turn to Annapolis Royal and the settlement at Chebucto Bay.

Yet the perennial problem of lack of funds and manpower retarded the execution of Philipps's design. He had to spend money elsewhere that should have been dedicated to blockhouses at either Minas or Chignecto. In March 1724, for example, he had to ask the Board of Trade to reimburse him for his substantial out-of-pocket expenses (£2,000) in fitting out the colony's schooner, the *William Augustus.* Despite earlier promises, the Admiralty refused to assign a station ship to Annapolis Royal as it had at Newfoundland, Massachusetts, New York, and Virginia. The commander of the navy's station ship at Newfoundland had to pull double duty and occasionally would sail to Nova Scotia waters to help his colleagues. In 1723, the *Soleby* had patrolled off Nova Scotia, and in 1724 the commander of the *Ludlow Castle* agreed to help with the Mi'kmaq.[48] Still, Philipps knew that his colony needed its own ship. But on the isolated frontier that was Nova Scotia, outfitting a schooner for naval operations was no small or inexpensive task. Despite a Board of Trade request to the treasury to reimburse Philipps, no monies were forthcoming.[49]

The funds that Philipps devoted to *William Augustus* proved money well spent. Captain Southack, its skipper, used it to patrol the fishery for Indian attacks and keep open a line of communication between Canso and Annapolis Royal. Philipps had wanted the

William Augustus to sail to Chebucto Bay and survey sites for settlements. But as was the case with so many things in Nova Scotia, the schooner could not be spared for nonmilitary activities. Perhaps sensing that an opportunity to make real changes in the management of Nova Scotia had slipped through his hands, Philipps, still in London, lashed out. He complained that he could not "think that Province to be in any way of being settled[,] it being not reasonable to imagine that any persons of condition will venture their lives and effects upon so precarious a footing."[50]

Matters looked troubling from Doucett's perspective in Fort Anne as well. The Abenakis had recommenced their raids and compelled Lieutenant Governor William Dummer of Massachusetts to order the evacuation of the Maine frontier. In Nova Scotia, Mi'kmaq had killed two British soldiers outside Annapolis Royal and burned several homes in the faubourg. Doucett responded by executing one of the Mi'kmaw captives.[51] It looked as if Maine and Nova Scotia had fallen into an inconclusive Indian war in which the Indians attacked in the spring, the British retaliated, and by the late fall and through the winter both sides waited for the action of the next season.

For a brief moment, however, the Yankees seemed to have won the war on the Maine frontier. In July 1724, a hundred Massachusetts rangers under Captains Johnson Harmon and Jeremiah Moulton, with three Mohawk mercenaries as scouts, marched on Norridgewock to assassinate Father Râle and destroy the settlement. The raid was a success: Râle died in the opening moments of the battle; one of the Abenakis' leading war chiefs, Mog (Heracouansit), was killed; and the rangers massacred nearly two dozen women and children. The survivors fled to Saint-François and Bécancour, and Massachusetts welcomed the news as a crushing blow inflicted on the Abenakis.[52]

The destruction of Norridgewock worried Vaudreuil. The French could expect the Wabenaki Confederacy to fight only until it could make the best peace possible with the Anglo-Americans. Perhaps after the leveling of Norridgewock and the death of Râle the Kennebecs would cut their losses and seek a return to the status quo antebellum with the Anglo-Americans. It would have been understandable if they had lost their will to fight.

Such was not the case, however. In October 1724, Vaudreuil reported to the Ministry of Marine that the death of Father Râle "n'a pas découragé" the Kennebecs; perhaps the subsidy of two thousand pounds that he gave them helped ameliorate their grief. The Kennebecs, at least, seemed to redouble their commitment to opposing the British.[53] New Englanders' inability to read the currents of events further discredited pro-peace factions that were emerging among the Abenakis. On December 10, 1724, Captain John Lovewell and his company of rangers, acting under the Massachusetts Assembly's promise of one hundred pounds for each Indian scalp, killed two Abenakis. In February, Lovewell's men killed another ten Indians near Lake Winnipesauke, further angering the Western Abenakis of New Hampshire. In the spring of the next year, Lovewell marched against the Pigwacket band of Abenakis, only to meet his end in an ambush near Saco (now Lovewell's) Pond. Although scalping and scalp bounties long had been a foundation of Anglo-Americans' way of war, Lovewell's actions had transformed the war into an intractable blood feud between New England and the various bands of the Abenakis.[54]

The Maliseets came to the assistance of their Abenaki allies and struck again at the New England frontier. In the summer, the French had heard that the Maliseets were inclined to make a formal peace with the British, but after the destruction of Norridgewock, they again raised the hatchet. They petitioned Vaudreuil to repair their arms and resupply them with powder and ball. Maliseet war parties then set out for the Maine frontier, where they burned five or six homesteads, killed eight or ten settlers, took some prisoners, and drove the remaining settlers into their blockhouses.[55]

With their success on the Maine frontier, the Maliseets considered expanding the war into Nova Scotia. The Maliseets certainly had to wonder how long the British would remain vulnerable. Construction of the blockhouse at Canso had changed the balance of power, and the Mi'kmaq skirmishes with Bradstreet's marines had gone badly. Perhaps more important, by early 1725, the Maine frontier had become a no-man's land; few targets remained for the Maliseets who wanted to make names for themselves as warriors. For the Maliseets who hoped to profit materially from this war, Nova Scotia offered better pickings. The time had come for them to act—they informed Vaudreuil that they and the Mi'kmaq would like to attack Canso.[56]

Over the course of the winter of 1724–25, rumors circulated among the British that the Acadians had supplied the Indians with war goods. Credible intelligence reached Annapolis Royal that two Acadians, Guillaume Godet and Paul Petitpas (whose father, Charles Petitpas, had collaborated with the British), had piloted and transported Indian warriors to Canso and had supplied the Mi'kmaq with one hundred pounds of powder and balls as well as eight or nine muskets.[57]

Lawrence Armstrong, having returned to Nova Scotia with an appointment as lieutenant governor, proposed to prevent Indian attacks by interdicting Acadian and French support for the Maliseets and Mi'kmaq. Without the manpower or means to blockade the colony, Armstrong directed Hibbert Newton, custom collector for the colony, and John Bradstreet to travel to Île Royale to demand that Governor Saint-Ovide stop supplying the Indians with war goods. Calling Saint-Ovide to task for the "many irregularitys clandestinely transacted by some of the people in your Government in order to disturb and annoy H.M subjects, by entertaining, prompting and encouraging the Indians to commit their barbarous and cowardly hostilities, in supporting them with presents and continual supplies of ammunition," Armstrong warned that he would take all French goods, ships, and traders in Nova Scotia as prizes of war, except for those the British authorized to trade in the province.[58]

Despite threatening Saint-Ovide with what amounted to essentially a declaration of war, Newton and Bradstreet also were to enlist the governor as a peace intermediary between the British and the Indians. The Nova Scotia Council had concurred with Armstrong that the primary condition of peace must be Indian reparations for the ships they had seized. In return for that admittance of culpability, the British would continue to allow the Indians to practice their Catholic faith, so long as they had among them only priests whom the council approved. Saint-Ovide was to pass on those terms to the Indians as proof that the British were "ready to receive their proposals." Of course, the diplomatic dance that Newton and Bradstreet were to undertake would be tricky. Armstrong directed that they were to give the overtures with care, "so that it may not appear that we [the British] are suing for peace."[59] A firm stand was the only kind that Lawrence Armstrong knew how to take.

Armstrong certainly did not lack for nerve. Saint-Ovide, who by then had a decade of experience in dealing with British demands and accusations, proved a skilled diplomat. Conceding that trading war stores to the Indians was forbidden, he noted that he was sure no French subjects had taken powder or lead to the Maliseets or Mi'kmaq. To sooth Armstrong's raw feelings, he promised to punish any Frenchman who armed the Indians and would direct that anyone who went to Nova Scotia to purchase cattle from the Acadians—a direct violation of British law in itself, because the only authorized trade house in the colony was at Annapolis Royal—would need to pass through Canso, where the British could search them for arms and ammunition. On the subject of giving presents to the Indians, Saint-Ovide noted that it was upon orders from France, not him, that the Indians received gifts each year. "The only way to redress it," Newton and Bradstreet reported the governor as saying, "was for the English government at home to represent the matter to that of France."[60] Last, concerning the prospect of peace with the Indians, Saint-Ovide said that he recently had spoken with the Mi'kmaw chiefs of Minas, Cobequid, Pisiquid, Shubenacadie, and Miramichi.

The question became whether Armstrong would see the glass as half full or half empty. At a time when the British had not heard from the Indians in nearly two years, Saint-Ovide on Île Royale was in regular contact with them, including the chiefs from as far away as present-day New Brunswick. Saint-Ovide then related that although the Mi'kmaq seemed amenable to peace, the Maliseets "would not so readily come into it, as being a people inured to war." If it would make the British feel better, however, he would speak to the Indians the next July, which was "the proper time to assemble the chiefs" (and eleven months in the future), "to continue for the best."[61]

Anglo-Indian Diplomacy to End the War

Certain that the French would do little to defuse the hostilities, the British held only the small hope that if Massachusetts could come to peace on its frontier, peace would spread to Nova Scotia. News had arrived that Vaudreuil had passed away; there was the possibility that his replacement as governor-general, Charles de Beauharnois de La Boische, marquis de Beauharnois, would look to unload the burden of supporting a clandestine war. In April, Massachusetts had sent a delegation to Montreal to demand that the French stop outfitting Indian war parties. In observing that by giving the Indians weapons and munitions the French had violated the Treaty of Utrecht, they made a less than subtle threat. Of course, at this stage in the conflict, Great Britain surely would not have gone to war with France over a few settlements in the Maine backcountry. Yet even the miniscule risk of war between New England and New France led Beauharnois to believe that the time had come to pull back from support of the Abenakis.

It was becoming increasingly difficult for the French to keep the Abenakis united. The Penobscots had come to realize that they could not defeat the Yankees without direct military support from New France, and in the summer of 1725 they sent a wampum belt calling for peace with the British to the Indians at Saint-Françoise. Although the Saint-Françoise Abenakis refused to take hold of the belt, the Penobscots pushed ahead with peace talks without them. If the Penobscots bowed out of the war, sooner or later the other Abenakis would, too, followed by the Maliseets and the Mi'kmaq. Thus, Louis XV's commendation to encourage Father Gaulin's efforts to foment war among the Mi'kmaq, actions that he deemed "most favorable," were overcome by events. The Ministry of Marine's decision to send Saint-Ovide specific orders to aid the Maliseets because they were "disposed to continue the war" similarly had become moot since the Penobscot Abenakis planned to sit down and talk peace with Massachusetts.[62]

The authorities in Nova Scotia watched the developing Yankee-Indian peace talks closely. Captain Paul Mascarene traveled to Boston to observe the Penobscot-Massachusetts negotiations.[63] In July and August and again in November and December 1725, he watched Massachusetts representatives and Penobscots led by Sauguaaram (Loron) hammer out the framework for a peace among the colonies and the eastern Indians. Most important for Nova Scotia, despite a Mi'kmaw raid on Canso in the summer that saw them take ten shallops, the Maliseets and Mi'kmaq who endorsed the treaty with New Englanders promised to travel to Annapolis Royal in the spring of 1726 to formalize their own treaty with John Doucett.[64]

Although the New Englanders had not won an overwhelming victory against the Abenakis but had merely survived the war and had grown as tired of it as the Indians had, they managed to gain and solidify their position vis-à-vis the Indians. The Yankees unfairly placed the blame for the war at the Indians' feet by making them acknowledge that they were "now sensible of the miseries and troubles they have involved themselves in." The Indians promised to "make our Submission unto" King George and "hold and maintain firm and constant Amity and Friendship with all the English, and will never confederate or combine with any other nation to their prejudice." The New Englanders again promised the Abenakis rights to hunt, fish, and take fowl as ratified in the 1713 Portsmouth treaty, while the Indians reiterated the terms of 1693 and 1713 treaties that gave British subjects rights to "peaceably and quietly enter upon, Improve, and forever enjoy" settlements, lands, and properties in Maine. Henceforth, Massachusetts would regulate all trade between the British and Abenakis. Of course, the Indian leaders had long wanted a regulated trade with the Anglo-Americans to restrain the trade in alcohol that was devastating their communities, but the assumption was that the Yankees and Britons would manipulate the trade to their, and not the Indians', advantage. Of greater consequence, it would be up to Sauguaaram and his confederates to enforce the provision of the treaty among the other Abenakis, to reduce them to reason should any of them want to continue the war against the British.[65]

Some might want to suggest that New Englanders pulled the wool over Sauguaaram's eyes at the treaty negotiations. This suggestion, however, is insulting to Indians in its implication that they could not understand the terms and nuances to which they had agreed; moreover, three oath-sworn interpreters—John Gyles, Samuel Jordan, and Joseph Baries—distinctly read and interpreted the terms of the treaty. Among the interpreters, John Gyles was adequately conversant in the nuances of Abenaki dialects. At the start of King William's War, when he was ten years old, Abenakis took him captive and moved him from village to village. When he was sixteen, his Abenaki captors sold him to a French priest who worked among the Maliseets of the Saint Lawrence River valley. Gyles stayed with the French priest and the Maliseets for four years and at the end of the war was repatriated to Massachusetts. He subsequently became one of the colony's leading authorities on the eastern Indians. The Penobscots greatly trusted him; following the war, they specifically asked that Gyles remain as commander of the fort near Saint George's River.[66]

What is more likely than that Sauguaaram allowed himself to be bamboozled is that he made a shrewd move to win more time and concessions from both pro-war Abenakis and the war-weary New

Englanders. After Father Lauverjat stressed that according to the treaty's final provision Sauguaaram's followers were to compel the other Abenakis to cease hostilities, Sauguaaram had his excuse and repudiated the treaty. The Penobscots' annulment of the treaty cut both ways. The New Englanders would see their much-sought-after peace slip away, while the pro-war Abenakis would see that although Sauguaaram had reneged on the treaty, the wall of Abenaki unity was crumbling. The Yankees, no doubt angered by more Jesuitical interference in their affairs with the eastern Indians, nonetheless opened a second round of talks with all the Abenaki factions. In the ensuing treaty of 1727, the New Englanders reinforced some and conceded other points from the 1725 treaty. The second treaty, with all the Abenakis, guaranteed Indian rights to their lands, use of those lands in perpetuity, and the right to have Catholic priests among them.[67] Sauguaaram's gambit for time had taken much of the pain out of the initial treaty.

The Maliseets and Mi'kmaq had no need for a ploy like Sauguaaram's. They received immediate satisfaction in their negotiations with the British in Nova Scotia in 1726. The agreement they signed favored them greatly. When the Maliseets and Mi'kmaq met with Armstrong to finalize the specifics of their treaty at Annapolis Royal in the summer, they made sure to make it clear that the British had not defeated them. In addition to the traditional gifts that came with the protocols of reciprocity, the Maliseets and Mi'kmaq demanded that the British sweeten the deal. Armstrong complained that he had to raise an additional credit of three hundred to four hundred pounds "to make those savages easey in firmly keeping the peace and if possible to resume their furr trade for H.M. interest."[68] Yet in return for that largesse, the Maliseets and Mi'kmaq gave up little. Unlike the Maine Indians, the Maliseets and Mi'kmaq refused to declare themselves in submission to the British monarchy. Although they acknowledged King George's "jurisdiction and dominion over the territories of the said Province of Nova Scotia or Accadie," they agreed only to make "submission to His said Majesty in as same a manner as we have formerly done to the Most Christian King [of France]."[69] Of course, the phrasing "jurisdiction and dominion over the territories" was only so many words to the Indians, as they had no comparable syntax for landownership. More important, they would have felt no need to have the British try to explain those terms to them. There would have been enough confusion in the translation of the treaty from English to French to Mi'kmawi'simk without complicating the mix over abstractions such as "dominion" and "sovereignty." Moreover, for years, the French officials had told the British that the Indians were French allies and as such were neither their subjects nor auxiliaries. Indeed, as one historian has stated, the "idea that he [the French king] had any claim on their lands, or that they owed him any more allegiance than they owed their own chiefs, was foreign to them."[70] While the British viewed such pronouncements as empty rhetoric, both the Indians and the French believed that the Indians were in fact independent entities. When the Maliseets and Mi'kmaq transferred their relationship of friendship (rather than subservience) with the French to the British, they in fact were giving the British very little. The treaty listed terms to which equals, not superiors and inferiors, could subscribe: the Indians promised to refrain from molesting British subjects; to pay restitution for robberies; to return British deserters to the officers of the garrisons; and in cases of quarrel between them and the British, to first seek redress in British law.[71]

No wonder then that Doucett found the Indians "extreamly well pleas'd with the peace."[72] Besides the three hundred pounds in presents and the lenient terms of the treaty, Doucett, seeing how ephemeral New England's peace had been, signed an additional protocol with the Indians. In return for the Maliseet and Mi'kmaw leaders' signatures or marks, Doucett further promised protection and friendship to the Indians, "who shall not be molested in their planting and hunting." As an added bonus, Doucett guaranteed the Indians' right to practice their Roman Catholic faith under the tutelage of priests, as long as the missionaries first asked British permission to live among them.[73]

The treaty of 1726, and a subsequent one in 1728 with the rivière Saint-John Maliseets that reaffirmed it, was as much an Indian victory as a British one. The Maliseet-Mi'kmaw War, albeit coinciding with the special circumstances of Father Râle's War, had forced British agents on the far reaches of the empire into acknowledging the Indians' essential right to possess their lands. Mascarene's Treaty, as the agreement between the Indians and British in Nova Scotia came to be called, was hardly a peace imposed.

While the terms of Mascarene's Treaty at first glance may seem only to have given concessions to the Maliseet and the Mi'kmaq, the British nonetheless had taken a large step toward their goal of strengthening dominion over Nova Scotia. For only a handful of deaths, relatively little disruption of the fishing operations at Canso, and several hundred pounds' worth of presents, four major benefits flowed from the treaty.

First, it dissipated the immediate threat of an Indian war. Although violence sporadically engulfed the Maine frontier for another year after 1726, Nova Scotia had forged a peace that Maliseets and Mi'kmaq eagerly accepted, in large part because it was on terms favorable to them. The British never fully trusted the Indians (and vice versa), but they had made peace, not conflict, their normative state of relations. After 1726, they never again faced widespread Maliseet resistance.

Second, the British had made huge strides in weaning the Indians from French support. At the peace negotiations, it must have been abundantly clear that the British officers at Annapolis Royal had become players in the Indians' trade network with the Europeans. In that sense, Mascarene's Treaty greatly complicated Maliseet and Mi'kmaw dealings with the French. The Indians had proven themselves active participants—rational actors—in managing a complicated French-Indian alliance. After 1726 they would have to navigate a more difficult course of trade relationships with not only the French but also the British and New Englanders.

Third, and of far-reaching importance, the British had in effect absorbed the Maliseets and Mi'kmaq into their empire. Prior to the war, the Maliseets and Mi'kmaq "continued to live in their world, outside the sight of European officials."[74] The seventy-seven Indians who signed their names to Mascarene's Treaty, however, had negotiated their way from the edges to the center of the emerging British Empire in Nova Scotia. The war was an initial step toward resolving the questions of Maliseet and Mi'kmaw sovereignty over the lands of Acadia. The British, in return for peace, essentially afforded the Indians the same rights that the Acadians had received in the Treaty of Utrecht. If the Acadians, in agreeing to live under British laws on British territory, were de facto if not de jure subjects of the empire, so too were the Mi'kmaq and Maliseets. It mattered not that the Maliseets and Mi'kmaq did not conceive individual landownership in the same terms the British did. Thereafter, the British considered the

Mi'kmaq and Maliseets as part of a composite empire, and the Indians in return would "have patterns of authority, reciprocity, obligation, custom, and privileges that their members used within the imperial framework."[75]

Last, and most important, by nipping a long-term war with Maliseets and Mi'kmaq in the bud before it could fully bloom, the British freed themselves to concentrate on other matters in Nova Scotia. Indeed, the Maliseets and Mi'kmaq had stood as only one part of a larger problem presented by an Acadian-Indian-French triad of opposition. With the option of placing Indian issues on the back burner, the British could focus on either the French or the Acadians. With the Crowns of Great Britain and France both holding firm to the Thirty Years' Peace initiated at Utrecht, Anglo-Americans in Nova Scotia could look anew at the Acadians.

3

Anglo-Americans and Acadians in Nova Scotia, 1720–1744

When Richard Philipps arrived in Nova Scotia in the spring of 1720, he undoubtedly expected trouble with the Acadians. The preceding decade of British rule had witnessed the Acadians generally treating Anglo-American claims to dominion with if not derision then apathy. The central point of contention in British-Acadian relations remained the oath of allegiance. A string of British officials had attempted to extract an oath from the Acadians, but other than handfuls of banlieu Acadians who lived directly under the nose of the garrison at Fort Anne, none had agreed to subscribe. The new governor's arrival changed none of that.

For ten years, the Acadians steadfastly had refused to swear an oath on anything but their terms. They, much more than the British, continued to define the parameters of the British-Acadian relationship in Nova Scotia throughout the 1720s and 1730s. By 1730 they had set the boundaries of their relationship with the Anglo-Americans, in which they became "the French Neutrals." The path and development of those relations points to an important aspect of the development of the British Empire. Their give-and-take with the Acadians on the oath issue suggests the extent to which Britons were willing to negotiate the terms of empire with peoples they supposedly had conquered. In their golden age, the period to which they would look after the grand dérangement, the Acadians flourished politically, socially, culturally, and economically.[1] The British—supposed overlords of Nova Scotia—proved unable to compel the Acadians to do more than merely tolerate the British presence among them.

Acadian forms of resistance in the 1720s and 1730s, and British reaction to them, are the focus of this chapter, which shows how individual personalities, to a much greater extent than policies, shaped the course of Anglo-Acadian relations on the Nova Scotia frontier. By the end of the first third of the eighteenth century, the British Empire in Nova Scotia was above all a product of negotiation, and its successes and failures ultimately depended on the personal character and qualities of the British governors—Richard Philipps, Lawrence Armstrong, and Paul Mascarene. For the Acadians, the negotiations ushered in their golden age, in which they forged what at the time seemed a lasting modus vivendi with the Anglo-Americans. By 1744, few Acadians would have conceived the grand dérangement as possible.

Philipps's First Administration

By 1720, nothing had changed since John Doucett asked the Acadians to swear loyalty to King George three years earlier. The Acadians from Minas and Chignecto presented Doucett with a list of reasons why they would not take an oath then or in the future.[2] When news reached them that Philipps—whom they figured would present them with an oath—had arrived in the colony, the Acadians turned to Governor Saint-Ovide on Île Royale. Fearing that Philipps would revert to previous British policy and demand that they vacate the province if they continued to refuse to swear allegiance to the British monarchy, the Acadians disingenuously reminded Saint-Ovide that they had "preserved the purest sentiments of fidelity to our invincible monarch" and requested that he send them an officer "of note and experience" to serve as their spokesman with the British.[3]

Although Saint-Ovide demurred to wade too deeply, or publicly, into the brewing British-Acadian contest over the oath, the Acadians were not totally without French support. Three days after Philipps's arrival at Annapolis Royal, the Recollet priest Justinien Durand appeared at the head of 150 "lusty young men (as if he meant to appear formidable)." When Philipps asked him why the Acadians had refused to take an oath, Durand told the governor that his parishioners had unanimously committed to remain subjects of France and would soon leave for Île Royale. Moreover, the priest said, the Acadians feared the Indians. Philipps was astute enough to see that debating with Durand would get him nowhere. "Arguments," he told the Board of Trade, "prevailed little without a power of enforcing: for the case is thus, they [the Acadians] find themselves for several years the only Inhabitants of a large Country, except the small Garrison of this place, which having been so much neglected they make no account of, and began to think they had as much right here as any other."[4]

The Acadians of Minas and Chignecto were, like their banlieu relatives, similarly uncooperative. Philipps dispatched James Blinn to inform them that he had arrived and they were to send deputies, their leading citizens who would receive instructions and direction from the newly formed colonial council.[5] The deputies, however, soon reported that they could not honor Philipps's request to take an oath. They repeated the excuses that other Acadians had given to Doucett, namely, that they feared "the fury of the savages" who "watched them everyday." They also claimed that Governor Nicholson had given them the option of remaining French subjects if they so chose. That was in fact true but lacked an important detail: Nicholson had allowed them to decide for themselves whether they wanted to stay French subjects, but those who did would have to leave the province within one year. To preempt Philipps when he would remind them of Nicholson's conditions, the deputies claimed that they had not emigrated because they had found no one to purchase their lands. Queen Anne had promised them title to their farms, as well as a valuation of the land that British officials had failed to make. The Acadians rhetorically asked Philipps if he expected them to up and leave their homes and receive nothing in return.[6]

His initial experiences with the banlieu and outlying Acadians convinced Philipps that he would have to negotiate the terms of an oath. There was much more at stake in Nova Scotia than soothing British pride over the Acadians' refusal to acknowledge King George publicly as their monarch. The governor, who was first and foremost a soldier, feared that relations between Great Britain and France could devolve into war at any time, and his men in Fort Anne remained vulnerable to attack from Canada. Alienating the Acadians would do little more than exacerbate that vulnerability. Because he feared that if the Acadians were "allowed to remain on this footing, they may be obedient so long as the two Crowns are in alliance, but in case of a rupture they would be enemies,"[7] Philipps identified several measures that offered the promise of defusing at least the local Acadian threat.

First, he would try to interdict communications between the Acadians and the French on Île Royale and in New France. Key to that program would be developing close relationships between the Acadians and the garrison. As such, Paul Mascarene, a Huguenot, became the conduit through which British communication reached the Acadians. Although the earlier plan to reward with land grants those Britons who married Indian women had drawn few soldiers or Indians, some of the men of the garrison had forged close ties to Acadian women. William Winniett, for example, had married Marie-Madeleine Maisonnat, daughter of Acadian privateer Pierre Maisonnat and Acadian Madeleine Bourg. Within the tight-knit Acadian community, Winniett's marriage to Marie-Madeleine gave him connections with her relatives, including the influential (at least among the Acadians) Prudent Robichaud.[8] The most important of the unions, from a military perspective, was the marriage of Lieutenant Edmond Bradstreet to Agathe de Sainte-Étienne de La Tour. La Tour was the granddaughter of Charles de Sainte-Étienne de La Tour, one of the founders of Port Royal, and her family name still carried a great deal of weight within the Acadian community.[9] Although her fellow Acadians increasingly came to identify Agathe as a British collaborator, probably because she converted to Protestantism and the British recognized her as the sole heir to the La Tour lands in Nova Scotia, her marriage to Lieutenant Bradstreet nonetheless opened a door to Acadian society. More important for the long-term history of British-Acadian relations, Edmond and Agathe had two sons, Simon and Jean-Baptiste, or John. John Bradstreet, not to be confused with his older cousin of the same name, became one of the most important figures in Nova Scotia during King George's War. In the 1740s, he proved a valuable cultural intermediary, based on his kin relations and his extensive network of trade with the Acadians, on the Nova Scotia frontier.[10]

Of course, affairs of the heart take time to develop, so Philipps suggested that the Board of Trade compel the French—he did not say how—to recall the priests currently in Nova Scotia and replace them with other, more tractable ones.[11] As long as hostile priests remained among the Acadians, the British would lose the contest for the hearts and minds of the local population. Yet too abrupt of a move against them, such as arresting or banishing them from the colony, would certainly alienate the Acadians, as well as being a direct violation of the treaty of Utrecht. Thus, Philipps personally could do little against the priests and needed the support of the home government. In the interim, each mass offered a meeting in which the priests, if they chose, could preach against the British. Controlling the church services was impossible. Even knowing what the priests said at mass was difficult, since they and the Acadians would have seen British attendance as an attempt to spy. Indeed, the British had to walk a very fine line in dealing with the priests, a line that they managed with only mixed success.

Finally, regarding the Acadians as a whole, Philipps directed that his men were to avoid any action that might anger them. Although he doubted that they would openly take arms against him, he remained concerned that they could emigrate and, on their way out of the colony, sabotage the dykes. But taking advantage of what he saw as their fear of the Mi'kmaq and Maliseets, he thought he could lure them into a promise to take up arms against the Indians if he allowed them to remain neutral in any Anglo-French conflict. The Acadians had asked for the same concession from Doucett in 1717. Philipps saw no reason not to give it to them. The Acadians could "live quietly and pleasantly in their houses, not to harbor or give any manner of assistance to any of the King's enemys," he wrote. In return, he would confer full title to their lands, the thing he believed they most wanted from the British.[12]

In trying to find a middle ground in Anglo-Acadian relations, Philipps had framed the terms of what in time would become known as the Convention of 1730, after which the British would know the Acadians as the "French Neutrals." But before the specifics of that Anglo-Acadian agreement could be reached, the British had to deal with Father Râle's and the Maliseet-Mi'kmaw wars. It took them until 1726 to quash the troubles with the Indians of Nova Scotia, and then they were successful only through bargaining and negotiation.

The Beginnings of Compromise

John Doucett and Lawrence Armstrong, after Philipps returned to London in 1722, generally adopted the governor's program for dealing with the Acadians. Although Armstrong implicated the two Acadians—Godet and Petitpas—in aiding the Mi'kmaq, the locals had for the most part stood aloof of the Indian war. Indeed, they remained quiet and went about their business, which meant supplying cattle and grain to the French garrison at Île Royale in open and flagrant violation of British law. Still, the Acadians' behavior was not so egregious, especially when an Indian war threatened, as to compel Doucett or Armstrong to take direct military action against them.

Avoiding conflict with the Acadians during the Indian war paid large dividends for the British in the fall of 1726. In the wake of Mascarene's Treaty, the fact that the Indians would no longer serve as France's cudgel became clear. Indeed, the Maliseets and Mi'kmaq had in effect pulled away from the French and were beginning to lean toward the British. Perhaps the Acadians thought it was time for them to make a similar move. Of course, they would not abruptly and fully break from the French, but with the wave of accommodation that seemed to be washing over Nova Scotia, maybe they could extract favorable terms from the British.

In September 1726, the banlieu deputies met with Lieutenant Governor Armstrong at Annapolis Royal. The Acadians were there supposedly to take the oath of allegiance—for "their own and children's future advantages," as Armstrong blustered.[13] He may have felt the need to appear as if he were fully in charge. The troubles with the Indians were a recent memory, and perhaps more important, Doucett, the British officer with whom the Acadians mostly had dealt, recently had died. Whatever the case, in dealing with a new lieutenant governor, the Acadians saw an opening to request more than the protection of their properties and religion. Upon translation of the oath into French, the deputies asked that "a clause whereby they may not be obliged to carry arms might be inserted" so that they would not have to fight for the British.[14] One can only assume that Armstrong paused to consider the implications of the Acadians' request. He knew that Philipps had considered offering them neutrality, and everyone could see that the British had treated them as neutrals during the Indian war. Armstrong had to act quickly so as not lose face with the Acadians or, worse, appear indecisive. His answer was as good as could have been expected, especially coming from the difficult position in which he found himself. He answered that he would grant the Acadians neutral status because under the laws of Great Britain, Roman Catholics were forbidden from serving in the army, although the law was rarely enforced. "His Majesty having so many faithful Protestant subjects first to provide for," Armstrong related to the members of the council, "and that all that His Majesty required of them was to be faithful subjects not to join with any enemy, but for their own interest to discover all traitorous and evil designs," he would allow the clause to be written in the margin of the French translation. The banlieu Acadians then "took and subscribed the same both in French and English."[15]

In the following weeks and months, Armstrong must have questioned whether conceding the neutrality point had been the proper thing to do. Significantly, he chose not to inform the imperial bureaucracy, either the Board of Trade or the secretary of state, that he had secured an oath of allegiance from the banlieu Acadians. Because the issue of the oath remained the most significant point of contention between the Acadians and the British in Nova Scotia, surely Armstrong, a tiny cog in Newcastle's patronage machine, would have reported his negotiations with the Acadians if he thought it would have boosted his standing in the duke's eyes. More telling, after securing the oath from the banlieu Acadians, Armstrong made no further mention of the neutrality clause in his discussions with the colony's other Acadians. When by the spring of 1727 the deputies of Minas and Chignecto had yet to present themselves before the council and take the oath, he sent Captain Joseph Bennett and Ensign Erasmus James Philipps (possibly Governor Philipps's nephew) to the distant villages to administer the oath. Bennett and Philipps were to remind the Acadians that it was their duty to take the oath because King George had gave them "the Enjoyment not Only of your Estates but Religion." They were to say nothing of neutrality, however, and instead pass on the lieutenant governor's stern warning that in case they did not comply, the Acadians had none but themselves to blame for "the Consequence of so much Disrespect and Disobedience."[16] In the end, Ensign Philipps reported, the inhabitants of Beaubassin flatly refused to take any oath but to the "bon Roy du France." Their priest, Joseph

Ignâce, had openly counseled them against promising anything to the British.[17]

Armstrong, more a reactionary than a forward-thinking administrator, thereupon reverted to the heavy-handed approach. In July, in an empty gesture that was mere bravado, he again forbade all trade between Anglo-Americans and those Acadians who had not taken the oath.[18] The outlying Acadians naturally continued to trade with the Indians and the French—a paper decree from Annapolis Royal would not have changed the trading patterns that had held for decades. One could, of course, see Armstrong's proclamation as an attempt to divide and rule. Indeed, after the few Acadians who lived on Cape Sable, distant from the centers of French-Acadian influence across the Bay of Fundy or at Louisbourg, agreed to take the lieutenant governor's oath, Armstrong revoked all trading and fishing prohibitions on them, provided that they avoided the area of Minas Basin "during the time of the disobedience of the inhabitants of those parts."[19] That change in policy, however, did nothing to encourage the Minas and Chignecto Acadians.

Developments in the metropolis compelled Armstrong to press the oath issue even more. In the immediate wake of Bennett's and Philipps's failed mission up the Bay of Fundy, the colonial council had begun to search for a compromise position with the Acadians and recommended that Armstrong pull back from confronting the Acadians. Cajoling them had gotten the British nowhere and in fact had irritated and alienated them. The council encouraged Armstrong to write the Acadians a "Civil letter to invite the principal men among them hither in order to reason with them on their undutiful behavior."[20] The outlying Acadians simply ignored the request for a meeting. Then Armstrong and the council received word that King George I had died and his son had taken the throne. Officers and subjects across the empire therefore would be required to take an oath of allegiance to the new monarch. Armstrong had little choice but to demand that the Acadians subscribe to an oath.

It was, however, up to him to decide how the oath read. Here was an opportunity for compromise. Yet the oath that Armstrong and the council developed was a throwback to the old oaths that was hardly likely to gain Acadian acceptance. Not only did it say nothing of neutrality, but it failed to address the Acadians' concerns about their religion or property. Although the council acknowledged that a Roman Catholic would have a difficult time taking any oath that did not allow him the free practice of his religion, Armstrong and his advisors consciously chose to focus on only the temporal. While it is unlikely that they hoped to "pass one by" the Acadians, they more likely expected the Acadians to follow the intent of Matthew 22:21 and "give back to Caesar the things that are Caesar's, and to God the things that are God's."[21] The new oath thus read: "I promise and sincerely swear that I will be faithful and will obey truly his Majesty King George the Second."[22]

Administration of the oath did not work out as well as Armstrong had hoped. First, the Minas Acadians refused to subscribe. On September 12, Armstrong summoned Alexandre Bourg, Charles Landry, François Richard, and Guillaume Bourgeois to receive the oath and then administer it to their neighbors. At first glance, this change in execution offered a small flicker of hope. If select Acadians rather than Britons proctored the oath, perhaps the rest of the Acadians would consent. Such, however, proved to be wishful thinking.[23]

The Acadian deputies refused to do Armstrong's bidding. "Instead of persuading them to do their duty by solid arguments of which they were not incapable," Armstrong reported, "they frightened and terrified them (their neighbors), by representing the Oath so strong and binding that neither they nor their children should ever shake off the yoke, so that by their example and insinuations the whole body of the people almost to a man refused them."[24] When called before the council to explain their behavior, the deputies remained recalcitrant and claimed that unless the oath contained provisions for the protection of their religion, neutrality, and property, concessions they felt they previously had won, they would not take it.

The council forced the Acadians' hand by offering the oath directly to them. The deputies defiantly refused. Armstrong ordered them arrested "for their contempt and disrespect."[25] Landry, Richard, and Bourgeois must have especially angered Armstrong—he ordered them laid in irons in the fort's jail. Bourg, who had developed an amicable relationship with Paul Mascarene, avoided imprisonment but was nonetheless banished from the colony with the orders to leave behind his personal property. After several days during which tempers cooled, Armstrong released Landry, Richard, and Bourgeois, but not before having done irreparable harm to the Britons' claim to being benevolent rulers.[26]

Armstrong's mood deteriorated further after Ensign Robert Wroth reported from Chignecto. Wroth was to collect the oath from the Acadians, but at each settlement he visited, he heard the same excuses for why they would not take it. When the Acadians told him that they would subscribe if he promised them the same conditions the Minas deputies had demanded, he acceded. He then went as far as to give them a fourth rider, stating that they were free to leave the colony and could sell their property to the British. The inhabitants of Chignecto gladly took that oath. Wroth then traveled to Minas, where word of his generosity had preceded him, and collected more Acadian subscriptions.[27]

Wroth had done little more than concede to maintain the de facto state of British-Acadian affairs in Nova Scotia. Since 1710, the British had allowed the Acadians the free practice of their religion and likewise had treated them as neutrals. Similarly, Queen Anne and King George I had granted them title to their property. Even his provision that allowed the Acadians to leave the province was nothing new; a similar clause had been included in the transfer of Acadia from France to Great Britain in the treaty of Utrecht. In that sense, Wroth's oath was a clarification of the principles agreed to at the end of the previous British-French war. Had Armstrong put aside his frustration with the Acadians, he would have seen that all they really wanted was an unambiguous statement that the British would continue to honor the agreements they had made with the French in 1714 and the Anglo-Americans afterwards.

Armstrong and the council naturally did not see it that way. They believed Wroth had undone fifteen years of British policy and upbraided him for overstepping his bounds. Wroth's actions, the council concluded, had been "unwarranted and dishonourable."[28] More important, and of a more pressing issue, Armstrong had to find a way to repudiate the concessions the ensign had made without enraging the Acadians. The council claimed that Ensign Wroth had spoken so far out of turn and beyond his mandate that his agreement with the Acadians carried no validity. Still, after the events of autumn 1727, the British no longer could claim that the Minas and Chignecto Acadians refused to subscribe to any oath.

The arrests, as well as the repudiation of Wroth's oath, led thoughtful Acadians and priests again to consider that little, short of money, was to be gained in dealing with the British. Sulpician missionary René-Charles de Breslay at least seems to have thought as much. Armstrong had to castigate him for taking too large a role in the "public affairs" of Annapolis Royal. Breslay had managed to maintain cordial relations with the British since his appointment in 1724. His church at "Fort Mohawk," the blockhouse from which Iroquois warriors had watched over the Acadians after the British first took possession of Annapolis Royal, had become a place for Acadians to gather but had not drawn too much British scrutiny. Indeed, having the church near the fort must have simplified the garrison's task of keeping tabs on the comings and goings of the Acadians. Thus, in the early days of the parish, one might have been inclined to see Breslay's agreement to build his church at Fort Mohawk as a symbolic gesture of accommodation. After the arrest of the deputies, however, the church on the old Mohawk blockhouse just as easily could have become a symbol of open defiance. Armstrong received reports that Breslay had taken to holding trials and courts in which he resolved disputes within the Acadian community. Such actions, Armstrong contended, showed that Breslay "endeavored to withdraw the people from their dependence on H.M. government by assuming himself the authority of a Judge in Civil affairs and Employing his Spiritual Censures to force them to a submission."[29]

Breslay refused to admit to usurping British civil authority and instead countered that the real issue between him and Armstrong was that he had refused to secure a personal loan for the lieutenant governor. That in fact may have been true. Armstrong fell deeply into debt during his tenure in Nova Scotia, and he continually complained about extraordinary expenses such as having to advance three hundred pounds of his own money to secure Mascarene's Treaty. Having lost his personal possessions and purse in the wreck of the British fleet in 1711, the lieutenant governor was never far from penury, which certainly contributed to his irascibility. Whatever the cause of the tiff between Breslay and Armstrong, the outcome was hardly satisfactory to the lieutenant governor; more important, it showed the impotency of British authority in even Annapolis Royal. Armstrong ordered the garrison's adjutant—the main administrative officer of the regiment—to bring the priest before the council. Before the British could arrest him, however, the Acadians warned Breslay, and he absconded to the woods to hide among the Mi'kmaq. Powerless to do much else, Armstrong, in another empty gesture, posted a notice on the church door at Fort Mohawk that directed the priest to leave the province within a month. Breslay ignored the order and remained in hiding on the outskirts of Annapolis Royal for fourteen months.[30]

The Convention of 1730

During approximately the same time that Armstrong was doing his best to alienate the Acadians, Philipps received orders to return to Annapolis Royal. It was an assignment on which he more than likely would have preferred to pass. Not only were the locals as troublesome as ever, but he would not have the resources to deal effectively with them. Moreover, Armstrong, his second in command, was a Newcastle man, not his. Perhaps that explains why he found it so easy to savage Armstrong's reputation and repudiate his policies.

After spending the summer and autumn at Canso, Philipps arrived at Annapolis Royal in November 1729. He must have been heartened when the Acadians greeted him warmly by complaining that they had suffered terribly under Armstrong.[31] He therefore sent messengers to both the banlieu and outlying Acadians informing them that although winter was almost in full swing, he hoped they would come to Annapolis Royal and take the oath. To encourage the Acadians that he was there to save them from Armstrong, he cynically extended his hand in friendship. Although in his correspondence he would later unfairly call the Acadians "rather a pest, and incumbrance than of an advantage to the Country, being a proud, lazy, obstinate and untractable people, unskillful in the methods of Agriculture, nor will be led or drove into a better way of thinking,"[32] he repudiated Armstrong's policies in a heartbeat. While at Canso, he had heard of Armstrong's run-in with Father Breslay. Philipps sent a clear message of where the lieutenant governor stood in his eyes when he reinstated Breslay as the priest of Annapolis Royal and gave him a certificate "of his good comportment."[33] In another act sure to raise questions among the locals about his confidence in his subordinate, Philipps made it a point to remind the Acadians that they were secure in their personal property and possessions.[34] Last, Philipps rehabilitated Bourg in both British and Acadian eyes by appointing him notary for Minas. To the Acadians, it must have looked as if Philipps was trying to apologize for the many insults that they had received during Armstrong's tumultuous administration.

Father Breslay and the Acadians meet with Philipps to take the oath in late 1729. In January 1730, the governor could report that he had extracted an oath from every banlieu male above age sixteen, and he expected the Minas and Chignecto Acadians to follow suit quickly.[35] The oath that he proffered in Annapolis Royal said nothing of neutrality, property rights, or religion: "Je promets et jure sincèrement en foi de Chrétien, que je serai entièrement fidelle, et obéirais vrayment sa Majesté, le Roy George le Second, qui je reconnois pour le souvrain Seigneur de la Nouvelle Ecosse et de l'Accadie. Ainsi Dieu me soit en aide." ("I promise and sincerely swear as a Christian, that I will be entirely faithful, and truly obey his Majesty, King George II, whom I recognize as the sovereign Lord of Nova Scotia and Acadia. So Help me God."[36] The Acadians, having previously won those terms at Utrecht, from Queen Anne, and from Lieutenant Governor Armstrong, naturally assumed that those provisions were implied in the oath. It was a shrewd move on Philipps's part. He gave the Acadians nothing new but had taken nothing away from them, either. It no longer needed to be said, or even debated, that the Acadians were neutrals, Catholics, and indeed owned their property.

In the early spring, Philipps traveled to Minas and Chignecto to complete "the entire submission of all those so long obstinate People."[37] In his report to the Board of Trade, Philipps self-servingly noted that for twenty years the Acadians had "continued stubborn and refractory upon all summons of the kind, but haeving essay'd the difference of Government in my absence they signify'd their readiness to comply with what I shou'd require of them."[38] Again, the issues of neutrality, religion, and property were not included in the oath, but Fathers Charles de La Goudalie (from Minas) and Noël-Alexandre de Noinville (from Pisiquid), who spoke for the Acadians, later declared that they had negotiated neutral status for their flocks with Philipps. The Minas and Chignecto Acadians then took an oath to the effect that that they would be "completely faithful" to King George, whom they also recognized as the sovereign lord of Nova Scotia.[39]

Richard Philipps was well pleased with himself. Because the Acadians were "a formidable body and like Noah's progeny spreading themselves over the face of the Province,"[40] he assumed that he had won a major victory for the empire and, no doubt, a ticket home to London. Unfortunately for Philipps, the devil was in the details. Although he noted that he had not "prostituted the King's honour in makeing a scandalous capitulation in his name and contrary to H.M. express orders, as has been done by one Ensign Wroth of my Regiment,"[41] the Board of Trade found something to criticize in the banlieu oath. The Board of Trade's secretary, Alured Popple, informed Philipps that the Acadians in fact had not promised to be faithful to the king. "The Oath," Popple wrote, "indeed seems intended to have been a Translation of the English Oath of Allegiance, but the different Idiom of the two languages has given it another turn." In the copy of the oath that Philipps sent the board, the participle "to" as in pledging "allegiance to King George" had been omitted in the French translation. Thus, the French translation promised fidelity without saying to whom. Popple continued that any priest trained in rhetoric would know "the word 'Fidèle' can only refer to a dative case and 'obéirai' governs an accusative." The priests would "explain this ambiguity so as to convince the people" that they were under no obligation to King George II. Popple and the Board of Trade would have preferred that the oath read "Je promets et jure sincèrement en foy de Chrestien que je serois [*sic,* serais] entierement fidelle [*sic,* fidèle] à sa Majesté le Roy George le Second que [*sic,* qui] je reconnois pour le Souverain Seigneur de la Nouvelle Ecosse et de l'Acadie et que je lui obeirais vrayment. Ainsi Dieu me soit en aide." (I promise and sincerely swear as a Christian that I will be entirely faithful to his Majesty King George the Second whom I recognize as the Sovereign Ruler of Nova Scotia and Acadia and that I will obey him truly. So help me God.")[42]

Popple's criticism took the wind out of Philipps's sails. Stung by their disapproval, Philipps wrote back that although he was sorry that the Board of Trade did not think the oath was adequate, he nonetheless had used his best understanding of other English oaths and French "in the forming of it." He had examined the oaths from neighboring British colonies and copied them. He then specifically had added the words " 'Je jure en foi de Chrétien' to make it stronger, and afterwards to make it more significant to the circumstances" of the Acadians. The ambiguous "fidèle," moreover, was the only word he could find in his French dictionary "to express allegiance." He even claimed to have spoken to several Francophones, and they had assured him that both "fidèle" and "obéir" were dative verbs and that the conjunction "et" between the verbs referred to the king. The oath he gave was therefore, in his opinion, "stronger than the original English." The bottom line, Philipps perhaps rightly observed, was that no matter what he offered to the Acadians, the priests "will make use of an argument more suitable to their principles that no oath is binding on a Papist, to obey what they call a Heretick Prince."[43]

Despite the Board of Trade's critique, Philipps's oaths (as subscribed to by the banlieu and outlying Acadians) effectively ended the controversy for almost a generation. Britons did not try to extract another oath from the Acadians until 1749. Although never approved by London, the Convention of 1730 framed British-Acadian relations for nearly a generation. In that sense, Great Britain's common-law tradition—one of the trademarks of the later empire—had found its way to Nova Scotia. Although there were no formal, written documents stating as much, after 1730 both Acadians and Britons understood that the Acadians were neutrals entitled to the free practice of their Catholic faith and the full possession of their property.

Following his French grammar lesson from the Board of Trade, a disgruntled and bitter Philipps merely bided his time until he could return to London. Over the next year and a half, he accomplished little in Nova Scotia and only sporadically communicated with the board. Short of a few memoranda in which he requested more troops and funding to build blockhouses across the colony, requests he surely knew the Board of Trade would table, Philipps did nothing to improve the British position in Nova Scotia.[44] Finally, in 1731, the Board of Trade recalled Philipps, and he traveled to England, never to return to Nova Scotia.

Armstrong and the Acadians: Round II

Lawrence Armstrong retook the reins of British control and almost immediately butted heads with the Acadians. One of his first acts was to settle scores with them. Armstrong rightly felt that the Acadians had betrayed him when they had greeted Philipps in 1729 with complaints that they had "unfortunately experienced on several occasions the great difference there is between your [Philipps's] benign and just administration and that [Armstrong's] from which we are just relieved."[45] Unfortunately for the Acadians, Armstrong held a grudge. While it would have been politically inexpedient to lash out directly at the Acadians and thereby draw attention to himself as a disturber of the peace, he clearly stated that he required a "Suiteable Behavior from all."[46]

It is tempting to see Armstrong, because of his surly personality, as the prime mover in nearly shattering the fragile accommodation between Anglo-Americans and Acadians. Yet the Acadians also bear some culpability for proverbially poking their fingers in Armstrong's eye. With Philipps gone, they returned to ignoring the British. First, they refused to acknowledge Armstrong's letter stating that he had taken over management of the colony and that he wanted to survey and assess the Acadians' lands—long a point of concern for the Acadians. Of more immediate and pressing concern, Armstrong had directed that the garrison would require two hundred quintals of beef and sixty hogshead of provisions annually. Armstrong noted that the British would pay for the supplies. He had worked out a deal with the Robichauds—the family that had been supplying the British with supplies since 1710—to purchase sheep and cattle on the hoof and march them to Annapolis Royal. He had sent his shopping list to the Minas Acadians through their deputy and notary—Alexandre Bourg—but again had heard nothing from them.[47] With Philipps gone, it was back to the same old ways for the British in Nova Scotia—ignored by Acadians and dependent on price-gouging New Englanders for the necessities of life.

The Mi'kmaq then added to Armstrong's frustration. The Board of Trade had directed him to build a storehouse at Minas. Armstrong wisely chose not to send British engineers on the task and instead contracted the construction project to two Acadians, René and Pierre Le Blanc, from a family with amicable relations with officers of the garrison. However, when the Le Blanc brothers set about building, three Mi'kmaq threatened them in "most villainous manners, and approbrious language." One of the Mi'kmaq, known as Andress, threatened that he "had a dagger" for René for agreeing to build a "fort" for the British. Wisely, the Le Blanc brothers walked away from the job. When Major Henry Cope, who was on scene to supervise the construction project, assured the Indians that the building was designed only as a storage facility and not a fort—and asked what did it matter if King George wanted to build a fort anywhere on his lands in Nova Scotia?—the Indians retorted that "King George had conquered

Annapolis, but not Menis." The three Mi'kmaq further noted that they had heard from Anglo-Americans, most notable William Winniett, that the Acadians would receive preferential treatment at the storehouse. The Mi'kmaq would not tolerate such a blatant show of disrespect in which Acadians received preferential trade terms.[48] The Mi'kmaq then robbed some British traders on Chignecto on the pretense that the Anglo-Americans owed them rent. Suddenly, it seemed as if the Mi'kmaq were reinvigorated to "obstruct the settlement of this Province."[49]

As troubles with the Acadians and Indians swirled about him, ill will between Armstrong and the priests began anew. Armstrong accused Father Antoine Gaulin, with whom the British had a long and troubled history, and Father La Goudalie (whom the bishop of Quebec recently had appointed to the post of vicar-general for British Acadia) of attempting to convert Protestants to Catholicism and (more damning and in direct violation of the treaty of Utrecht) concealing a British deserter. Undoubtedly the priests were engaged in the former and probably the latter. As the French authorities observed, Catholic priests and Protestant clergymen were waging a contest for the hearts and minds of the peoples of Acadia.[50] Armstrong found the French proselytizing "audacious" and personally resented it.[51]

Relations between the priests and Armstrong only deteriorated from there. On the heels of Armstrong's confrontation with La Goudalie, the banlieu Acadians requested a new parish priest.[52] Father Breslay, who had represented the Acadians with Philipps, had returned to France in 1730, and they had been without a priest since then. In turning to Armstrong, they may have been offering an olive branch; at least they had not gone directly over his head to Saint-Ovide or the bishop of Quebec. Naturally, Armstrong overplayed his hand; instead of accepting the Acadians' small measure of obedience, he took it as an opportunity to remind them of the kind of behavior he expected from the priests. When he forwarded the Acadians' petition to Saint-Ovide, he noted that he would allow priests to enter Nova Scotia provided they were of "known probity, that will Behave themselves in the Execution of their Ecclesiastical Office, with Such Discretion as may be agreeable to the laws of Great Britain."[53] Saint-Ovide only needed to read further to understand why Armstrong had authorized two new missionaries. Not only was the parish at Annapolis Royal open, but so too was Minas. Armstrong had banished

La Goudalie from the colony. The lieutenant governor seemed to have had enough of the priest, especially in the wake of their exchange of letters over the previous spring. Perhaps Armstrong also wanted La Goudalie out of the province because the priest had negotiated the terms of the Minas oath of allegiance with Philipps. Father La Goudalie refused to leave the colony, however, and remained the parish priest at Minas until 1740. The Acadians must have interpreted all this as proof that Armstrong had it in for their clergy.

The new priest at Annapolis Royal, Claude de La Vernède de Saint-Poncy, proved in the short term more tractable to British interests than either La Goudalie or Gaulin. In November 1732, Armstrong sent a dispatch to the bishop of Quebec reporting that Father Saint-Poncy had arrived safely. When the priest presented himself to the council, Armstrong told him that all priests were expected to behave like "men of Honour and not prove the fomenters of Discord, and as I may say Rebellion."[54]

Saint-Poncy, however, soon drew Armstrong's wrath. The brigantine *Baltimore* had wrecked off Cape Sable, and Mi'kmaq had pillaged the vessel. Armstrong ordered that either Saint-Poncy or Claude-Jean-Baptiste Chauvreulx, the head priest at Pisiquid, immediately travel to Pobomcoup (Pubnico), the small settlement on Cape Sable, to demand restitution from the Mi'kmaq. The problem was that Father Saint-Poncy had previous plans to go to Cobequid, and Chauvreulx seemed content at Pisiquid. When Saint-Poncy and Chauvreulx appeared before the council so that Armstrong could lecture them on their duties as priests who served at his favor, the fathers gave as good as they got. They addressed Armstrong and the council in "a most insolent, audacious, and disrespectful manner" and said that they had nothing to do with the Mi'kmaq who took the *Baltimore.* When asked how they dared ignore a direct order from an officer of the king's government, Chauvreulx answered, "Que je suis ici de la part de Roy de France" ("I am here on the part of the King of France"). Saint-Poncy made a statement to the same effect, and then the two priests stormed out of the council chamber "in a very great passion, slamming and throwing the doors in a most rude and insolent manner."[55]

The council, shocked by the priests' behavior, demanded that they appear again. The British intended to order them to remain in the presbyter at Annapolis Royal until an opportunity arose to deport them to Île Royale. When Saint-Poncy and Chauvreulx appeared before the council the second time, they demanded chairs upon which to sit, claiming that they were not criminals required to stand before accusers. They then reminded Armstrong that they had "no business with things temporal" and came to the council of their own free will. Of course, that was unacceptable for the council, and Armstrong ordered them arrested and banished from the colony. Father Saint-Poncy avoided immediate deportation; 107 banlieu Acadians signed a petition asking that Armstrong pardon him, and the council agreed to allow him to stay through the winter provided that he held mass only at Fort Mohawk.[56] The British sent Chauvreulx to Île Royale, where he promptly turned around and reentered Nova Scotia. Ironically, he took refuge among the few Acadians and Mi'kmaq at Pobomcoup.[57]

The pressures, frustrations, and near penury that came with his posting in Nova Scotia finally proved too much for Lawrence Armstrong. Since Philipps's first return to England, Armstrong had been in a spat with Major Alexander Cosby (Philipps's brother-in-law) over who should serve as lieutenant governor. Cosby was well connected with the Acadians: he was the husband of Anne Winniett, the oldest daughter of William Winniett and Marie-Madeleine Maisonnat. Cosby became a thorn in Armstrong's side and worked covertly against Armstrong's initiatives. Then, in the spring of 1737, Armstrong's houseboy Isaac Provender burned the lieutenant governor's residence to the ground. In the postfire investigation, Armstrong learned that his disgruntled servant—one can only imagine what it must have been like to have been beholden to Armstrong—had planned on murdering Armstrong and his wife while they slept.[58] On December 6, 1739, Armstrong snapped. He stabbed himself to death in his bed.

Mascarene's Administration

It is a tragic but true statement that the death of Armstrong opened a door to a British-Acadian rapprochement in Nova Scotia. After an initial struggle within the council to determine who was entitled to Armstrong's office, Major Paul Mascarene won his fellow councilors' support to assume the role of lieutenant governor.[59] Among the many British officers who served in Nova Scotia in its early years, Mascarene is certainly the most appealing. Hailing from a Huguenot family, he passed his early years receiving an education in the classics before taking a commission in the British Army. Following a twenty-year career (capped by his success in forging Mascarene's Treaty in 1726), he retired to Boston to look after his motherless four children. While in Boston, he prospered as a merchant and trader and become one of the leading citizens of the city's French-Protestant community. Upon Armstrong's death, he returned to Nova Scotia. Unlike his immediate predecessor, he was determined to meet the Acadians halfway and worked tirelessly not to alienate them from the British.[60] He was no ideologue. "As long as there are men," he eloquently noted, "there will be different opinions and sentiments on certain points. It is enough that the Churches, which are all members of the Universal church can agree on the fundamental points of the doctrine of Jesus Christ and do not impose on each other the terms of communion as being articles of faith."[61] Thus began a period in which Anglo-Americans and Acadians came closer together.

Mascarene had seen too many failures of British policy resulting from knee-jerk reactions that gave little thought to long-term impact. He therefore wrote the secretary of state to request explicit instructions for dealing with the Acadians. His most pressing issue revolved around Acadian land rights. "The increase of the French Inhabitants," he wrote, "calls for some fresh instructions on how to dispose of them."[62] In the absence of the epidemics of diseases that wracked other colonies, the Acadians had seen a huge population growth.[63] As long as they remained in the British Empire where King George technically owned the land, they potentially faced a Malthusian crisis. They continually had divided and subdivided their lands among their burgeoning families, forcing some to settle on "the skirts of this Province, pretty far distant from this place." Some Anglo-Americans had favored breaking up the new Acadian settlements by force, because under the letter of the law the Acadians were not entitled to any lands other than those they had held in 1713. However, Mascarene knew that such a policy was impracticable and, more important, morally bankrupt. "If they are debarred from new possessions," he argued, "they must live here miserably and consequently be troublesome, or else they will continue to possess themselves of new tracts contrary to orders, or they must be made to withdraw to the neighboring French Colonies of Cape Breton or Canada." Mascarene strove to preclude any mass exodus of Acadians by convincing them of the benefits that they would accrue as subjects of the British Empire. He devoted his time and energies to explaining to the Acadians the benefits of British rule "by administering impartial justice to them and in all other respects treating them with lenity and humanity."[64]

The case of the Tibogue Acadians exemplifies Mascarene's judicious approach. In July 1740, eight banlieu Acadians determined to stake out better lives for themselves and moved to Tibogue, which technically sat on royal land. Mascarene summoned them before the council and chastised them for leaving Annapolis Royal without permission and, what was more important, for squatting on the king's property. The Acadians responded that they were becoming destitute in the banlieu, and if they could not settle new lands, they would have to emigrate to Île Royale or Canada. Mascarene realized that the Acadians were in a difficult position. He therefore allowed them to winter at Tibogue and gave them permission to hunt and fish on those lands. The Acadians, however, were to build no dykes until ownership of their land could be sanctioned by the home government.[65]

Mascarene's evenhanded and fair-minded approach to dealing with the Acadians carried over to his relations with the priests. When Father Saint-Poncy, who remained on house arrest in Annapolis Royal, asked for a passport to travel to Minas and then to Île Royale, Mascarene granted him one.[66] With Armstrong perhaps gone to a better place, Father Chauvreulx likewise returned to his parish at Pisiquid. His replacement during his time at Pobomcoup, Father Jean-Baptiste de Gay Desenclaves, took over the parish at Rivière-aux-Canards. Chauvreulx's confrontation with Armstrong and his subsequent internal exile certainly piqued Desenclaves's interest. Desenclaves thereupon engaged Mascarene in an exchange of letters in which the two men cordially discussed the meaning of Matthew 22:21. The priest observed that the spiritual is so often connected with the temporal "as sometimes not to be able to be divided." Mascarene responded that theological debates were fine, but the real issue was how any position would affect the Acadians. "Under the pretence of this connection," he wrote, the missionaries had assumed the power to make themselves "the Sovereign judges & arbitrator of all causes amongst the People." "Consider Monsieur," Mascarene wrote, "how this tends to render all civil judicature useless, & how easy it will be for the Missionarys to render themselves the only distributors of Justice amongst people bred up in ignorance and of what consequences it is for the maintaining of his Maj'tys authority to restrain that Power."[67] When the church excommunicated an Acadian for some petty offense, Mascarene judged that the priests had deprived the man "of all assistance and necessaries of life without any legal process and consequently contrary to the Laws of Great Britain."[68] He reminded Desenclaves that he would expel any missionary who crossed the spiritual-temporal line; he then allowed the priests to remedy the excommunication.[69] It is difficult to imagine Armstrong taking a similarly well thought-out approach to dealing with the priests.

Events in the counting houses of London, however, threatened to shatter the calm that Mascarene had worked to build. The city's leading commercial interests hankered after war in the belief that it would fill their accounts. Prime Minister Robert Walpole managed to keep them at bay through the War of the Polish Succession (1731–38), a dynastic war between France and Austria in which the British had no vital national interest but which the hawks saw as an opportunity for commercial gain. In 1739, pro-war factions in Parliament manipulated the nearly decade-old encounter between Captain Robert Jenkins and a Spanish customs officer into a casus belli. In the spring of 1740, Mascarene received word that Great Britain and Spain were at war.[70] For the next several years, the War of Jenkins' Ear remained centered in the Caribbean and in Florida and Georgia. Nonetheless, the potential of the two major Catholic monarchies of western Europe, France and Spain, joining forces against Great Britain seemed real. Mascarene therefore had to direct a more watchful eye toward the Acadians, Indians, priests, and New France.

Through the autumn and winter of 1740–41, Mascarene found it necessary to show the priests a firmer hand. In September, he learned that Father Saint-Poncy had returned to Chignecto from Louisbourg and was offering a "scheme to the prejudice of the Government." Mascarene immediately issued an order expelling him.[71] When the Acadians of Chignecto requested that Saint-Poncy remain their priest, Mascarene refused. He would allow them a missionary, but it could not be Saint-Poncy. More important, any new priest they received had to first report to the lieutenant governor at Annapolis Royal. In the fall of 1741, the council learned that Father La Goudalie had arrived in the province as Saint-Poncy's replacement but had failed to present himself in Annapolis Royal. After he finally appeared, Mascarene grilled him. Although La Goudalie affirmed that King George was the lawful sovereign of Nova Scotia, Mascarene clearly did not trust him. Mascarene allowed La Goudalie to remain at Minas, but only if the moderate Father Desenclaves accompanied him.[72]

Managing the priests increasingly consumed Mascarene's time. In November 1742, Jean-Pierre de Miniac arrived from Quebec, purportedly to assist Father La Goudalie as grand vicar of Acadia. The French authorities understood that if war broke out with Great Britain, the Acadians' neutrality would be tested. They hoped that one of their most experienced missionaries, La Goudalie, with Miniac's assistance, could bring the Acadians to the French side.[73] Mascarene and the British did not know the exact details of the French plan, but they were nevertheless suspicious. Thus, when Miniac failed to appear at Annapolis Royal, warning bells sounded. The priest claimed that the lateness of the season prevented him from traveling there, but the council believed that he was in the province in an "irregular manner" and warned him that if he did not appear immediately, he would be expelled. Miniac reported to the council and temporarily defused another confrontation between the priests and the British.[74]

Despite the priests' continually pressing the limits of Mascarene's patience, most Acadians wanted to avoid confrontation with the lieutenant governor. His policies of accommodation had convinced the Acadians that there was more to be gained in helping the British than in confronting them. Thus, when in the spring of 1742, Mi'kmaq at Grand Pré seized a ship belonging to a New England trader named Trefry, the Minas Acadians reclaimed Trefry's boat, and their deputies told the council that métis Jacques Momquaret and Thomas Wonitos had committed the crime.[75] Mascarene returned the Acadians' goodwill in the Trefry affair when in April, Acadians Jean Terriot and his brother Joseph found themselves arrested by a sergeant of the garrison. It seems that some of the men of the garrison still looked to pick fights with the Acadians. The sergeant had seized the Terriot brothers because they had approached the council without first reporting to the officer of the day. It was indeed a minor matter but one that could have created a rift between the Acadians and British. Mascarene moved quickly to smooth over Acadian anger and released the Terriots. He used what could have been an embarrassing moment for the British to reassure Acadians that as long as they "held fast to their Duty and allegiance" to King George, the British would protect them in their "in their Properties and Libertys."[76]

Still, Nova Scotia was, as the Board of Trade observed, a British colony in name only. Except for the garrisons at Annapolis Royal and Canso, there were no other Anglo-American settlements in the province.[77] The sheer size of their population in proportion to the occupiers gave the Acadians the upper hand in their dealings with the Anglo-Americans. Despite the occasional flaring of tensions between individual Acadians and priests with the British, the Acadians for the most part had found a place of peaceful coexistence with the Anglo-Americans. Indeed, they had worked hard to build amity with the British.

Unfortunately for the Acadians, such efforts toward amity proved to be worth very little when King George's War came to Nova Scotia in 1744. In that conflict, the Acadians found themselves caught between powerful competing French and Anglo-American interests. Over the course of the next decade, Anglo-Americans switched from searching for negotiation with the Acadians to violently imposing their imperial will upon them. In hindsight, for the Acadians of Nova Scotia, the golden years between 1720 and 1744 stand as little more than the calm before the storm.

F. R. Schell's pastoral Dyke Lands suggests all the elements of prosperity—rich fields, healthy livestock, and the promise of a prosperous trade via the sloop—that drew Anglo-Americans to Nova Scotia. Courtesy of Nova Scotia Archives and Records Management (NSARM).

Although painted in the early nineteenth century, William Eagar's landscape offers a sense of the lay of the land when Anglo-American forces marched from Halifax into the Minas Basin. *Cornwallis, Grand Pré and Basin of Minas from the North Mountain,* by William Eagar, 1830–35. Courtesy of NSARM.

Paul Mascarene sought to find a middle ground with the Acadians. He spent many years among them, first as an officer in the garrison in Annapolis Royal, then as lieutenant governor of all of British Nova Scotia, and finally as a member of the Nova Scotia Council. Although the closest thing to a friend that Acadians had among the British, Mascarene adopted harsh measures, when required, to bring the Acadians under British rule. Courtesy of the Los Angeles County Museum of Art.

This circa 1924 photograph of Fort Edward (Windsor), Nova Scotia, shows a blockhouse (on the left). Blockhouses were the first step in establishing effective British control over Nova Scotia. Anglo-American rangers built them as forward operating bases from which to control Indian and Acadian populations. Courtesy of NSARM.

Edward Cornwallis became governor of Nova Scotia in 1749. He would brook no opposition from the Acadians, although he realized the need to placate the Indians before dealing with the Acadians. He personally disliked the Gorham brothers but enthusiastically unleashed them and their rangers on Indians and Acadians alike in Father Le Loutre's War. Courtesy of NSARM.

This highly dramatized illustration shows Anglo-American soldiers herding Acadians to the transports. It is difficult to tell whether the troops are British regulars or Yankee provincials. From F. O. Darley's "Illustrations de l'Acadie d'Évangéline." Courtesy of NSARM.

General Robert Monckton served as the field commander of the Anglo-American forces in Nova Scotia from 1755 to 1758. He is best known for his services as a brigadier during the campaign outside Quebec in 1759, which this portrait by J. Watson (after Benjamin West) commemorates. In Nova Scotia, he proved himself an effective counterguerrilla leader and led his forces in a ruthless pursuit of Acadian refugees and fighters across the peninsula and into present-day New Brunswick. Courtesy of NSARM.

Thomas Davies's *North View of Fort Frederick Built by Order of the Honourable Colonel Robert Monckton* (1758) depicts the outpost that the British established at the mouth of the St. John River. From it, Anglo-American forces advanced up the river and destroyed Acadian refugee settlements, effectively driving the Acadians from New Brunswick. Courtesy of the National Gallery of Canada, no. 6269.

Thomas Davies's *View of the Plundering of and Burning of the City of Grymross* (1758) shows the fate of the Acadian villages during the Anglo-American operations to drive the refugees from present-day New Brunswick. Courtesy of the National Gallery of Canada, no. 6270.

4

King George's War, 1744–1748

France's declaration of war on Great Britain on March 4, 1744, and Great Britain's reciprocal action three weeks later, proved a watershed in Nova Scotia's history.[1] King George's War, as the North American part of the War of the Austrian Succession was known in the colonies, fundamentally changed the nature of empire in Nova Scotia. By its end in 1748, the war had profoundly altered the dynamic nature of the complex web of Anglo-American–Indian–Acadian–French relations in ways that few contemporaries could have imagined or contemplated only four years earlier.

Events essentially unconnected to North America thoroughly undermined Mascarene's and the Acadians' efforts at accommodation. When King George's War began, the well-being of the empire in Nova Scotia was of comparatively minor concern for the British. Not only had Britons seemed to have reached an acceptable level of accommodation with both the Indians (following the Maliseet-Mi'kmaw War of the early 1720s) and the Acadians (with the Convention of 1730), but British politicians and leaders had more pressing concerns. Since 1739 Great Britain and its North American colonists had been mired in a stalemated conflict with Spain (the Anglo-

Spanish War or the War of Jenkins' Ear) over trade in the Caribbean and the expansion of Georgia. Maintaining the balance of power in Europe, meanwhile, proved increasingly difficult. Since the death of Emperor Charles VI of Austria in 1740, European diplomacy and statecraft had become almost unmanageable. Frederick II (the Great) of Prussia used Charles's death and his failure to leave a male heir as pretext to invade Silesia in an attempt to wrest it from Empress Maria Theresa, thus igniting the First (1740–42) and Second (1744–45) Silesian Wars. With Austria bogged down in a war with Prussia, King Louis XV of France eyed the Austrian Netherlands as easy Hapsburg fruit for the picking. In line with the traditional British practice of guaranteeing the neutrality of the Low Countries as a means of protecting the English Channel, as well as Hanoverian concerns over the security of their realm, in the summer of 1743 King George II, in his capacity as Hanoverian Elector of the Holy Roman Empire, led a British force to the continent to defend the Dutch republic. In June, the "Pragmatic Army" of Britons, Hanoverians, and Austrians defeated a French army at Dettingen in western Germany. France's declaration of war nine months later thus plunged the peoples of Nova Scotia into a "shifting complex of wars with multiple causes and multiple objectives," as well as multiple loyalties.[2]

At first glance, it would seem that Nova Scotians had little at stake in another dynastic war in Europe that threatened their precarious peace. The struggle that wracked Nova Scotia between 1744 and 1748, however, took a distinctly American face. New Englanders who had imperial designs of their own on Nova Scotia were moving away from the British-Acadian accommodation that had characterized the previous decades. Throughout the war, American rather than British concerns shaped the empire's course in Nova Scotia. French officials in both Canada and Paris, moreover, saw the war as an opportunity to regain Acadia. The armies they sent into Nova Scotia, however, accomplished little except straining Acadian–Anglo-American relations. Acadians lost the most in the war. On one hand trying to maintain their independence from the French in the Anglo-French imperial conflict, and on the other hand struggling against New England's imperial designs, the Acadians fell victim to forces that they could not control. In the end, King George's War brought a screeching halt to the Acadians' golden age and set the stage for the horrific violence of the following decade.

Canso and Le Loutre's Siege of Fort Anne

The French struck the conflict's first blow in Nova Scotia in May 1744. Soon after reports of France's declaration of war on Great Britain reached Louisbourg in April, Jean-Baptiste-Louis Le Prévost Duquesnel, commandant of Île Royale, ordered François Du Pont Duvivier to drive the British from Canso. After several weeks of preparations, Duvivier's force of 350 *troupes de la marine* (France's regular soldiers, who garrisoned the North American colonies) struck on May 24. The British commander at Canso, Captain Patrick Heron, had only 87 men under his command, and he was not interested in fighting. The ensuing events reflected poorly on him. In preparation for a landing of Duvivier's army, two French privateers opened their guns on the old British blockhouse. Heron immediately rushed from his fortifications to offer a white flag of truce. The French commander demanded the surrender of the blockhouse, to which Heron agreed, and then set it and a British man-of-war tender afire.

Once in Louisbourg as prisoners of war, Heron and most of the British captives hardly comported themselves better. Several of the troops deserted to the French side and served on a French privateer, and Heron lobbied incessantly for his release.[3] Fortunately for him, a shortage of provisions at Louisbourg led Duquesnel to agree to parole the British troops to Boston, provided that select officers remain as hostages. Ensign John Bradstreet, son of Edward and Agathe Bradstreet of Annapolis Royal, agreed to stay behind when the majority of the British contingent sailed in September. Bradstreet spent the next several months reconnoitering the fortress under the cover of message bearer between Louisbourg and Boston. Upon his release in a prisoner exchange, he presented Governor William Shirley of Massachusetts with a detailed plan for its capture. Still, in the early days of the war, the French had seized the initiative.[4] Only Fort Anne at Annapolis Royal stood in the way of a total French reconquest of Acadia.

Paul Mascarene, from his post at Annapolis Royal, correctly suspected that the French would move against Fort Anne at the first opportunity. He therefore set about preparing the garrison as best he could. He evacuated the men's families to Boston and put his soldiers and the artificers that Governor Shirley had sent to work repairing the fort's dilapidated walls. He turned to the banlieu Acadians to supply the British with the building materials and provisions and was heartened when they "show'd themselves ready, not only to get the timber necessary for that kind of work, butt to be employed in the Repairs."[5] Near the same time, he sent an urgent request to Shirley in which he asked for a reinforcement of troops to augment the one hundred effectives he had on hand. Since the British had taken Nova Scotia in 1710, they had kept only the understrength Philipps's Regiment in the colony. Duvivier had taken nearly 40 percent of the regiment prisoner at Canso. Mascarene also understood that he probably would have to face the Maliseets and Mi'kmaq in a bush fight in which his remaining regulars would be outmatched. He therefore requested that Shirley put out the word across New England that backwoods fighters were needed in Nova Scotia.[6]

Father Jean-Louis Le Loutre moved on the British before Mascarene could get Fort Anne fully ready.[7] In July, Le Loutre (who resided among the Indians at the Shubenacadie [Tatamagouche] mission) appeared outside Annapolis Royal with three hundred Mi'kmaw warriors. In hindsight, it should have come as no surprise that Le Loutre would have taken such a bold and belligerent step. Le Loutre's original posting had been to the parish at Annapolis Royal, where he was to replace Father Claude Saint-Poncy, with whom the British had so much trouble. The Séminaire des Missions Étrangers instead sent him to the mission among the Mi'kmaq at Shubenacadie. After a brief internship to "learn the savage tongue" under fellow Jesuit Pierre Maillard, Le Loutre went native. (It seems natural that Le Loutre—"the Otter"—would become the most militant of the priests in Nova Scotia. Within woodland-Indian cosmology, otters possess a keen sense of justice, which often leads them to be revolutionaries and rebels. They are active and altruistic creatures to whom friendship and solidarity are of paramount importance.) While he labored at his mission, Le Loutre had no outside supervision and was free to do as he wished. He wrote in 1740, for instance, that he had received no news from Canada or France for the previous year, save the occasional letter from Father Miniac.[8] Perhaps it was then that he first dreamed of taking back Nova Scotia for his adopted Mi'kmaw flock. The three hundred warriors whom he assembled in the summer of 1744 points to his ambitions; it was the largest gathering of Indians to date to take arms against the British in Nova Scotia. The warriors must have trusted Le Loutre, and they just as likely offered a frightful sight.

Indeed, no Acadian risked his scalp to warn the British when the Indians were right on top of them; upon the arrival of the Mi'kmaq at Annapolis Royal, the banlieu Acadians "intirely left" the Anglo-Americans to their own devices.[9]

Despite outnumbering the garrison nearly three to one, the Indians proved unable to take Fort Anne. Their only realistic chance for victory lay in surprise; perhaps if they could have caught the garrison unawares and rushed into the fort, they might have succeeded. However, the soldiers' headlong retreat to safety upon spotting the Mi'kmaq effectively doomed the siege from the start. Although they captured and scalped two regulars who foolishly ventured from the fort to tend the gardens, the Mi'kmaq could do little else. They temporarily cut off another squad of soldiers who had made a sortie to burn an outbuilding, but the squad made its way back to safety under the covering fire of the fort's swivel guns. Indeed, the Indians soon learned that they could accomplish little in the face of the British guns. Several Mi'kmaq approached the fort under cover of the outlying barns and stables, for instance. Although they managed to get to the foot of the glacis—the earthen slope that ran outward from the base of the fort—and sniped at the sentries, cannon fire forced them to retreat.[10]

With the element of surprise lost, the best for which Le Loutre and the Mi'kmaq could hope was a miraculous turn of events, such as the French appearing with cannon or the garrison losing its nerve and surrendering. Although the first possibility was unlikely, the Mi'kmaq would have been encouraged had they known the goings-on inside the fort. Surrounded by three hundred Mi'kmaw warriors, the New England laborers almost broke under the pressure. They loudly declared that they had come to Nova Scotia to work, not to fight and die. Their questionable judgment—surely the Indians would not have differentiated between laborers and soldiers had they breached the walls—"caus'd a backwardness and dispirtedness amongst their fellows."[11] However, someone (perhaps Mascarene or Captain Edward How of the garrison) convinced them that they would have to fight if they wanted to live. When Mi'kmaq attempted to immolate a sergeant and several soldiers who had been cut off in a small guardhouse about a quarter mile from the fort, Edward How drafted the workers into a rescue party. Using the cannon on the fort's ordnance tender in the river to supply covering fire, How and the artificers sallied to the guardhouse. The tender's guns kept the Indians pinned down long enough to allow How's men to rescue the regulars and to tear down a fence that offered the Indians cover. Upon returning to the fort, How requested permission to take his men to tear down the barns and stables behind which the Indians were hiding. The success at the guardhouse appeared to have fortified the workers' spirit. Mascarene "would not baulk them" and again sent How forward under the cover of the cannons. The Indians, driven from the immediate vicinity of the fort and with nothing to protect them, withdrew to about a mile distant and spent the next several days looking for the British to drop their guard. The first "siege" of Fort Anne was effectively over, and the Indians, Mascarene reported, gave the garrison "no great trouble" except for stealing some sheep and cattle. When seventy Massachusetts troops aboard the *Prince of Orange* fortuitously arrived, the Indians knew the game was up. They ransacked a few buildings in the faubourg and then retreated for their homes by way of Minas Basin.[12] Le Loutre traveled with them and kept a low profile in the colony until the autumn of the next year.

Duvivier's Siege of Fort Anne

Although the British had repulsed the Mi'kmaq at Annapolis Royal, the French threat remained. The French had several hundred troupes de la marine on Île Royale, and they had long been formulating schemes to take Fort Anne. In 1739, Isaac-Louis de Forant, governor of Île Royale, had crafted a plan for an amphibious attack on the fort. His concept of operations called for two frigates to sail from Louisbourg with two hundred regulars, which would trap the British inside the fort and prevent it from being reinforced. In short order, two hundred additional regulars would arrive with siege engines and sappers in tow. The French troops would then take the guns from their ships and use those to batter the fort's walls. When Duquesnel replaced Forant in 1740 and war between France and Great Britain seemed imminent, the new governor considered executing the plan, only to have the Ministry of Marine inform him that because Great Britain and France were not yet at war, he was to limit his actions to defensive measures.[13] Still, the French at Louisbourg had given a good bit of thought to how they would take Fort Anne—more important, they were itching for a fight.

Encouraged by the victory at Canso and what he mistakenly saw as widespread Indian support, Duquesnel dusted off Forant's plan and set it in motion. On July 29, the Duvivier brothers, François and Joseph, left Louisbourg at the head of fifty troupes de la marine, around a hundred Île Royale Mi'kmaq—the Nova Scotia Mi'kmaq had little interest in returning to Annapolis Royal—and seventy Maliseets under the guidance of Father Maillard. François would command the army, and his brother would assist him. Supporting Duvivier were the French frigates *Caribou* and *l'Ardent*. The combined French and Indian force would land on Chignecto, then set out by land through Minas Basin to Annapolis Royal. Duquesnel hoped that by his "showing the flag" among the Indians and Acadians, more would join Duvivier's army.

When the French force arrived at Beaubassin on August 8, however, it did not receive a particularly warm welcome from the Acadians. Although Duvivier recommended that they join "their ancient friends,"[14] the Acadians seemed reluctant. Two important issues may have been at play. First, the appearance of the French put the Acadians in a difficult position. They had long held steadfast to their neutral status, which had been won from the British through a long and often danger-fraught process. In that light, their cousins' inactions at Annapolis Royal during Le Loutre's siege in July could be explained, both to the British and to the French. Second, the Acadians would have seen the French soldiers as invaders as much as liberators. Most of the rank and file of the troupes de la marine were conscripts from metropolitan France, and thus outsiders in the closely knit Acadian community. At the same time, although mostly Canadians, the officers of the French forces shared little in common with the Acadian farmers. The Canadian aristocracy of New France's Saint Lawrence Valley heartland dominated the army's officer corps. They hailed from a militarized society in which only the church rivaled the power and prestige of the army.[15] Acadians, by contrast, had made a society dominated by subsistence farmers in search of a basic "competency."[16] It is not difficult to imagine the tension between the aristocratic French officers and the simple, though certainly not simple-minded, Acadians. Although François Duvivier was nominally an Acadian because he had been born at Port Royal, he had spent his entire adult life in the army, where he had made a fortune in trading ventures spread across France's Atlantic empire. He was certainly no more a friend to the Acadians than were the soldiers he commanded.

Whatever the cause of the Acadians' aloofness, Duvivier could not afford to allow it to derail his campaign. He reacted as one would expect from an aristocrat used to having his way. After ten days in Beaubassin (where his army consumed the Acadians' stores and requisitioned supplies for its march on Annapolis Royal), Duvivier moved to the Minas Basin. His terse handling of the Acadians there did little to further the French cause. Besides demanding horses and teamsters from the villages of Minas, Pisiquid, Rivière-aux-Canards, and Cobequid, he directed that deputies from each village "shall be assembled, to pledge fidelity for themselves and all the inhabitants of the neighborhood." He "ordered [the Acadians] to acknowledge the obedience they owe the King of France" and threatened that those who "contravene the present order shall be punished as rebellious subjects, and delivered into the hands of the savages as enemies of the state."[17] Father Miniac questioned Duvivier's orders and suggested that he was placing the Acadians in a very difficult position. Duvivier dismissed the priest, and the Acadians had little choice but to offer up the horses and teamsters. Yet, all told, only a dozen Acadians—led by Joseph Leblanc *dit* Le Maigre ("the Skinny"), Joseph-Nicholas Gautier *dit* Bellair ("Handsome"), and Joseph Broussard *dit* Beausoleil ("Bright Sun") and his brother Alexandre—openly supported the French. In the later development of romantic legend of Acadian resistance after the grand dérangement, Le Maigre, Bellair, and Beausoleil came to be seen as early "freedom fighters." Whatever one's views of their actions, their decision to join the French would cost both them and their communities dearly.[18]

It is safe to say that when Duvivier and the regulars left for Annapolis Royal on August 30, the golden age of the Acadians had ended. For the preceding decade and a half they had managed to keep both the British and French at arm's length. Henceforth, they would be caught in the middle of the French–Anglo-American struggle for their homelands, a struggle in which they had nothing to gain and everything to lose.

Duvivier found more frustration with the Indians. On the whole, they showed little interest in breaking the peace with the British. In May, several Saint-Jean Maliseets traveled to Annapolis Royal to ask Mascarene whether they and the British were still at peace. "We are sensible we Cannot Live without the assistance of the English," they said, "and if They and the French do Go to war our designs are to Lye

Quite and meddle on Neither side."[19] The French clearly had miscalculated the extent of Acadian and Indian support that they would find in Nova Scotia.

Historians have observed that the Indians of the Northeast often fought conflicts driven by concerns over captives, booty, and individual prestige in wars that ran parallel to the Anglo-French conflict. The focus on individual glory led to an aversion to taking casualties; native warriors therefore were loath to risk costly assaults on Euro-American fortifications and open-field battles. That interpretation, however, seems incomplete as an explanation for why the majority of the Mi'kmaq chose to shun Duvivier in the autumn of 1744. There emerged a syncretism among the Indians between their and European motivations for warfare. Since the British conquest of Nova Scotia in 1710, both Maliseets and Mi'kmaq had been very particular in choosing when they would, and when they would not, fight. During the war of the 1720s, for instance, community-wide concerns such as John Doucett's holding of Indian captives and British attempts to establish a permanent presence at Canso shaped Mi'kmaw actions, more so than the impulses of individual concerns. When war returned to Nova Scotia in 1744, the Mi'kmaq surely gave thoughtful debate to the benefits and dangers of an open alliance with the French. It is likely that the exhortations of Father Le Loutre and the force of his personal standing among the Mi'kmaq motivated them to raise the hatchet in the summer. But it is just as likely that the Mi'kmaq who had been to Annapolis Royal in July saw something that gave them pause. They certainly were astute enough to know that they could not breach Fort Anne's walls without artillery. They also knew that the Anglo-Americans would seek terrible retribution against any Indians who aided the French. That alone would be enough reason to sit out the second siege of Annapolis Royal.

Of course, the British were in even worse straits than the French regarding Indians and would have to depend on assistance from the Acadians or New England. The Acadians, however, clung hard to neutrality and were not inclined to offer help. At the same time, the support from New England was not all that was hoped for. Although forty Bay Colony militiamen arrived to reinforce the garrison, they came without guns and ammunition. Because most of the firearms in the British armory were "for the most part defective," the militia offered little more than labor and mouths to feed. Mascarene put them to work building barracks while the fort's overworked smiths worked to repair as many of the guns as possible.[20]

Time seemed to have run out for the defenders of Fort Anne when, on September 6, Duvivier and his army appeared on the brow of a hill about a mile from town.[21] The French immediately set about erecting shelters for what all assumed would be a siege. The next morning, a French party approached Fort Anne. The British responded by unlimbering one of their cannons and shot a ball, which "graz'd" the French and encouraged them to withdraw. That night, "when they could not be much exposed to our artillery," Mascarene recorded, Duvivier sent small parties to reconnoiter the British position. The ensuing sniping and skirmishing "kept the whole garrison in alarm all night, none being able to sleep."[22] Mascarene's main concern was that the French would discover the fort's weak spot: a hollow that offered them cover all the way to one of the parapets, where Duvivier's men could set fire to hastily thrown-up fir timbers.

On the morning of the seventh, Duvivier sent his younger brother, Joseph, to the fort under a flag of truce. Joseph told Mascarene that resistance was futile. The French, he claimed, expected the arrival of several heavily armed ships of the line. While the *Caribou* and *l'Ardent* were hardly the powerful men-of-war that Joseph claimed, Mascarene knew that French warships passed in and out of Louisbourg regularly. Joseph boasted that the approaching armada also included transports that carried 250 regulars. Thus, if Mascarene would consent to surrender at this time, his brother in turn would promise benign treatment of the garrison. The alternative—a long siege followed by perhaps captivity among the Indians or, worse, slaughter—did not need to be said.[23]

Mascarene civilly dismissed Joseph and reported to his officers. Among them, there was a consensus that they "were not reduc'd to such straits as to talk of a surrender." Mascarene then informed the French that he would not give up the fort, but if the French fleet "should be in our Basin," he would "consider what we were to do." Clearly unsatisfied with the initial British response, the elder Duvivier again sent his brother to Mascarene asking for a twenty-four-hour truce so that the British would have time to fully consider their predicament.[24]

During those early stages of the *siège en forme,* the facade of British resistance began to crack. Most of the company officers in the garrison were, in Mascarene's words, "very ready to accept the proposal [for the truce and a reconsideration of the surrender terms], the dread of being made prisoners of war having no small influence with most." Some of the officers saw little benefit in fighting a doomed battle for the honor of the empire. "Some things were spoke," Mascarene reported, "in regard to the condition of the Fort, the temper of our men, the little support or even intelligence we had from the other such as gave me a great deal of uneasiness."[25] Thus, Mascarene reluctantly agreed to send three officers to negotiate preliminary terms with Duvivier, but he resolved to himself "not to sign any articles without extremity brought me to it." Duvivier, however, responded that he would deal only with Mascarene and dismissed the British officers out of hand. They returned to the fort and reported that the truce would expire at noon on September 8. Mascarene thereupon seized Duvivier's curt dismissal of the officers to convince them that the French had "no other intention than to entrap us by sowing division" among the British. The officers, perhaps with their pride slightly bruised by both Duvivier and their commander, agreed to break off all parlays with the French. At that point, some of the regiment's privates and noncommissioned officers, those who could not expect as benevolent treatment in the hands of the French and Indians as the officers could, "threatened to seize their officers for parleying too long with the Enemy." When Mascarene gathered the men of the garrison to say that they would fight rather than surrender, they "press'd their assent by three cheerful Huzzas to my great satisfaction."[26]

Duvivier waited until the ninth to begin his formal siege. It proved not much of one, because he lacked the heavy guns to batter the fort into submission. The commanders of the *Caribou* and *l'Ardent* had not arrived. They feared the coming of a British naval squadron that was rumored to be riding in the Bay of Fundy and would trap them in the river.[27] Still, every night, French troops and Indians poked and prodded at the walls of Fort Anne. The garrison found "little more harm accruing to us than the disturbance in the night." The battle for Fort Anne thus became a twenty-four-hour affair as the French searched for a weak spot in the fort each night and the artificers spent their days strengthening walls and avoiding French snipers. On September 15, Duvivier again asked Mascarene to surrender, which he refused.

The battle for Fort Anne continued along the same lines until late September, when a British brigantine and sloop with twenty New England rangers and twenty-two Maine Indians arrived from Boston.[28] There was insufficient room in the barracks for the rangers—one can speculate that the New England militia and workers were reluctant to share their quarters with Indians—so Mascarene pointed the rangers to the lower town. Because the rangers had arrived without adequate arms and ammunition, Mascarene stripped the men inside the fort of their serviceable firearms and issued these to John Gorham's company. With weapons in hand, the rangers occupied a large building in the town. Protected by the swivel guns that they placed along each side of the building, the rangers had little to fear from the French and Indians. Using Gorham's personal sloop, the rangers slid up and down the river and harried the French behind their lines. They also escorted the artificers in the necessary but particularly unglamorous task of collecting firewood for the garrison. Several days after their arrival, the rangers ambushed a party of French-allied Indians, killing several and scattering the rest. On the whole, their patrols "kept off the Indian Enemy who in small Partys rov'd continually about us with fire wood, materials, and other necessarys."[29]

By the end of September, it was clear that the French siege had failed. The banlieu Acadians, who had been nowhere to be seen for the last several weeks, reappeared and inquired why their houses had been destroyed (the British had razed them to prevent the French from using them). The Acadians also reported that several companies of Frenchmen had marched to Minas, and they informed Mascarene of "the dread they had been kept under by the French Commander."[30] Then, on October 2, Captain Michel de Gannes de Falaise arrived in the French camp carrying orders from Île Royale to terminate the campaign. Four days later, in the midst of a rainstorm, the French army broke camp and moved toward Minas. The rangers had just arrived back in camp after having been out on a foraging party. Mascarene had planned on using them as an escort "to pay a visit to Mons. Duvivier in his Camp." "I suppose," he noted with apparent satisfaction, "that Mons. Duvivier did not care to stay for it."[31]

All involved learned important lessons from the siege. On September 25, for example, when most of the rangers were out skulking around the French lines, a "wild Indian" whom Gorham had left behind wandered into a French ambush. Mascarene immediately ordered a party of regulars to rescue the Indian. In the ensuing firefight, a British sergeant was killed and a private was wounded. Though Mascarene believed that the damage his men had done to the French was "not inconsiderable," the firefight convinced him "how necessary it is to set Indians against Indians; for tho' our men out do them in Bravery yet being unacquainted with their sculking way of fighting & Scouting to fight under cover, expose themselves to[o] much to the Enemy's shot."[32] Meanwhile, the Maliseets and few Mi'kmaq who accompanied the French army went away from the siege frustrated. Not only did they have few war trophies to show for their efforts, but they had placed themselves openly at war with the British and Yankees. More ominously, the British had taken to enlisting the support of Maine Indians and New England frontiersmen to do their fighting for them in Nova Scotia. The war with the Anglo-Americans had started badly for the Indians and might get worse. For the French, until they could send an army with siege guns and cannon against Annapolis Royal, there was little to gain from exposing their forces in a siege. The key to the French campaign in Acadia depended on the navy's ability to supply the army. Of far greater significance, the Acadians had been thoroughly uncooperative. It should have been clear to the French that their assumptions about French-Indian and French-Acadian relations had been grossly wrong and their strategy for the reconquest of Acadia needed thorough revision.

Duvivier reached Minas on October 7 and spent the next ten days resting his army there. The locals could not ask him to leave, nor could they too openly support him for fear of Anglo-American retribution. Fortunately for them, Duvivier had little interest in staying on the peninsula. With his expedition a total failure, he needed to return to Île Royale to explain his actions. When he learned that Governor Duquesnel had died and that his uncle, Louis Du Pont Duchambon, had become became acting governor, Duvivier had the excuse he needed. He rushed to Louisbourg and left Captain de Gannes, who had been born at Port Royal and therefore possessed Acadian credentials, with a small detachment of troops at Beaubassin to clean up loose ends among the troublesome Acadians. Surely the Acadians breathed a sigh of relief.

Mascarene and the British Settle Scores with the Acadians

With the French gone, Anglo-Americans and Acadians could set about repairing any damage that the French invasion had done to their relationship. The banlieu Acadians pointed out that they had been the real victims during the siege, and they reminded Mascarene that not one of them had taken arms against the British. The Acadians of Minas Basin made it similarly clear what they thought of the French army and the war. They presented Mascarene with their polite suggestion to Duvivier that the troupes de la marine that he had wanted to leave in Minas would be better off on Chignecto.[33] They then showed Mascarene a memorial that they claimed they gave to de Gannes in which they asked him to remove his "savages and troops from our districts." In what must have been a shock to de Gannes and a relief to Mascarene, the deputies told him, "We live under a mild and tranquil government, and we have all good reason to be faithful to it. We hope therefore, that you will have the goodness not to separate us from it; and that you will grant us the favor not to plunge us into utter misery."[34]

Mascarene thanked the Minas deputies for their continued loyalty to King George. He later wrote that the colony owed its preservation to the "French Inhabitants refusing to take up arms against us."[35] Nonetheless, he needed to settle some accounts. Those who were "suspected of being implicated in the designs of the enemy," Mascarene stated, would have to "vindicate" themselves. Furthermore, those Acadians who traded with Louisbourg would have to cease immediately. Mascarene was particularly bothered to learn that a large cattle drive had been undertaken to Louisbourg. Pierre Terriot and Claude Pectre implicated only Le Maigre for the Acadian animals that found their way to the French.[36] Mascarene further judged that the Minas Acadians who actually took arms against the British, Le Maigre and Bellair particularly, were guilty of rebellion and "must leave the country before tranquility can be restored."[37] He threatened that if anyone offered Le Maigre and Bellair refuge, Mascarene would send troops to Minas, and those who sheltered the rebels "must unavoidably share in the trouble that military people generally bring with them."[38] In a closing aside, he assured the residents of Minas that his warm feelings toward them had not changed, and as long as

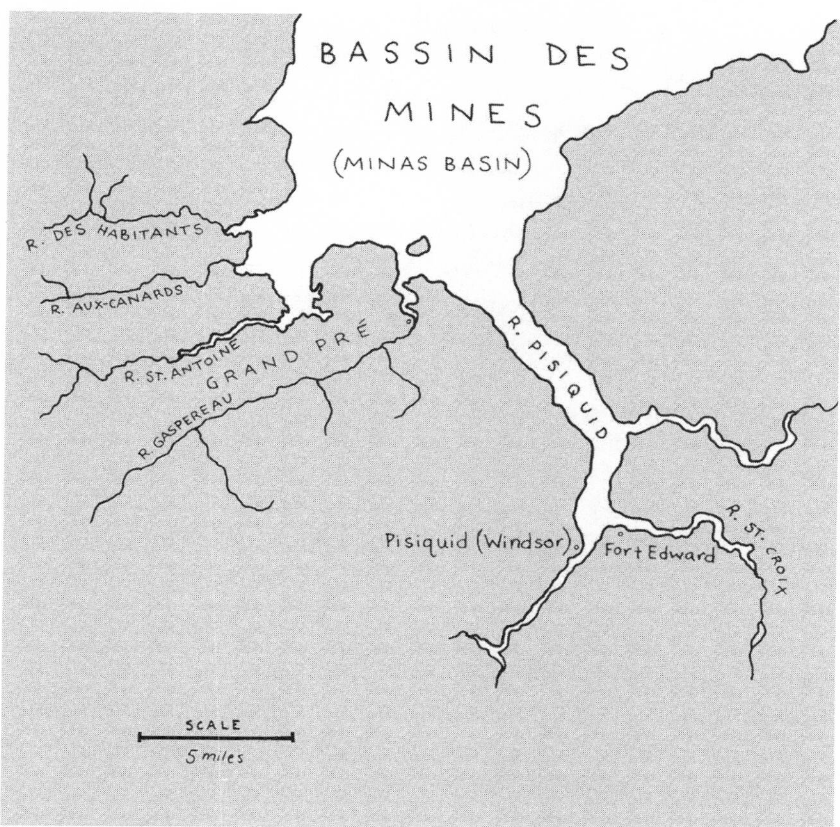

The Minas Basin.

they behaved with fidelity toward King George, they would always have in Mascarene "a good friend and servant."[39]

Le Maigre avoided deportation by presenting himself before the council. In January, he traveled to Annapolis Royal with Alexandre Bourg to protest his innocence. Le Maigre presented a letter from Duvivier in which the French commander asserted that the former had not taken arms against the British. The question of the cattle drive that Terriot and Pectre had mentioned, however, remained. It soon became clear to the council that if Le Maigre in fact had not taken up arms, he was at least guilty of going out of his way to supply the French with beef on the hoof. The council's punishment was severe. First the council relieved Bourg from his duties as notary for his failure to prevent Le Maigre from helping the French, then demanded that Le Maigre post a hundred-pound bond for his future good behavior.[40] Bellair eluded British authorities, but Mascarene arrested his wife and son and locked them in the jail at Annapolis Royal.[41]

Because the inhabitants of Chignecto had not "resisted" the French to the degree that most of the Minas Acadians had, Mascarene judged some of them "criminals against whom sentence is about to be pronounced."[42] Although the Acadians at Beaubassin in practice had not openly sided with the French, Mascarene felt that he had to make an example of someone. He therefore sent a summons to their deputies demanding that they present themselves before the council. "I am in a position to execute what I have so often said would happen to you, if you failed in the allegiance which you owe to his Britannic Majesty," Mascarene wrote.[43] When the deputies responded that they had little choice but to supply the French army with supplies, Mascarene found their excuses entirely unsatisfactory. "You owe no assistance, no obedience to any authority that does not emanate from his Britannic Majesty," he thundered, "and you have the strongest reason for abstaining from giving any assistance to his enemies."[44]

It was at that moment, when British-Acadian relations most needed a man devoted to compromise, that John Gorham stepped to the forefront of the colony's affairs with the Acadians. Although the British had repulsed the French at Annapolis Royal, Gorham believed the colony was far from secure. For him, the real threat to Nova Scotia came not from the French or Indians but from the Acadians. While Mascarene may have been content or at least politic enough to accept the banlieu and Minas Acadians at their word that they had resisted the French as best they could, Gorham did not trust the Acadians in the least.

Self-interest, more than principle and commitment to the empire, fueled Gorham's antipathy of the Acadians. He hailed from Barnstable on Cape Cod, one of the poorest regions of New England.[45] The traditional means by which Gorham men made their way in the New World had been as Indian fighters. But during New England's peace that followed Dummer's War, John had to look elsewhere to make his name. In his twenties, he went to sea. Throughout the 1730s, he traveled extensively throughout the Bay of Fundy region; in 1737, when he was thirty-one years old, he took command of the brigantine *Greenland.* The relative prosperity of the Acadian farms that Gorham saw in the Minas Basin and Chignecto fired his imagination. In 1738, he and Reverend Andrew Le Mercier, pastor to the Huguenot community in Boston and a close friend of Mascarene's, petitioned Lawrence Armstrong for proprietary rights to settle Sable Island.[46] Gorham and Le Mercier envisioned transporting French Protestants and livestock to Nova Scotia, where they would build a provisioning base for the fishing fleets on the Scotian shelf. It was an unrealistic plan that held little chance of success, yet it suggests that Gorham suspected that the path to his future prosperity traveled through Nova Scotia. By the outbreak of the war in 1744, John and Elizabeth Gorham had yet to obtain the competency that graced most of the Acadians. He understandably looked to military service and the Nova Scotia frontier as a place to make a better life for himself and his family.

In December 1744 he presented Mascarene with a proposal to take his rangers to raid Minas and Chignecto. Beyond issuing warnings, Mascarene had done little to punish the Chignecto Acadians for their disloyalty in aiding Duvivier. In addition, the banlieu Acadians reported that they had heard that a large party of Mi'kmaq had assembled between Chignecto and Minas. With Gorham confident of success and "well Inclined to do anything that Might tend to the distressing [of] the Indian Enemy,"[47] Mascarene authorized a raid. Mid-December thus saw Gorham making preparations for a campaign into the Acadian homelands. Because the rangers were short of supplies and Gorham's personal sloop could not survive a trip up the Bay of Fundy in the harsh winter seas, Mascarene outfitted the raiders with clothing, provisions, and arms and ammunition from the fort's stores for an overland trek to Minas Basin and Chignecto.[48]

Mascarene gave Gorham permission to draft "guides" from among the banlieu Acadians. The Acadians rightly reacted with concern; rumors floated about that Gorham's force was "to destroy all the Inhabitants that had any Indian blood in them & scalp them." They told Mascarene that "there was a great Number of Mulattoes amongst them who had taken the oath" and that news of the rangers' raid "had Caused a terrible Alarm."[49] They petitioned Mascarene for an exemption from having to serve, based on their status as neutrals. Such a request, the Acadians told Mascarene, did not reflect their disloyalty. Rather, it was only the commitment to neutrality that led them to shy from service with Gorham.

Mascarene would hear none of it, although on the surface this was a legitimate argument. He told them that he had not ordered them to take up arms but only to serve as pilots and guides as "the fair rules of war allowed." If the Acadians did not choose the guides among themselves, moreover, he would press them into service. It was hardly an answer that reassured the Acadians. If forced to guide the rangers to Minas and Chignecto against their kin, the Acadians responded, the Mi'kmaq "would assassinate them every day," especially since the British were unable to supply any "succor from the Gov't."[50] Rather than serve with or for Gorham, several banlieu men fled into the woods, while those who remained asked for a passport promising "security" against the rangers. Mascarene responded that he had given the rangers orders not to harm any Acadians who were loyal to the king.[51]

Fortunately for the would-be guides, before Gorham could draft them, Joseph Young's brigantine sailed into the harbor. If Gorham could use Young's ship, he would not need the Acadian guides. Gorham therefore postponed the raid as he negotiated with Captain Young to sail himself and his ship into harm's way. He even promised Young a 12 percent share in any booty the rangers took and thereby acknowledged that the mission had as much to do with privateering as with security of the colony. The negotiations proved moot, however, when Gorham grew tired of trying to make a deal with the reluctant Young and instead used his influence with the Nova Scotia Council to have Mascarene draft Young's vessel into provincial service. But with the addition of the brigantine, Gorham could send a larger force against Chignecto. In January, he put the expedition on hold and sailed for Boston to recruit more rangers and requisition supplies.[52] Within only ten weeks of having arrived in the colony, John Gorham—through force of personality, charisma, and sheer will—had begun to dominate the Anglo-American war effort in Nova Scotia.

New England's campaign against Louisbourg in 1745 further sidetracked Gorham's design for Minas and Chignecto. John Bradstreet had returned from captivity on Île Royale and planted a bug in Shirley's ear that Louisbourg was ripe for the taking. The garrison contained only seven hundred men, and many of them were Swiss mercenaries of questionable loyalty, Bradstreet reported. Bradstreet's intelligence proved accurate when in December the Swiss troops mutinied.[53] In addition, Bradstreet observed that provisions were short on all of Île Royale thanks to the efforts of New England privateers who had cut the island off from outside support, and the morale of the town dwellers had suffered considerably. After Shirley expressed only minimal interest in his plan to take Louisbourg, Bradstreet joined with William Vaughan, who owned one of New England's largest fishing operations, and the two of them lobbied Shirley to present the Massachusetts Council with their proposal. In January, Shirley met with the General Court in secret session. At first, the court was reluctant, but after the continued exhortations of Vaughan and council president William Pepperell of Kittery, it conceded to launch New England's largest expeditionary military undertaking to date.

Most of New England's military manpower, including the Gorham family, would be needed for the campaign. The General Court approved funding for three thousand troops from the Bay Colony alone. Shirley commissioned John Gorham's father, Shubael, colonel and commander of the Seventh Massachusetts Regiment and with General Pepperell called upon John's support in recruiting troops for the army. Pepperell and Shirley also expected him to leverage his contacts within the maritime community to procure the whaleboats that would serve as landing craft during the assault. Besides rank as a lieutenant colonel in his father's regiment, Shirley and Pepperell gave the younger Gorham operational and tactical command over all the expedition's whaleboat operations. Gorham would be the officer most responsible for making sure the Anglo-American provincials got safely from their ships to the shore.[54] It was a position of tremendous responsibility. With preparations for the campaign against Louisbourg consuming the great majority of his time, Gorham had little choice but to postpone his movement against Minas and Chignecto indefinitely.

Acadians and Mi'kmaq and the Louisbourg Campaign

The story of New England's siege of Louisbourg in the spring and summer of 1745 has been told many times and does not need recounting here. Two important aspects of the campaign that affected Nova Scotia, however, require attention. First is the role of the Acadians. Throughout May and June, with the Yankee army bivouacked at Canso, the Acadians went about their lives as if nothing out of the ordinary had happened. Because the New Englanders had come with a force of nearly four thousand men, discretion no doubt was the better part of valor. No Acadians took to the woods to wage a partisan war on the Americans' communication and supply lines, and none risked hurrying to Louisbourg to warn Governor Duchambon of the force he would soon face. The only direct support the Acadians gave to the French, the support of a few partisans, was to Lieutenant Paul Marin de La Malgue's force at Minas.

On January 19, Marin (one of New France's most renowned frontier soldiers) had left Quebec for a campaign against Annapolis Royal at the head of a three-hundred-man-strong party of troupes de la marine, Canadian militia, Abenakis, and sauvages domiciliés.[55] The welcome the Acadians offered was not dissimilar to the one they had given Duvivier the previous year. On May 25, five Minas Acadians appeared before the council in Annapolis Royal to tell of recent events. It was a bold act on their part, because Marin had forbidden any contact with the British. Nonetheless, the deputies reported that Marin had taken to requisitioning supplies from them and had confiscated much of the community's cattle and carts. He especially wanted to make an example of the deputies. Marin demanded that the Acadians provide three head of cattle a week, and if they failed to supply the animals, he would burn their homes and kill all their livestock.[56]

Marin dallied at Minas, then made his move toward Annapolis Royal. He arrived outside Fort Anne with no artillery with which to breach the walls just in time to learn that the Yankees had laid siege to Louisbourg and that he and his small army were needed there. By the time he was in a position to reach the besieged garrison, however, the French inside the fort were well past waging an effective defense. Duchambon capitulated on June 17. By August 1, Marin had returned to Quebec after spending the better part of the summer tromping back and forth across Nova Scotia. Although he reported to Governor-General Beauharnois that he felt the Acadians "were desirous of returning under French control,"[57] the reality on the ground was much different. The Acadians wanted nothing to do with the French army and its two forays into Minas, where it had accomplished nothing but eating Acadian crops and complicating their affairs with the Anglo-Americans.

Mascarene and the council assessed guilt and punishment for those Acadians who had helped Marin. It "was notorious that there were several among them that had been officious towards the enemy," the council observed. Moreover, someone had fired on a party of rangers near Goat Island, at the mouth of the Annapolis River. The council called Le Maigre to appear. When he protested his innocence (and lacking any hard evidence with which to indict him), Mascarene turned to Jean Terriot for information. Terriot told the British that only a handful of Acadians, perhaps members of the Raymond family (Terriot was unclear whether it was François, Jacques, or Joseph) and François La Basque and his son-in-law, had helped Marin. Moreover, Terriot claimed that he did not know who had shot at the rangers at Goat Island.[58] Mascarene would not arrest a man based on innuendo and hearsay alone. Le Maigre and members of the Raymond and La Basque families could be thankful that the rule of law and the rights of Englishmen were so dear to Mascarene and the British officers at Annapolis Royal. Even if the Acadians were not Englishmen per se, Mascarene would not violate his principles in the name of mere expediency.[59]

The second key point regarding the Louisbourg campaign in Nova Scotia centers on the participation of the Mi'kmaq. Beauharnois believed that the Mi'kmaq were "irreconcilable enemis of the English" and that they greatly feared becoming refugees in Canada or along the south side of Baie des Chaleurs. Thus he expected them to fight on Île Royale.[60] Yet most Mi'kmaq chose not to fight in 1745, and those who did, did so only halfheartedly. In their first engagement with the New Englanders at Port Toulouse (present-day St. Peters), the Île Royale Mi'kmaq put up virtually no resistance and allowed the Yankees to burn the settlement. They then refused to link up with Marin's force and instead withdrew up the East Bay of Bras d'Or Lake, where they hoped they would be safe from New England raiding parties and patrols. In late May, they consented to join a hundred Frenchmen under Philipe Leneuf de Beaubassin, a former officer of the troupes de la marine. Leneuf thought that the Mi'kmaq and a handful of volunteers from Louisbourg could wreak havoc behind the New England lines. But after a brisk skirmish near Petit Lorembec (Little Lorrain) that cost the Mi'kmaq sixteen wounded, the Indians had had enough. Although the French fort held out for another three weeks, the Indians abandoned Leneuf and traveled to New Brunswick. The fight at Petit Lorembec, meanwhile, motivated Commodore Peter Warren, commander of the British armada that had blockaded Louisbourg during the New Englanders' siege, to issue a stern warning to Duchambon. Warren wanted to forestall any French or Indian partisan activity that might complicate matters for the Anglo-American occupying forces. He instructed Duchambon to tell the Indians to leave the island; otherwise the British would "be obliged to put them, and all such French as shall be found with them, to the sword."[61] By that time, however, there were few Indians remaining to whom Duchambon could pass on the warning. In one final bit of frustration for the French, when Marin finally moved toward Louisbourg, the Mi'kmaq at Shubenacadie refused to help him drive off the three armed New England vessels that blocked his crossing of Northumberland Strait.[62] Indeed, in August, Acadian Pierre Landry appeared before the council to relate that the Mi'kmaq wanted a cease-fire, to which the British consented.[63] Clearly they, like the Acadians, wanted no part of the fight over Louisbourg.

Beauharnois and the Ministry of Marine realized that they needed to act quickly to defend New France. The Yankees had kicked open the eastern door to Canada, and the Indians and Acadians had stood by and watched them do it. That the British would approach Montreal and Quebec from Lake Champlain while a seaborne force would push up the Saint Lawrence from Louisbourg seemed almost certain. Because he could not hope to fight the British on the Saint Lawrence without significant reinforcements from the French navy, which could not sail to North America until the spring after the Anglo-Americans would have already set out anyway, Beauharnois chose to despoil the American frontier in New York and New England. Raids on the New York frontier also would help convince the Iroquois League that New France was far from conquered and would help quash what seemed to the French the Mohawks' worrisome drift from neutrality toward allegiance to the British. It was hardly an original plan, but that made it no less effective. The French had used the Indians and raids by the troupes de la marine to keep the English off balance in both of the two previous imperial wars. Yet the Anglo-Americans were unprepared. In August, seven hundred troupes de la marine, Canadian militia, and Indians overwhelmed the Bay Colony militia stationed at Fort Massachusetts.[64] In November, Marin (with four hundred troupes de la marine and sauvages domiciliés, plus Maliseets and Penobscots from Acadia) attacked Saratoga, New York. Marin's raiders ransacked the village and took more than one hundred captives, thereby pushing New York's frontier settlers into panic.[65]

Whereas the capture of Louisbourg, as historian Ian Steele has observed, "had done nothing to calm New England frontiers," it did deflect Indian activities outside Annapolis Royal.[66]

Meanwhile, all was not well for the Yankees inside Louisbourg. Although they had avoided both a major bloodletting in taking the fort and an Indian and French uprising following its capture, disease took a terrible toll on the New England troops. They were amateurs when it came to large-scale operations, and they knew little of the proper procedures for camp sanitation and health. By mid-January 1746, 500 of the New England troops had died, and another 1,100 were sick. The diseases that ravaged the Yankees struck regardless of rank. John Gorham's father died in the epidemic, and Gorham replaced him as commander of the Seventh Massachusetts Regiment.[67] In February, Mi'kmaq from Le Loutre's mission presented two letters for Shirley that they had intercepted in which the Anglo-Americans at Louisbourg requested 1,000 to 1,200 reinforcements to replace their dead and sick. In April, Le Loutre further reported that the Yankees had withdrawn from Canso and that disease and illness continued to wrack the army.[68] It remained questionable whether the Yankees could hold Louisbourg for the long term.

Beauharnois hoped to capitalize on the Americans' suffering. In the spring, several parties of Abenakis and Maliseets had approached him offering their services. If Beauharnois would promise bounties on British scalps—a practice that French and Anglo-American officials long had used to get their Indian allies and frontiersmen to go against the enemy—they would march on Nova Scotia. In May, François Duvivier and 300 Abenakis and Maliseets left for Acadia.[69] In late summer, after word that the Anglo-American invasion force that had mustered at Albany for the land invasion of Canada was collapsing on itself because of gross incompetence by its commanders and organizers and that a French fleet was on its way to North America, Beauharnois reinforced the French troops in Acadia with nearly 1,800 Canadian militia under Jean-Baptiste-Nicolas-Roch de Ramezay.[70] Ramezay replaced Duvivier as commander of the French forces, but the sauvages domiciles consented to join the French only as allies, not as auxiliaries. The armies of New France and its Indian allies stood posed to retake Nova Scotia, if only they could get the support of the heavy guns of the French navy.

D'Anville's Expedition

From inside Annapolis Royal and Louisbourg, the situation in Nova Scotia looked increasingly bleak as the summer progressed. The British held those two posts, to be sure, but the rest of Nova Scotia and Cape Breton Island were out of their control. The blockhouse at Canso, meanwhile, was "little better than a heap of rubble."[71] At the same time, rumors trickled in of the large French and Indian forces at Beaubassin on the Isthmus of Chignecto and in the Saint-Jean Valley. The vast majority of the Acadians had yet to rebel, but one could only guess how long they could keep the French at arm's length. In the late summer, the most troublesome news for the Anglo-Americans arrived from Europe. A French armada of ninety-seven ships commanded by the duc d'Anville, Jean-Baptiste-Louis-Frédéric de La Rochefoucauld de Roye (marquis de Roucy), had eluded the British navy's blockade and headed for North American waters. No one in the Anglo-American colonies knew for sure where the French would strike, and in the whirl of rumors that followed, some suggested that the French might be so bold as to attack Boston.[72]

D'Anville's fleet barely made it to North America. After its departure in June, storms wracked it off the Azores and scattered it across the North Atlantic. By August 24, the fleet had been at sea for over two months yet was still more than three hundred leagues (nine hundred statute miles) from Nova Scotia. On September 10, lead elements were within sight of the Nova Scotia coast, but three days later, a violent gale descended on them and damaged many of the vessels, which then returned to France. On September 27, second-in-command Constantin-Louis d'Estourmel and his ships joined those vessels that had managed to beat into the safety of Chebucto Bay on the east coast on the peninsula. The indefatigable Father Le Loutre was there to meet them. The authorities in Quebec had entrusted the priest with the secret semaphore codes that d'Anville would look for to know that the harbor was safe to enter. When d'Estourmel finally made landfall, he learned that d'Anville had died that morning. Three days later, d'Estourmel decided that the proper course of action while his fleet and sailors probably faced a battle with the British was to run himself through with his sword. Command of the expedition then fell to Jacques-Pierre de Taffanel de La Jonquière, marquis de La Jonquière, governor-general designee of New France. La Jonquière wrapped the French navy in further ignominy when contrary winds and fog compelled him to abandon a thrust against Annapolis Royal and ordered the fleet to sail for the West Indies. A report at the end of the disastrous expedition listed 587 dead and nearly 2,300 sick out of a complement of just over 11,000 sailors and soldiers. Luck and the gross incompetence of the French navy had spared Nova Scotia a major battle, and the French navy had again proven itself unable to support the army in Acadia.[73]

While d'Anville's armada sailed to its destiny, Gorham refocused on Nova Scotia. He left Louisbourg in the early spring after it had become clear that he could do nothing of merit while watching the soldiers of his regiment die. He first returned to Boston, where he stayed only for a brief period, just long enough to form another ranger company. With the Louisbourg operation finished, Gorham became almost single-minded in his desire to take the war to the Acadians and Indians in what increasingly looked like a French sanctuary in Minas and Chignecto. Upon the rangers' arrival at Annapolis Royal, Mascarene handed responsibility for military affairs outside Fort Anne to them.[74] Gorham and his men, who were at that time primarily Yankee frontiersmen, quickly set about procuring provisions and equipment for a punitive raid on Minas and Chignecto.

Before unleashing Gorham on the Acadians, Mascarene hoped that one last attempt at accommodation would avert bloodshed.[75] Basing his opinion on his many years among them, he believed that the great majority of the Acadians would commit to neutrality. Mascarene, with his many trading connections with the Acadians, believed that the key to British success in Nova Scotia depended on treating the locals as much as possible as partners in governance. But time was running out for both sides. He therefore directed Gorham to administer to as many Acadians as were willing to accept it an oath of allegiance to King George II. Because the French twice had used Minas as a staging area and the Acadians would expect the British to provide for their safety in return for taking the oath, Mascarene also instructed Gorham to build blockhouses in Minas and on Chignecto. He had set the table for one of the Yankees' worst military defeats in the eighteenth century.

The Battle of Grand Pré and Its Aftermath

Mascarene sent mixed messages to the Acadians. The British had not tried to place a permanent structure outside Canso or the banlieu since 1732. The fact that Mascarene gave the Yankee rangers—troops whom the Acadians viewed as "far more terrible than European soldiers"[76]—the mission of building the blockhouses worried the Acadians greatly. Many Acadians began to wonder what the British had in store for them. The Yankees at Louisbourg had made several bellicose pronouncements about deporting the Acadians. When Gorham reached Minas, he reported that the Acadians openly feared that the British intended the oath "only to make them easy until we can get them in our power to Remove them."[77] Indeed, on November 8 of the previous year, Mascarene and the council had sent their version of Nova Scotia's history to the Board of Trade, in which they judged that since the Acadians "cannot be accounted less than unprofitable Inhabitants," perhaps "the said French Inhabitants may . . . be transported out of the Province of Nova Scotia and be replac'd by good Protestant Subjects."[78] Despite a formal proclamation written in French that the British had no intention of harming the Acadians, few were relieved. Gorham undoubtedly exacerbated Acadian angst when, as "punishment" for several Acadian families who had fled in the face of the rangers and "Lodge[d] in the Woods at Nights for fear," he burned their houses and fields.[79] The Acadians were so distraught that they asked Mascarene directly if the British intended to deport them. He responded "by assuring them that if his Majesty had had any Such Intention, he would have heard of it" and assured them that their fears were "without Foundation."[80]

Gorham, meanwhile, had bigger fish to fry. The rangers learned of French movements on the peninsula from an Acadian they had abducted. The captive reported that d'Anville's fleet had wrecked, and more important, Ramezay had spread his forces along a line from Chignecto through Minas. Gorham rightly suspected that Ramezay would withdraw those forces once he learned of d'Anville's fate, and as the French pulled back to Chignecto, they would be open to ambush. The rangers, Gorham claimed, would "so Annoy & Surprise this Army as to oblige them to make as precipitate and Lucky Retreat as Monsieur Du Vivier did before in the Like Case."[81] But in what was surely a major disappointment for Gorham, Ramezay disengaged and slipped across the isthmus and to Beaubassin without making contact with the rangers.

Nonetheless, the British again had bested the French in Nova Scotia. Mascarene took that opportunity to tell the Acadians how costly d'Anville's disaster had been and rhetorically asked them what they had gained from it. Henceforth, he advised, they should avoid all "deluding Hopes of Returning under the Dominion of France."[82] Bellair took Mascarene's suggestion to heart and fled to New France.[83]

The autumn and early winter saw Nova Scotia abuzz with Yankee military activity. The Bay Colony had taken over management of the war. Gorham's Rangers arrived in Minas Basin, where they glared at the Acadians. Although they did not engage the Indians (or, for that matter, the Acadians or French) in any fights, their presence surely disconcerted the locals. William Shirley then sent Lieutenant Colonel Arthur Noble's regiment of 460 Yankee militiamen to Nova Scotia in November to relieve Gorham's Rangers of occupation duty. When it came time for the regiment's movement from Annapolis Royal to Minas Basin, however, only two Acadians stepped forward as guides. Mascarene thereupon summoned Paul Doucett (no relation to John Doucett) and Charles Pelerain, but they fled into the woods. The Acadians could not afford to betray their Acadian kin or violate their neutrality and become enemies of the Indians. Mascarene had to call back a party of rangers to serve as guides for Noble. The rangers led the Yankees to Grand Pré, then familiarized them with the area of operation before marching back to Fort Anne.[84] While the rangers showed the Yankees around Minas, Mascarene, who finally had grown tired of the Acadian disobedience, ordered the estates of Bellair, Doucett, and Pelerain confiscated.[85]

The residents of Grand Pré were less than pleased to find an entire Yankee regiment in their midst. The rangers had been bad enough, but the Acadians' frustration rose when Mascarene warned them to "seriously consider their Interest and to Animate the Inhabitants to their Duty" and directed that they had to provide provisions and supplies for the regiment. Moreover, the town lacked barracks, and because the rangers had made only a halfhearted effort at building the blockhouses (which at any rate would have offered inadequate shelter for an entire regiment), Noble dispersed his men in individual homes throughout the town. He even commandeered the town's stone-walled mill as his headquarters. The citizens of Grand Pré responded by placing "many Difficulties" in the way of the men's comfort by being parsimonious with food and firewood.[86]

Ramezay could see that the New Englanders were overextended and vulnerable at Grand Pré. On January 23, 1747, he sent nearly 240 Canadian militia, led by Captain Nicholas-Antoine Coulon de Villiers and Chevalier Louis de La Corne, with a party of Maliseets, to attack Grand Pré.[87] After a grueling but stealthy march on snowshoes and sleds down the north side of the isthmus, then through Cobequid, Shubenacadie, and Pisiquid, they found themselves on the eastern approaches to Grand Pré late on January 30. Coulon prepared for a pre-dawn attack by dividing his force into ten teams. He hoped to strike the dispersed British outposts simultaneously and put them quickly to flight. To the Canadians' and Indians' advantage, a howling snowstorm kicked up and covered the noise of their advance into the village. After receiving absolution in the pre-dawn darkness from Father Maillard, the Canadians struck around two o'clock the next morning. They surrounded "almost every officer's quarters within a few minutes," Benjamin Goldthwait recalled, "and after killing the sentrys, rushing into several of the houses and destroying many in their bed, so that before daylight they had killed about seventy, and taken upwards of sixty prisoners and wounded others," including Colonel Noble. Although first taken by surprise, the New Englanders rallied around the headquarters building. They held out for most of the day through repeated attacks and several truces that allowed both sides to remove and care for their wounded. Finally, as the sun began to set, the New Englanders ran low on ammunition, food, and water and raised the flag of surrender. In the fight, 6 New England officers, including Noble, and 124 privates had died. Another 34 were wounded, including Edward How, who had fought so well at Annapolis Royal in 1744. The French also took 53 Yankee prisoners. The French forces suffered only 6 killed (an Acadian from Port Toulouse, 2 Indians, and 3 Canadian militiamen) and 14 wounded. La Corne, who led the French forces after Coulon had been wounded, gave Goldthwait, the ranking New England officer still standing, generous terms. The Yankees were to march to Annapolis Royal, where they were not to bear arms for one year, and the French would transport the New England wounded to Rivière-aux-Canards, where they would be cared for until the British could provide adequate and safe transportation.[88]

Upon hearing of the action at Grand Pré, Mascarene rushed the rangers there. They were too late; the French did not intend to stay long. The French spiked the small cannon that the New Englanders had placed in the town and burnt the frames to the blockhouses. The rangers could do little but escort the shocked New Englanders to Annapolis Royal. Mascarene tried to bolster the Yankees' spirits by reminding them that their "misfortune at Mines was one of those things to which we are liable in war" and "that it is nothing but the surprise that has given them any advantage over you."[89] The truth of the matter, of course, was that a relatively small force of French partisans had effectively destroyed an entire provincial regiment.

Following Noble's defeat at Grand Pré, both Mascarene and Shirley abandoned hope of defending Nova Scotia with the New England militia. Clearly, static positions such as the one they had established at Grand Pré were of little value. Posting New England occupation forces outside Annapolis Royal offered little more than isolated outposts that the French could pick off at their choosing. Without enough soldiers to occupy all of Nova Scotia, both to overawe the French and to provide security for the Acadians, Shirley and Mascarene logically turned to the rangers.

They believed that the rangers were key to intercepting and destroying the French as French forces moved in and out of Nova Scotia. To date, however, the rangers had been too small in numbers to defeat the large forces that the French had sent into the colony. Shirley therefore proposed to raise two thousand of them. Of course, the money for such a force would have to come from elsewhere, so the governor dispatched Gorham to the duke of Newcastle to lobby for the formation of several new ranger companies.[90] "I think the great service which Lieutenant-Colonel Gorham's Company of Rangers has been to the garrison at Annapolis Royal," Shirley wrote in Gorham's letter of introduction, "is a demonstration of the usefulness of such a corps."[91]

John and Elizabeth Gorham sailed for London in the spring of 1747. British officials gave him a warm welcome. Gorham made a positive impression on John Russell, duke of Bedford and secretary of state of the Southern Department; Gorham's Rangers were, in Bedford's estimation, "more than ever absolutely necessary for the immediate preservation of the Province of Nova Scotia."[92] In April, King George II granted John and Elizabeth an audience. The king likewise was impressed with Gorham and granted him a captain's commission in the regular British army.[93] While neither the king nor Bedford said anything about giving Gorham two thousand men to command, the man who had entered the war in 1744 in hopes of bettering his and his family's lives certainly had done well.

Captain Gorham of the British army (he also held the rank of colonel in the Massachusetts militia) returned to Nova Scotia in late 1747 to learn that the war had effectively ended. With Gorham in London and the Massachusetts militia still reeling from the shock of the battle at Grand Pré and the men of Philipps's Regiment best suited for garrison duty, Mascarene had put offensive operations on hold. The French, meanwhile, had withdrawn toward Quebec. Thus, Gorham spent the winter of 1747–48 again recruiting rangers and stockpiling supplies for what he hoped would be his first real offensive operation into Minas and Chignecto, not the building and oath-delivering errand that Mascarene had sent him on in 1746.

In Gorham's absence, the French had had the opportunity to operate with impunity in Chignecto and Minas. Nothing came of that chance. French military efforts had to focus on the threat posed by Anglo-American forces on the New York front. In the spring, La Corne returned to Quebec with plans for an invasion of Canada that he had learned from the Anglo-American prisoners. New Englanders had set aside nine hundred men for a springtime attack against Fort Saint Frédéric (Crown Point) on Lake Champlain, and Commodore Warren had set sail for England to muster naval forces for a drive up the Saint Lawrence. At the same time, the British had just enough offensive striking power in Nova Scotia to keep the French off guard. In April, Captain John Rous sailed the twenty-four-gun *Shirley* and two transports with three hundred men to Minas Basin. Rous occupied Grand Pré for four days in a show of British resolve. Matters then became progressively worse for the French. In May, word arrived in Quebec that Commodore Warren had reached Boston with fifteen warships. Just then, the French officers from Beaubassin reported that their forces, posted on the extreme far end of a slender tether of supplies, were succumbing to hunger and disease. Further intelligence came in that fourteen warships were en route to Louisbourg and two British corsairs were patrolling off the Gaspé Peninsula, thereby isolating Nova Scotia from any French reinforcements by sea.[94]

The key to all the intelligence of the British movements around the colony had become the Acadians. After the Anglo-American campaign into the Minas Basin in the winter of 1746–47, the Acadians seemed to once again look more favorably on the French. Only a few Acadians had openly sided with the French, but many more were amenable to passing the French intelligence and warnings of British troop movements. Indeed, the banlieu Acadians had passed on news of the arrival of Warren's warships in Boston. In September, the inhabitants of Beaubassin requested that the French send them supplies, because they had been cut off from trade with the outside world. The Acadians were drifting dangerously close to the French. If the British could prove the Acadians' willingness to share information with the French, as well as their requests for French aid, there would be hell to pay.

News that British and French negotiators had reached preliminary terms of peace at Aix-la-Chapelle in the spring of 1748, however, put an end to all military operations in Nova Scotia and postponed the Yankees' settling accounts with the Acadians. The war was a stalemate in Europe, and the British debt had ballooned. Clearly seeing that the two Crowns were looking for ways out of the war, Mascarene extended an olive branch to the Acadians.[95] He sent Joseph Gorham, John's younger brother, to Grand Pré to pay the Acadians for the provisions that they had supplied to Noble's troops. Gorham probably could not believe what he heard, but Mascarene, if it meant keeping the peace between the Anglo-Americans and Acadians, was willing to forgive the locals for any potential wrongdoing. He also suggested that John Gorham send the rangers on furlough to New England, where they could see their families and rest. Gorham grudgingly agreed but used his time on leave to recruit more rangers for his companies. He offered a fifteen-pound advance in pay to anyone willing to enlist for what the captain was sure would be the next war in Nova Scotia.[96]

5

Father Le Loutre's War, 1749–1755

The peace of Aix-la-Chapelle offered only a lull in the fighting in Nova Scotia. The terms that ended the War of the Austrian Succession in Europe failed to resolve the reasons for King George's War in North America. New Englanders had embraced the third of the imperial wars as a means to complete the conquest of Acadia, take Louisbourg, and rid themselves of the menace posed by French Canada and its Indian allies. At the end of four years of fighting that saw as many disappointments as successes, however, the Yankees were no nearer to reaching any of those ends. Indeed, regarding the northeastern frontier, the British profoundly disappointed them at the end of the conflict by returning Louisbourg to the French in return for Madras, India, and the maintenance of the balance of power in Europe.[1]

Although New France still stood, the French likewise had suffered a string of defeats. The failure to capture Annapolis Royal, the temporary loss of Louisbourg, the wreck of the French fleet, and the inability to win Mi'kmaw and Acadian hearts and minds and employ them as allies all had reflected poorly on French arms. Even an amateur of strategic thinking could see that the eastern reaches of New France were vulnerable and needed reinforcing.

For the Acadians, the war had been a disaster. Both the French and the Anglo-Americans questioned their neutral status and endangered their prosperity and security. Indeed, Anglo-American doubts about Acadians' commitment to neutrality became a sword of Damocles hanging over their heads.

The war brought still more ambiguities and confusion for the Indians. The Mi'kmaq, after an initial foray into the conflict in 1744, tried their best to stand above the Europeans' war, while the Maliseets joined, albeit halfheartedly, with the French. The extent of the Indians' devotion to the French in the next conflict, however, remained open to question. In the spring of 1748, then, all involved in Nova Scotia must have been unsure of what the purported peace meant and, more important, how long it might last.

John Gorham and Jean-Louis Le Loutre determined that the peace would be short-lived. Neither Gorham nor Le Loutre was content with the return to the status quo antebellum to which their respective monarchs had agreed, and both did their utmost to settle what they viewed as the fundamental question in Nova Scotia: to whom did the colony belong? On the distant frontier of North America, both had free rein to settle that question without interference from the London or Paris. That suited their preferences. Neither possessed the slightest reservation about doing whatever was necessary to completely rid Nova Scotia of his enemies. Any means justified their ends, and neither would permit outside interference with or internal opposition to his designs for the colony. In the end, they thrust Nova Scotia into a brutal war from which others proved unwilling and unable to pull back.

Father Le Loutre's War—the war takes his name because he, more than anyone, wanted the Anglo-Americans out of Nova Scotia—possessed the worst characteristics of modern warfare: indiscriminate violence inflicted on noncombatants, the creation of large refugee populations, guerrilla operations, terrorism, fierce insurgency and equally vicious counterinsurgency, and most ominously, ethnic cleansing. The brutality that Father Le Loutre's War unleashed in Nova Scotia developed an inexorable momentum that pushed the French, Anglo-Americans, Acadians, and Indians to a point at which the accommodation and peaceful coexistence that had defined the late 1720s and 1730s no longer seemed possible. At the midpoint of the 1750s, Anglo-Americans—both Britons and Yankees—threw away the modus vivendi of the previous decades. They used Father Le Loutre's War as a pretext to drive the Acadians from their homelands. The proscription and deportation of the Acadians was, from the Anglo-American perspective, a necessary and logical act of the frontier war for empire in which they found themselves.[2] Indeed, one cannot remove the Acadian dispersion from the context of Father Le Loutre's War.

Hostilities Surface

The tempo of events in Nova Scotia quickly outpaced developments in Europe. On April 30, 1748, French and British negotiators had agreed to preliminary terms to end the war, and in May, the French Crown ordered a suspension of military activities at sea.[3] But to give time to overcome opposition to the treaty—William Pitt had stated as early as 1746 that he "would never restore Cape Breton . . . while any resource remain'd" to vigorously prosecute the war against France[4]—the signing of the formal declaration of peace did not occur until October. All the maneuvering and geopolitical concerns in London, however, were mere distractions to John Gorham. The ranger captain believed that Anglo-Americans needed to impose their authority over first the Acadians and then the Indians. He also held that force was the only measure that the Acadians and Indians would respect.

Paul Mascarene came out of the war essentially agreeing with Gorham. The fighting had convinced him that the British possessed little real authority over the Acadians and Indians, and all his careful and fair handling of them had resulted in only a minuscule level of obedience without allegiance. "I cannot possibly avoid being moved to find so small a Correspondence between your words and actions," he told the Acadian deputies in late August 1748, "which may undoubtedly Cause the Sincerity of your Promises to be much suspected and consequently render all my Endeavours to promote your happiness abortive."[5] Mascarene thus was disinclined to offer more carrots and instead preferred more sticks. Gorham's Rangers, who loathed the Acadians and whom the locals equally despised and feared, fanned out across the colony to collect oaths of allegiance. If Mascarene wanted Gorham to send a clear and unambiguous message of British power to the Acadians, he was not disappointed.

In September, Gorham took his company to the French missions and small Acadian settlements in present-day New Brunswick to inform the locals that they were required to send deputies to Annapolis Royal. Although the Acadians—long accustomed to receiving such demands from the British—agreed, the Maliseets refused. When Gorham insisted that they comply, matters quickly deteriorated. After an exchange of harsh words, the Maliseets opened fire on the Yankees and killed two rangers. Gorham was enraged. He seized two Indians who did not have the luck or good sense to avoid his rangers, and he put a Maliseet village to the torch. Roland-Michel Barrin de La Galissonière, the marquis de La Galissonière, who was governor-general of New France, wrote to both Shirley and Mascarene to excoriate Gorham and warn them that if they did not rein him in, there would be war. Mascarene and Shirley had no interest in being lectured, and they responded that they supported their officer fully.[6] No one on the Anglo-American side seemed overly concerned that war with the Indians was imminent.

Indeed, by 1748 it was clear to many Anglo-Americans that war was the only means to make good their claims to Nova Scotia. The Yankees particularly had grown tired of half measures, waffling, and the general lack of support. Despite estimates that showed between five hundred and one thousand Mi'kmaw men sprinkled across Nova Scotia and Acadia,[7] the Yankees must have thought they could settle affairs, at least in an open fight, with the Indians. At the same time, other Anglo-Americans had come to see the Acadians as posing as much of a threat as the Indians. William Vaughan, who had encouraged Shirley to attack Louisbourg in 1745, wrote in London's *Gentleman's Magazine* that the Acadians would be the ruin of the British in Nova Scotia. They controlled the wealth of the colony, and their numbers overwhelmed the British. It was not a new argument. Richard Philipps had warned twenty years earlier that the Acadians were like the progeny of Noah and would smother the British in the colony. Vaughan gave that argument fresh support and estimated that when Great Britain took possession of Nova Scotia in 1710, there had been between three thousand and four thousand Acadians, but since then their numbers had exploded to twenty-five thousand. Acadia was "already more populous in proportion to its extent, than any part of Canada," he correctly observed. Even if he did overestimate the size of the Acadian population at both dates, the fact remained that the

British had yet to establish an effective civil government in the colony, and few Anglo-Americans, except for the small community in the faubourg, had risked moving there. As the British population scratched out a living constrained to the vicinity of Annapolis Royal and the summer fishing camps at Canso, the Acadians spread across Chignecto, Île Royale, and even the Gaspé Peninsula.

The French, if the British could not, understood the value of Nova Scotia, Vaughan believed. "Thus we see [that] the French are unwearied in their efforts to recover this place," he warned. The loss of the sole remaining British outpost in the colony, Annapolis Royal, would be an unmitigated disaster. The French could garrison four thousand to five thousand men around Fort Anne and make it, with Louisbourg, an impenetrable barrier that would hem in New England at the Maine frontier and cut off British trade and fishing in the western North Atlantic.[8] Settling the colony with Protestants therefore seemed to offer the solution to all the British problems in Nova Scotia.

In 1749, the Board of Trade finally addressed the concerns that those on the ground in Nova Scotia had raised. The board agreed to establish a new settlement, which it called Halifax (in honor of George Montagu Dunk, second earl of Halifax and president of the board), on Chebucto Bay. The Board of Trade had been interested in Chebucto Bay as early as Charles Davidson's aborted scheme to send settlers there in 1724 but had been unwilling to devote the resources necessary for a settlement. The navy, however, left King George's War convinced that it needed better port and repair facilities in western North Atlantic waters. Its only careening yards in the Atlantic outside Europe were in the West Indies, and those could not keep up with the demands of the fleet.[9] Thus the board, at the Admiralty's urging, again looked at the Atlantic side of the Nova Scotia peninsula. As an alternative to a new settlement and base at Halifax, the British of course could have turned to Louisbourg. There remained, however, the significant detail that the diplomats had returned that locality to France at Aix-la-Chapelle. In addition, as a port it was inadequate for the navy's purposes, and the Yankees had shown how difficult it was to provision (as well as the overrated estimate of its defenses). While some opponents of the Halifax plan claimed that it was a gigantic boondoggle—thirty years after its founding, for example, Edmund Burke called Halifax an "ill-thriven, hard-visaged, and ill-favored brat" that had cost Great Britain £700,000[10]—the decision was in fact the proper one for the navy, the security of Nova Scotia, and the prosperity of the empire.

Halifax Changes Everything

The typically parsimonious Board of Trade set out to build the settlement as cheaply as possible. The board hoped to draw settlers from the British soldiers, marines, and sailors who served in North America. In 1719 it had authorized Richard Philipps to grant fifty acres of land in fee-simple, with no quit rents, to any serviceman who agreed to stay in Nova Scotia once his enlistment was complete. The offer attracted very few takers, because the Indians had little motive to join the Anglo-Americans. In March 1749 the board provided more inducements. To any enlisted troops who agreed to settle in the province, it promised fifty-acre land grants plus ten-acre head rights—titles to land given in return for paying for the transportation of persons, such as laborers and family members, to the colony. Noncommissioned officers would receive eighty acres and fifteen-acre head rights. Officers did even better: besides thirty-acre head rights, ensigns would get two hundred acres, lieutenants three hundred, and captains four hundred, while field grade officers would receive six hundred for settling in the colony. In addition, the Crown would provide the settlers with arms and ammunition to defend themselves.[11]

In May 1749, over 2,500 Protestant settlers sailed for Chebucto Bay. On June 28, after what one propagandist judged "a short and pleasant passage of between five and six weeks," they landed.[12] Companies of British regulars from the Twenty-ninth (Hopson's), the Forty-fifth (Warburton's), and the Fifty-sixth (Horseman's) Regiments soon joined them.[13] The regulars had been at Louisbourg, and upon returning the fortress to the French, they sailed south to link up with the settlers at Chebucto Bay.[14] The arrival of the British at Halifax thus had as much the flavor of an amphibious invasion as a landing of settlers. Gorham's Rangers marched from Fort Anne and took a position outside the beachhead from which they could look over the settlement and intercept any attacks on it. There was even talk that some of the defeated Highlanders from the Jacobite Rebellion of 1745, who had a reputation as fierce backwoods fighters, might be of use to the empire in Nova Scotia.[15]

Edward Cornwallis, Halifax's protégé (to whom he had given the governorship of the colony), wasted little time in taking a firm stand with the Acadians. A mere two weeks after the landing, Cornwallis convened the Nova Scotia Council. There were no openly pro-Acadian voices on it: members included Cornwallis; Nova Scotia experts John Gorham, Paul Mascarene, and Edward How; Yankee Benjamin Green as treasurer; Hugh Davidson as secretary; and John Salusbury—a client of Lord Halifax—as register and receiver of rents.[16] Cornwallis's first declaration to the Acadians signified that a new British administration had arrived. After informing them that King George had decided to send a "considerable number" of subjects to Nova Scotia and advising that it was the Acadians' duty to "give all countenance, assistance and encouragement" to them, Cornwallis spoke directly to the locals' past behavior. Despite having given the Acadians the free exercise of their religion and possession of their land, the British had "not met with a dutifull Return, but on the Contrary divers of the said Inhabitants have openly abetted or privately assisted His Majesty's Enemies in their attempts, by furnishing them with quarters, Provisions and Intelligence and concealing their designs." The only remedy to that situation was for every Acadian to take an unqualified oath of allegiance within three months.[17]

The council considered options on how best to handle the expected Acadian refusal. Mascarene, whom Cornwallis upbraided for allowing the Acadians too many liberties, read past versions of the oath to provide context on British-Acadian relations. By that point in his career, and no doubt stung by Cornwallis's criticism, even he had tired of the Acadians' intransigence. Thus, he did not fight for incorporation of his suggestion that the British tack the phrase "& ce Serment Je prens sans réserve" ("and this oath I take without reservation") onto its end. The Acadians would have to swear unreservedly, "Je [nom] promets & Jure sincèrement, en foi de Chrétien que Je serai entièrement fidèle & obérai vraiment Sa Majesté Le Roi George le Second qeue Je reconnois pour Le Souverain Seigneur de l'Acadie ou nouvelle France." ("I [name] promise and swear sincerely, as a Christian, that I will be entirely faithful and will obey absolutely His Majesty King George the Second, that I recognize him as the Lord Sovereign of Acadia, or New France.")[18] There would be no room for the Acadians to maneuver. Cornwallis demanded nothing less than absolute obedience to King George II and his appointed representatives in North America.

The Acadians responded with little more than the warmed-over arguments of years past. On July 29, banlieu, Minas, and Chignecto deputies presented themselves to the council and answered that they could not take the oath, because it contained no provisions for the protection of their properties, religion, or neutral status. The council responded that there would be no negotiations. On the question of their properties, the council informed them that as British subjects their titles to their lands were guaranteed implicitly. Concerning their Catholic faith, the council would accept past practice and allow the Acadians priests, provided that the clergy received licenses from the governor. The council would say nothing of religion, however, in the oath itself. Last was the issue of neutrality: "It was the unanimous Opinion of the Council that no Exception should be granted them, but that they should be told peremptorily That they must take the Oath of Allegiance as offer'd them." Any Acadian who refused to subscribe would forfeit his land. Moreover, because the British could not trust the deputies to deliver the oath, Crown officers would travel to the Acadian regions to present it to the entire community. All within the colony had until October 26 to subscribe or face the consequences.[19]

The Acadians would not concede the last word on the matter. On August 1, they presented the council with the canard that they would emigrate from the colony and take their movable property with them if forced to take an oath not to their liking. Rather than express concern that the Acadians actually may have emigrated, Cornwallis forbade those who chose to leave the province from selling or removing their property. The establishment of Halifax had changed everything. There were thousands of settlers in place, and more on the way, who could easily move into Acadian homes and work their farms and livestock. So much the better, then, if the Acadians evacuated their lands. He dismissed the deputies with the reminder that they had until October 26 to take the oath or forfeit their property.[20]

With their first bullet—the threat to leave the colony—spent to no effect, the Minas Acadians turned to the Indians as an excuse. In obsequious language, they reminded Cornwallis that they had sworn allegiance to the Crown during Richard Philipps's administration.

Asking them to publicly recommit to another oath "would expose our [the Acadians'] lives to great peril from the savage nations, who have reproached us in a strange manner, as to the oath we have taken to His Majesty. This one binding us still more strictly, we should assuredly become the victims of their barbarous cruelty." The Acadians nonetheless found it within themselves to concede that they would reswear to the terms of allegiance that Philipps had given them in 1729. If the British were unable to grant that "liberty," they would leave Nova Scotia.[21]

Cornwallis and the council were near the end of their patience. They homed in on the Acadians' arguments like sharks on blood in the water. "We have cause to be much astonished at your conduct," they said. Noting that this was the third time that the Acadians had questioned the oath, they chastised the deputies for thinking themselves "independent of any government." The council told them that those who chose to remain in the colony after the window to leave Nova Scotia with their property had closed in 1714 had conceded to become British subjects. It was "contrary to common sense, also, to suppose that one can remain in a province, and possess houses and lands there, without being subject to the Sovereign of that province." The council then lectured the Acadians that they were deceiving themselves if they thought they were neutrals. In giving them neutral status, Philipps "did not do his duty," and no one in Great Britain had approved that oath. The bottom line was that "for more than thirty-four years past," all the Acadians had been "the subjects of the king of Great Britain." At that, Cornwallis dismissed the deputies and told them that on their return to Minas they would find a detachment of British troops sent there for their "protection."[22]

New Brunswick Interlude

The status of present-day New Brunswick temporarily distracted British attention from the issue of the Acadians and their oath, however. William Shirley, then in Paris to serve as a British representative to the British-French boundary commission appointed to resolve the debate over the territorial limits of Acadia, decided that he would from afar test the postwar waters. He wrote to Governor-General La Galissonière, the lead French negotiator, to remind him that the Maliseets who resided along the Bay of Fundy could expect the same protection and treatment as any of the king's subjects. Although the treaties of the mid-1720s had said nothing explicitly of the Maliseets becoming British subjects, Shirley's statements implied that the British considered them as such. More ominously, the tone of Shirley's letter made it clear that the British would use force to bolster their claims. In July, Ensign Charles des Champs de Boishébert, whom La Galissonière had stationed with 180 men at the mouth of rivière Saint-Jean, encountered the fourteen-gun sloop *Albany,* commanded by John Rous.[23] Rous had parlayed his reputation as New England's foremost privateer in Nova Scotia during King George's War into a commission in the Royal Navy. As the navy's ranking officer in the colony, he commanded the Nova Scotia "sea militia" of five armed vessels. Soon after landing at Halifax, Cornwallis sent Rous to conduct a "survey" (a reconnaissance) of the valley. With Rous, Cornwallis dispatched Edward How with orders to remind the Indians that they would have to make a proper submission to the British.[24]

With building Halifax and the Acadians occupying most of his time, however, the last thing Cornwallis needed was a shooting war on the other side of the province. He quickly recognized that he may have acted too aggressively toward the Maliseets, especially if they were under French influence. Thankfully, How was an experienced Indian negotiator with whom the Maliseets had traded and whom they trusted. First, How reached an agreement with Boishébert that the latter could remain in the valley but could not fortify the mouth of the Saint John River until the boundary commission had reached an agreement. Boishébert moved upriver to the mouth of the Nerepis River, where he constructed Fort de Nerepice, also known as Fort Boishébert.[25] Neither How nor Boishébert saw the need for a fight at that moment. More important, How also convinced some of the Maliseets to travel with him to Halifax to speak face-to-face with Cornwallis. On August 13, the governor and council met with a dozen Maliseets and several Mi'kmaq from Chignecto. All confirmed their commitment to the terms of Mascarene's Treaty.[26] How then carried the renewed terms of friendship to other Maliseet leaders in the Saint-Jean Valley. The "1749 Articles" went far toward not kicking the proverbial sleeping dog. Despite Gorham's claim that the Maliseets had "insulted" him—one of them had discharged a musket in his general direction, and the ball had sailed over Gorham's head too close for his comfort—Cornwallis would not antagonize them. The

Indians explained that they had been intoxicated, and what may have seemed like a potshot at Gorham in reality had been an accident. It was a good enough explanation for Cornwallis.[27] Still, it should have made the point that there was much to learn in overseeing the Yankees and the Indians.

Le Loutre Starts His War

Jean-Louis Le Loutre could not let the Anglo-Indian rapprochement stand. Since his return to the colony in 1749—he had left Acadia with the remnants of d'Anville's fleet and had tried to return in 1747 and 1748, both times to have British warships capture him—he had been La Galissonière's point man in Nova Scotia.[28] The governor-general's plan revolved around protecting Acadia by containing the Anglo-Americans on the peninsula and keeping them busy in their own settlements. Chevalier Louis de La Corne would strengthen the border between the French and the Anglo-Americans at Pointe-à-Beauséjour, which overlooked rivière Missaquash. Boishébert would build a blockhouse (Fort Menagoueche) at the mouth of the Saint-Jean. Le Loutre, meanwhile, would lead the Mi'kmaq in a petite guerre behind Anglo-American lines.[29] "As we cannot openly oppose the English venture," Le Loutre wrote, "I think that we cannot do better than to incite the Indians to continue warring on the English; my plan is to persuade the Indians to send word to the English that they will not permit new settlements to be made in Acadia. . . . I shall do my best to make it look to the English as if this plan comes from the Indians and that I have no part in it."[30] The British refused to buy the last part of that bill of goods, however. One correspondent wrote that Le Loutre "put all in fire and flame, and may be justly deemed the scourge and curse of this country."[31] It thus was his eagerness to accept the mission as partisan fighter that started the war which bears his name.

No guarantees existed that the Mi'kmaq would take up the hatchet. Reverend William Tutty, the Halifax settlers' Anglican minister from the Society for the Propagation of the Gospel in Foreign Parts (SPG), noted that upon the landing, Mi'kmaq initially warmly greeted the British. Mi'kmaw men brought their families to the camp and traded with the settlers. They "seemed not in the least dissatisfied with our settling here." "But," Tutty continued, "they vanished all at once, summoned as we learned afterwards by their priest."[32] Le Loutre grasped that "the founding of Halifax—with its clear implication that Nova Scotia was to become an important British settlement colony—had substantial effect on the native population, particularly the Micmacs [Mi'kmaq]."[33] The Acadians, more so than the Indians, worried the priest. If they saw the British succeed, the French would forever lose them to Anglo-American influence. War between the Anglo-Americans and Mi'kmaq thus would serve dual purposes: it would complicate the British settlement of the colony and remind the Acadians that they had better choose carefully with whom they sided.[34]

Although the Mi'kmaq had maintained at least peaceful if not amicable relations with Anglo-Americans for the previous four years, they threw caution to the wind in the summer of 1749. On September 18, several Mi'kmaq and Maliseets killed three Englishmen at Chignecto, though at a cost of seven dead to themselves. Although the affair at Chignecto "might have been a private pique," more a robbery than an act of war, there remained a feeling among the Anglo-Americans that the French were engaged in "sinister dealings" to encourage the Mi'kmaq to raise the hatchet.[35] Intelligence that partially calmed those fears arrived on September 19 when Joseph Gorham—John's younger brother, who served as an officer in the rangers—reported that he had recently met with Father Pierre Maillard at Canso. Maillard, who had taken over the Shubenacadie mission from Le Loutre (who was then at La Corne's camp at Pointe-à-Beauséjour), had assured Gorham that the Indians at his mission were committed to peace. It seemed that the priest could be trusted. The younger Gorham had been at Canso to escort a party of hay cutters when Mi'kmaq had captured twenty of the foragers and took them to Louisbourg, from where Governor Charles Des Herbiers de La Ralière released them. Gorham assumed that Maillard's intercession had something to do with Des Herbiers's rapid handover of the prisoners. In reality, Maillard was straddling the fence. Although he had staked out a reputation among the British as a moderate voice and key to negotiations with the Indians, he was at the same time in contact with his old friend Le Loutre.[36] Four days later, on September 23, the Mi'kmaq threatened war on the British in a letter that Maillard wrote. The letter was an attempt to negotiate, but one backed by the threat of violence.[37] Maillard explained his apparent about-face by claiming that the Indians were "forced to defend themselves as they can and to prevent the British from becoming entirely the masters of the interior of Acadia."[38]

While properly concerned about the outbreak of war with Mi'kmaq, Cornwallis and his officers did not panic. The senior leaders of the colony were military officers, and war was the thing they knew best. Although Cornwallis made the obligatory complaint that he had only the six companies of Philipps's Regiment and Gorham's Rangers to protect hundreds of miles of front against Indians intent on "greatest mischief," by late September, the British were in fairly good shape to deal with the Indians.[39] Annapolis Royal, then under the command of Captain John Handfield, still had its cannon and walls that guaranteed its safety.[40] Halifax, meanwhile, was more than secure. It was a heavily defended camp with three hundred buildings, two blockhouses, and a complete palisade.[41] At the same time, Gorham's Rangers were building another blockhouse, which would become Fort Sackville, at the head of Bedford Basin and the terminus of the road to Minas. As a bonus, the day before the Mi'kmaq declared war, the British had received an envoy from the Maliseets, who swore that they would remain British friends. The strength of their defensive positions and the diplomatic isolation of the Mi'kmaq only reinforced the Britons' strategic estimate that Mi'kmaq alone "could not essentially hurt" them.[42] To make sure that the Maliseets remained committed to the British, the council sent How and Gorham with a party of rangers to deliver a thousand bushels of corn as further evidence of British goodwill. The Maliseets' dependence on Anglo-American food subsidies had become close to an addiction. It was no coincidence that the more moderate Edward How traveled to the Saint-Jean Valley with Gorham. Cornwallis could not afford any rash actions on the ranger's part that might work contrary to the message of British benevolence.[43]

Cornwallis waited to see whether the Mi'kmaw declaration of war had been mere bravado. When Mi'kmaw warriors with the Acadian Beausoleil attacked workers at Dartmouth—the small settlement that had sprung up across the bay from Halifax—and killed five settlers, Cornwallis had his answer.[44] The French and Mi'kmaq, Cornwallis reported to the Board of Trade, "had begun their usual game—their Missionary to the Indians De Loutre [*sic,* Le Loutre], the same that led them before Annapolis Royal, has once more persuaded

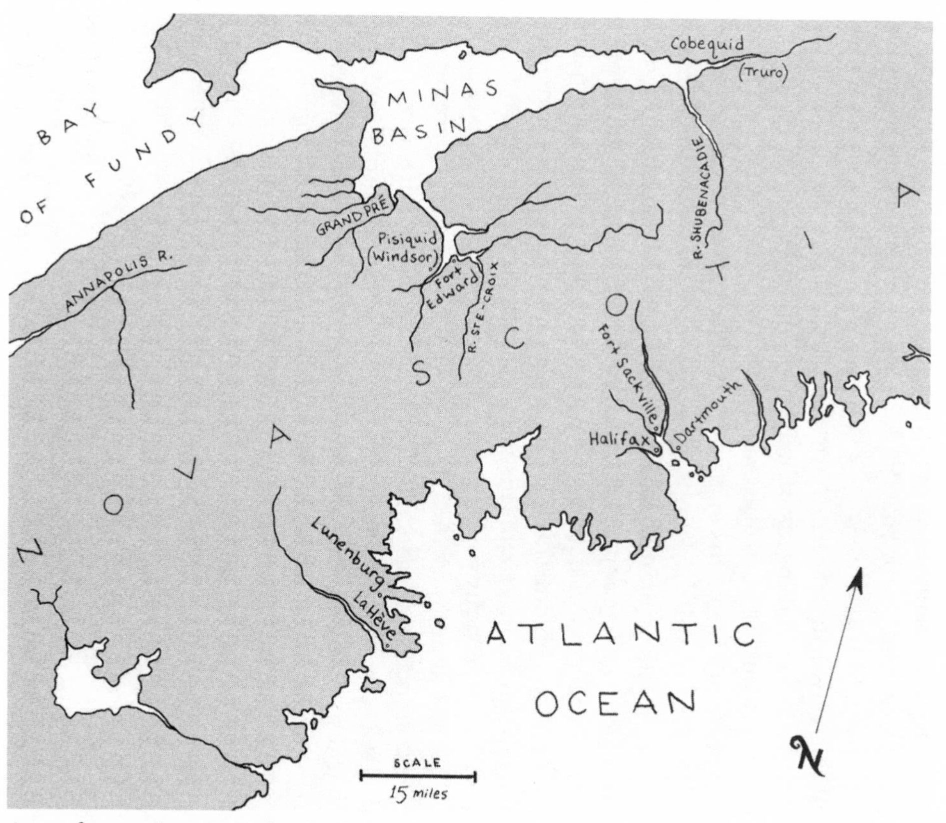

Area of operations in Father Le Loutre's War.

them to begin hostilities." The next day, he and the council declared that the Mi'kmaq were "bandit Ruffians"—to declare war against them would be to acknowledge them as a "free and independent people."[45] The British administrators of Nova Scotia were extremely legalistic in the dealings with both the Indians and the Acadians. According to Britons' understanding, the Mi'kmaq were rebels for having violated the terms of Mascarene's Treaty, in which they had become subjects of the British king. As such, their actions denied them any rights as legal combatants and allowed the British to employ any means to suppress them. Thus, on October 1, the council formally placed a ten-guinea bounty on each Indian killed or taken prisoner.[46] Reverend Tutty, with more than enough unintended irony, acknowledged that "this may seem to civilized people an extraordinary way of making war, but is the only effectual way of fighting such an enemy with the prospects of success. To offer premiums for the destruction of whole bodies of men sounds harsh to humanity, and it was not without difficulty the Governor assented to it; but such is the cruelty and cowardice (always inseparable companions) of these savages, that there is no safety without their extirpation."[47] The next day, Cornwallis called for volunteers to serve in ranger companies under Captains William Clapham and Francis Bartelo. With Gorham's Rangers taking to the hinterlands to hunt Mi'kmaq, the governor needed more rangers to patrol the environs of Halifax and Dartmouth. Three days later, he ordered the sea militia to Mirligueche Bay, about seventy-five miles southwest of Halifax, to destroy the Mi'kmaw village there.[48]

While Cornwallis and the British prepared to take the fight to the Mi'kmaq, their October 26 deadline for the Acadians to take the oath or have their properties confiscated approached. On October 22, the deputies from Minas arrived at Halifax, no doubt concerned that they were in for a potential confrontation with the British. Yet when the two sides met, Cornwallis chose not to press them. Because the British had troubles with the Mi'kmaq on their hands, he met with the Acadians briefly and then dismissed them.[49] Once again, the Acadians had dodged a British bullet.

Despite the mustering of Clapham's and Bartelo's Rangers and the patrols of Gorham's Rangers, the British made no contact with the Indians in November. Cornwallis quickly learned the lesson that so many Americans already knew: the Indian enemy was extremely difficult to bring to battle and could strike and then escape as quickly and unexpectedly as it emerged. This became painfully clear on December 8 when three hundred Mi'kmaq surprised Captain John Hamilton and eighteen men at Grand Pré. The British troops surrendered without firing a shot. The council found it "strange that a party should be thus surprised" and began to question whether the Acadians had played a role.[50] Near the same time, Captain Handfield's command discovered around three hundred Mi'kmaq (and, it was erroneously reported, Maliseets) skulking around Fort Anne. The banlieu Acadians had not warned Handfield of the Indians' approach. They spent a week "besieging" the fort but, as expected, could do no damage.[51]

Cornwallis looked to bring his forces to bear as soon as possible on the Indians. On December 10, he ordered all the adult males of Halifax (around 850 men) mustered into a militia. Although the militiamen did not perform as well as Cornwallis would have liked—they seemed grossly unmilitary—they freed the rangers for offensive operations.[52] On December 21, Gorham had returned from an extended patrol toward Minas and Chignecto and reported that he had failed to make contact with the Indians. He found only a dozen abandoned Indian canoes. After allowing him only a brief rest, Cornwallis ordered Gorham out again on Christmas Day, 1749. John Salusbury noted in his journal that Gorham had again "gone after Indians" and hoped that "good luck [would] attend Him."[53]

The Indians remained difficult to find. While at Pisiquid (present-day Windsor), however, Gorham abducted three Acadians and transported them to Halifax for questioning. They had nothing specific to say about where the Mi'kmaq were, but they did claim that the Indians had threatened them if they supported the Anglo-Americans. The captives also implicated eleven other Acadians in the ambush of Hamilton's forces in Minas.[54] On the whole, however, British intelligence remained "very dark," and Salusbury was convinced that "somebody Knows more of the matter [of Mi'kmaw intentions] than they will tell." Worries of Mi'kmaw and Acadian attacks began to take their toll on the settlers' morale. "It is hard," he wrote, "that one poor French priest [Le Loutre] should give us this disturbance."[55]

Cornwallis hoped to capture Le Loutre and thereby put an end to the troubles. He thought that he had an ideal fix to his problem in hand. In late 1749, he had drafted Captain Silvanus Cobb and his sloop *York and Halifax* (80 tons) into the sea militia. Cobb was well known in Nova Scotia. He had served as a company commander under Gorham in the Seventh Massachusetts Regiment during King George's War and had made many trips up the Bay of Fundy as a messenger and merchant. Cornwallis held high opinion of him as a man who knew "every Harbour and every Creek in the Bay [of Fundy], a man fit for any bold enterprise."[56] The governor therefore directed that Cobb covertly sail the *York and Halifax* to Chignecto and arrest Father Le Loutre; while there, he should seize some Acadian women and children as hostages for the Acadians' good behavior.[57] Although the Indians would see Gorham's troops coming overland and warn Le Loutre, perhaps Cobb could move quickly and stealthily enough to take the priest.

Cobb's preparations, however, left much to be desired. Upon receiving his orders from Cornwallis, he traveled to Boston to provision his ship and recruit men for the mission. With no apparent concern for operational security, Cobb advertised throughout the town that he was planning a "cruise" up the Bay of Fundy. Although British intelligence collection was ineffective, such was not the case with the French. Word of Cobb's plan quickly reached Nova Scotia. If everyone in Boston, Halifax, and Annapolis Royal knew of it, then the Acadians, Mi'kmaq, and Le Loutre surely did too. Cornwallis called off the raid, and Salusbury sourly wondered what might have been had Cobb taken care "not to blast it at Boston."[58]

The British needed to push back the veil that covered the enemy's intentions. Cornwallis therefore ordered Bartelo to take his rangers to Cobequid and arrest the town's priest (Abbé Gerard), who had refused to present himself before the council. Cornwallis had grown tired of Gorham, whom he described as "good for nothing," insisting that it was "impracticable" to march against the Acadian-Indian stronghold. Bartelo managed to bring the priest and deputies to Halifax, but he found no Indians. Cornwallis treated Father Gerard well, lodging the priest in his own house "to show regard to the character but likewise to pick out some further intelligence from him."[59]

Gorham had the opportunity to rehabilitate himself in Cornwallis's eyes when the latter ordered his company to march to Minas Basin to build a small blockhouse at Pisiquid.[60] He set out for Pisiquid in mid-March and soon ran into a party of Mi'kmaq and Acadians at the Saint Croix River, about twenty-eight miles from Halifax. The rangers commandeered two Acadian houses and a sawmill as a defensive position but soon found themselves in danger of being overrun. Gorham, whom the Indians slightly wounded in the thigh in the firefight, sent a runner to Halifax for reinforcements but had to wait a day for the relief party to reach him. The arrival of Clapham's Rangers and a company of regulars and their two field pieces compelled the Indians and Acadians to disengage.[61]

The rangers' failure to destroy the Acadians and Indians added to Cornwallis's growing frustration. He believed that Gorham had "advantages in this engagement seldom found with Indians." He had the upper hand in men and firepower, and if Gorham had somehow notified Captain Handfield at Minas, the latter could have attacked the Indians from behind, which would have produced a "total rout."[62] Instead, Gorham, in Cornwallis's view, allowed the enemy to slip away to fight another day.

British Operations in Chignecto

Cornwallis and his advisors chomped at the bit to take the offensive. They believed that if the British could establish a fort on Chignecto, they could "continue for some time to harass and hunt" the Mi'kmaq "by Sea and Land" until they had to "either abandon the Peninsula or come in upon any Terms we please."[63] On March 30, Cornwallis directed Major Charles Lawrence of the Fortieth Regiment to take three hundred regulars, rangers, and volunteers to Chignecto and build a blockhouse there. The operational piece of the plan included having Lawrence march overland to Minas Basin, where he would link up with the sea militia. Rous's ships would then carry the party into Chignecto Bay and land the infantry at the mouth of rivière Missaquash. An amphibious assault offered both surprise and security. If the Anglo-Americans had gone overland, they would have had to march to Cobequid at the head of the basin, then cross the Cobequid Mountains along the Planches (Boards) River road, which would open them to innumerable areas of ambush.

Lawrence's force mustered at Fort Sackville on April 5, then marched to Pisiquid. Discipline was the order of the day. With Gorham's Rangers in the vanguard and flanking the party, the troops marched and, Salusbury wrote, "never went out of our ranks lest the Enemy might have taken advantage and truly in Millions of places twenty men might have anoy'd us greatly."[64] The Anglo-Americans met no resistance, however; on April 8, Lawrence was in Pisiquid. The next day, the troops joined John Handfield's company, which had marched to Grand Pré. With the arrival of the Anglo-American force, many Acadians abandoned their homes, which led the British officers to suspect that the Mi'kmaq and French were "at Hand."[65]

The British plan then began to unravel. Captain Rous in command of the *Albany,* the *York and Halifax,* and six transports had left Halifax the same day as Lawrence's land force. But it took them ten days to reach the Minas Basin and pick up the infantry. Finally, on April 18, all the troops had been embarked and the transports were ready to sail for the isthmus. The small fleet exited the basin past Cape Split on the outgoing tide but could not clear Cape Chignecto when the currents and winds shifted in the Bay of Fundy. For the next two days, the Anglo-Americans made little progress. Once they had finally rounded the cape, the tides within Chignecto Bay drove them into the mouth of rivière-aux-Pommes (Apple River). Rous pressed his command ahead; hugging the coast, the fleet made a difficult run directly toward the mouth of the Missaquash, where it managed to disgorge the troops.[66]

The French were waiting for them. Lawrence had completely lost the element of surprise. Upon leaving Minas Basin, the Anglo-Americans had observed smoke rising into the air. Someone had set fires to warn the French that an army was on its way. More ominously, the troops, as they approached the landing zone, observed large clouds of smoke rising above Beaubassin. Lawrence sent Bartelo's Rangers forward as pathfinders for the landing and to investigate. In a scene that must have been reminiscent of his experiences in Europe, Bartelo, who had commanded a British irregular unit in Flanders during the War of the Austrian Succession and had come to Halifax as a soldier of fortune, saw that the village was totally in flames and devoid of inhabitants.[67] Father Le Loutre had ordered the Mi'kmaq to burn the Acadian homes, as he was determined that no Acadian over whom he had control would live on British soil.[68]

Lawrence and La Corne faced each other under a white flag on April 22. La Corne, who had kept his men on the French side of the Missaquash River, informed Lawrence that he had reached the border and should proceed no farther. La Corne pointed out the large dyke where he had entrenched his men and Acadians behind pickets. "We

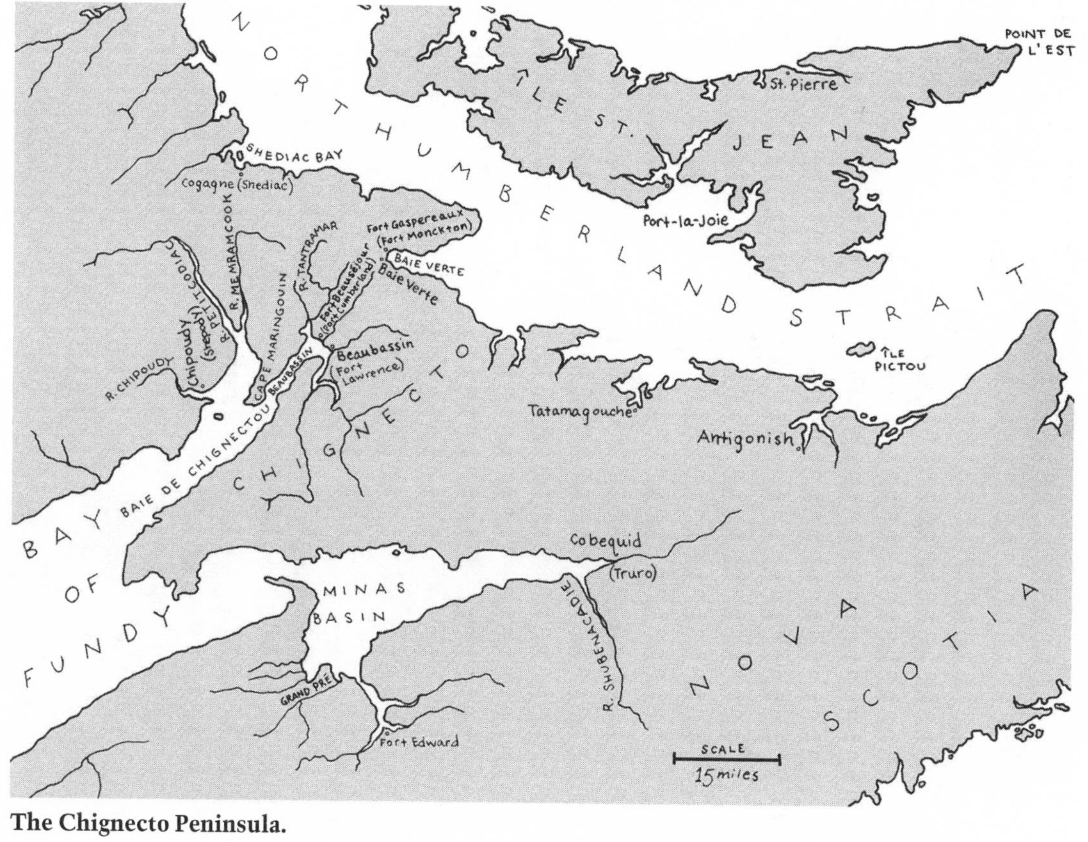

The Chignecto Peninsula.

found the enemy ready to receive us in all form," Salusbury recorded in his journal.[69] With the Indians lurking nearby in the woods, and not authorized to start a war with France, Lawrence chose to withdraw. Around four o'clock that afternoon, the Anglo-Americans marched through Beaubassin on their way to taking up a more defensible position. Parts of the village were still burning, which inspired Salusbury to worry that "the Inhabitants are certainly irreconcilable to burn All—and in this fury Hope they will not join the enemy."[70] The next morning, Lawrence held a council of war, and his officers concurred unanimously to return to Halifax.

If there previously had been any doubt, it was now clear that the Chignecto Acadians had taken up arms against the British. That was not all. During its short stopover in Minas, Lawrence's army had angered some of the Grand Pré Acadians. What at the time had seemed like justified complaints over the Anglo-Americans' confiscation of some Acadians' firearms to equip the rangers took on a more ominous meaning after the warning fires and the burning of Beaubassin. Lawrence understood that he needed to make a symbolic display of British might and therefore chose to lead his men overland to Halifax, despite the risks that entailed. Over four hundred British soldiers and the Yankee rangers marched down the Planches River road from Beaubassin to Cobequid, then turned to the southeast, to Pisiquid. As a reminder to the Acadians that the British intended to stay their course in Nova Scotia, Lawrence completed a blockhouse, which he called Fort Edward, at Pisiquid.[71]

Cornwallis was committed to staking out a forward base of operations on Chignecto, and in the late summer he ordered a second descent on the isthmus. Lord Halifax rushed Cornwallis reinforcements in the form of the Forty-seventh (Lascelle's) Regiment from Ireland. Halifax had done all that he could to help his protégé in Nova Scotia. On August 19, Rous led the sea militia to Minas Basin while Lawrence, recently promoted to lieutenant colonel, marched with nearly seven hundred men and several small artillery pieces for Grand Pré via Pisiquid. The land and sea elements linked together without incident, and on August 31 the fleet set out for Chignecto.[72]

With Rous, Lawrence, and Gorham in the lead, the troops went ashore east of Beaubassin on September 3. Because they had landed away from the Missaquash this time, there were no Frenchmen waiting for them. Instead, it was Le Loutre and his Mi'kmaq and Acadians, who had thrown up a breastwork from behind which they opposed the landing. After a fight that cost the landing party twenty casualties and several Mi'kmaq their scalps, Le Loutre's force withdrew and burned what remained of the Acadian fields and buildings on the British side of the Missaquash. Lawrence did not cross the river but instead set about putting up prefabricated blockhouse and barrack frames amid the ruins of Beaubassin.[73] Fort Lawrence, as the picketed bastion came to be called, gave the British a post in the heart of the most recalcitrant Acadian area.

The presence of Fort Lawrence, however, did not mean that the British had pacified the colony. Instead, Nova Scotia erupted into a difficult and costly petite guerre. At Chignecto, Edward How lost his life when someone, probably the métis Etienne Bâtard, killed him under a flag of truce after How had sallied forth to meet what he thought were French officers for prisoner exchange.[74] Soon, the Anglo-Americans needed more rangers for Nova Scotia, and advertisements appeared in Boston newspapers that offered five hundred pounds "for every *Indian* Scalp or Prisoner brought in."[75] The Indians and Acadians also killed Bartelo, who had led several hunter-killer missions directed against the Mi'kmaq. On his last operation, thirty-five Mi'kmaq and Acadians ambushed him and his sixty rangers. The Indians killed Bartelo and five or six of his men and captured another seven. The captives' bloodcurdling screams as the Mi'kmaq tortured them throughout the night had a steeling if not chilling effect on the Anglo-Americans. Gorham and thirty of his rangers, a little later, crossed the international border to raid the Acadian village on the rivière Petitcodiac on the French side of Chignecto Bay. The Mi'kmaq and Acadians repulsed the rangers. Throughout the autumn, Mi'kmaq and Acadians continued to harass, capture, and kill British soldiers on Chignecto. On September 28, the Acadian vessel *Jacob Maurice* arrived at Port Toulouse with thirty-seven British prisoners. Two days later, Mi'kmaq and Acadians struck Dartmouth and killed five more settlers.[76]

Fortunately for Cornwallis and his advisors, Le Loutre could not keep his forces in the field. Although Cornwallis dismissed the French claim of being unable to manage the Indians, who were "not their subjects but Allies," that was indeed true.[77] Mi'kmaw warriors traditionally had a strong antipathy to waging winter campaigns because Mi'kmaw groups normally broke into family units from which the men spent the winter hunting. The hunting parties then came back together in the spring.[78] It thus was difficult for the Indians to coordinate a year-round military operation. The Acadians, meanwhile, watched the winter approach with trepidation. The fighting over the course of the spring, summer, and autumn had disrupted much of their planting and harvesting in Beaubassin, and with large refugee populations among the Acadians—over 1,100 Beaubassin and Minas Acadians had fled to La Corne's camp at Pointe-à-Beauséjour—the winter was shaping up as a long one. The Beaubassin Acadians had nowhere to go, and many of the Minas Acadians refused to return to their homes and "raise the fury of the Indians."[79] They were stuck in the middle between the Mi'kmaq and the British. Le Loutre and the Mi'kmaq, not the British, had burned Beaubassin, after all.

Late 1750 thus saw a de facto cease-fire because the Indians had left the fields of battle. Although in November, Lord Halifax noted "that if the French & Indians were reduced the Province could be perfectly secured," that was easier said than done.[80] In the petite guerre around Chignecto, Anglo-Americans had killed only seven or eight Mi'kmaq. The Indians were nowhere to be found, and with them headed for their winter hunting grounds, the rangers were unlikely to be able to find any more. Most of the Acadians, meanwhile, had not risen up against the British and therefore had yet to become the full focus of their wrath.

The cease-fire, however, evaporated in the spring. Whereas the Acadians had suffered a long winter across the Missaquash, the Mi'kmaq had regrouped and were ready for action come the first thaws.[81] On March 26, Mi'kmaw warriors raided Dartmouth and killed fifteen people and wounded another seven, three of whom later died in Halifax's hospital. They took six captives, and the regulars who pursued the raiders fell into an ambush in which they lost a sergeant killed. Indians abducted another three settlers from Dartmouth two days later. In mid-April, Mi'kmaq struck the outskirts of Halifax. They managed to scalp two men but could do little against the main settlement. John Salusbury noted that losses were "trifling," which was a determination relatively easy to make from the security of Halifax. On May 13, sixty Mi'kmaq and Acadians led by Beausoleil again fell on Dartmouth. They killed twenty Anglo-Americans and took more prisoners. Both the regulars and the settlers were thoroughly demoralized. Salusbury noted that the soldiers were constantly drunk and of no use in protecting the outpost. The Indians, he observed, would "never cram themselves" into a blockhouse to wait for an attack but instead would actively pursue their enemies. Indeed, the regulars preferred "the Flanders discipline"—that is, attempting to contain an elusive and mobile adversary with a string of outposts. The Mi'kmaq "so intimidated the inhabitants" that they deserted Dartmouth. Cornwallis and the council eventually paid the Mi'kmaq £886 to repatriate some of the captives.[82]

The fear of Indian ambushes came to overshadow all Anglo-American tactical, operational, and strategic decisions. In May the Minas deputies appeared in Halifax to request support in driving the Indians from their villages. Some Acadians had concluded that Le Loutre's Mi'kmaq posed as much a threat to them as did the British. Cornwallis and the council immediately demanded that if the Acadians wanted the British to fight on their behalf, they would be required to take an oath of allegiance. While the Acadians demurred, Cornwallis nonetheless agreed to send one hundred regulars and rangers to reinforce the small garrisons at Forts Sackville and Edward despite fear that the Acadian request for assistance was a trap. Caution was warranted after the previous experience in Minas Basin; the council feared that Mi'kmaw spies, at the direction of Governor-General La Jonquière of New France, had instructed the Acadians to lure the British into an ambush.[83] Locked in their strongholds and at a loss for what to do with the Mi'kmaq, the British lost perspective on the task at hand. It remained difficult for them to imagine that the Mi'kmaq could fight the war without the support of the French, let alone for their own reasons and motivations.

The Fragile Cease-Fire

Yet the Mi'kmaq were inclined to stop the war. They had profited handsomely from the ransoms for the captives, and they essentially had contained the British at Halifax. The establishment of Fort Lawrence had not radically upset the military scene. The French responded by building a fort at the site of La Corne's camp. Fort Beauséjour, which would hold thirty-two small cannon, one mortar, and a garrison of around seventy men, as well as the smaller supporting fort at Baie Verte, which the French called Fort Gaspereaux, began to take shape in the spring and summer.[84] Those forts offered the Mi'kmaq more than trading spots with the French; they provided a strong barrier against further Anglo-American advances into Mi'kmaw hunting grounds across the Missaquash. There was little more for the Mi'kmaq to gain in continuing the war. Moreover, when Le Loutre left for Quebec and then Paris to garner support for the Mi'kmaq and the Acadian refugees whom he had driven to Baie Verte, the primary advocate for a continuation of the war was out of the province. Perhaps most important, Le Loutre had given the Acadian refugees the trade goods that had been set aside for the Mi'kmaq. Upon being denied their presents, many Mi'kmaq lost interest in risking their scalps in fighting the rangers and regulars.

The British, at the same time, needed an end to the fighting. The war had bankrupted the colony. Parliament had authorized £39,000 for Nova Scotia in 1750, but Cornwallis had spent nearly £174,000 fighting the Mi'kmaq and trying to put the colony on a secure footing in the face of Indian attacks. The rangers alone accounted for 7 percent of the expenditures, yet had proved unable to defeat the Mi'kmaq.[85] Cornwallis knew that the Board of Trade would hold him responsible for the budgetary crisis. In his scramble to reduce costs, Cornwallis naturally saw a huge savings in disbanding the rangers. At that point, John Gorham requested leave to travel to London to put his financial affairs in order. Gorham and Cornwallis increasingly had come to dislike one another and had clashed over what the ranger commander thought was his proper monetary due. During King George's War, Gorham had paid out of his own pocket to outfit two schooners, the *Anson* and *Warren,* to ferry his rangers around the Bay of Fundy. Cornwallis thought that the monthly rent on the schooners of £185, plus the £90 that Gorham charged for the use of his whaleboats, was "most extravagant."[86] Undoubtedly, Gorham was profiting handsomely from the war, even if his accounts had been in disarray since he had first formed the rangers in 1744. Thus, he had the perfect excuse to request leave to travel to London, where he of course could lobby above the governor's head for continued support for his rangers.[87] John Gorham never returned to Halifax. In late September 1751, the ranger captain (who had survived numerous fights with the Indians and French) died of smallpox.

The British felt out the Mi'kmaq on the subject of peace in the summer of 1751.[88] Although the man best suited for that mission, Mascarene, was close to retirement and his most trusted second, Edward How, had been murdered the previous year, the British had to do little other than wait for the Indians. In late 1751, the Mi'kmaq broke for their winter hunting camps, but come spring, they did not appear on the warpath. Such was the situation when Cornwallis's replacement, Peregrine Thomas Hopson, returned to the colony from a short absence in England. Cornwallis, who resigned in disgust over the budget battles with the Board of Trade, was more than happy to be done with the troubles of Nova Scotia. Hopson, of course, still feared that a renewal in fighting could befall the colony at any moment, even though peace seemed to be at hand. He thus directed Lieutenant Colonel Robert Monckton, upon the latter's taking command of Fort Lawrence, to be particularly aware to "defend British subjects against hostilities on the part of the Indians, and, if he consistently can, to try to chastise such insolence."[89] But the Mi'kmaq did not appear even at Chignecto. Rather than fighting Indians, Monckton spent his time at Fort Lawrence corresponding with his French counterpart at Fort Beauséjour, Jean-Baptiste Mutigny de Vassan, and exchanging livestock and deserters with him.

Finally, in the late summer, the Shubenacadie Mi'kmaq emerged from the woods and suggested that they were amenable to formalizing the peace. Their "chief," Jean-Baptiste Cope, whom the British suspected of murdering Edward How, approached the British as a long-lost friend. Many in the British camp loathed Cope, but nothing would be lost in signing a treaty with him. With much fanfare, the Shubenacadie Indians and the British "renewed" the friendship first elucidated in Mascarene's Treaty and then reconfirmed in the 1749 Articles. The treaty stated that "All Transactions during the Late War shall on both sides be buried in Oblivion with the Hatchet, and that the said Indians shall have all favour, Friendship & protection shewn them from this His Majesty's Government." In return for flour, tobacco, and sundry trade goods, the Shubenacadie Mi'kmaq would cease harassing and killing Anglo-American settlers and do their best to bring the other Mi'kmaw bands to the peace table. Few Anglo-Americans believed that Cope would keep his word if it did not suit his advantage, however. Salusbury went as far as to describe the entire course of negotiations as "a foolish piece of formality."[90]

As was so often the case on the early American frontier, violence begot more violence and threatened to shatter the general peace. In May 1753, James Grace and John Connor escaped from the Indians and returned to Halifax with the scalps of six Mi'kmaq. Cope found himself in a difficult position. The governor of Île Royale, Jean-Louis de Raymond, had castigated him for his treaty with the Anglo-Americans. With Grace and Connor's scalping of Mi'kmaq, Cope had little choice but to respond. In May, he sent his son Joseph to Halifax to request provisions, upon which Governor Hopson sent a detachment of eight men with supplies to Shubenacadie. On May 19, Cope and his followers ambushed that party. They killed all of the teamsters except Anthony Casteel, who avoided death by posing as an Acadian but nonetheless suffered torture at the Indians' hands. Cope, in front of his followers, then burned a copy of his treaty with the British and proclaimed that the British were to blame.[91]

Hopson did not overreact. He understood that quelling all acts of Indian violence was impossible and that Cope did not speak for all the Mi'kmaq. The Le Hève (La Have) band of Mi'kmaq under Claude Gisiquah had agreed to peace on April 12, and they seemed committed to it despite the actions of Cope and his followers. Hopson thus refused to back away from his earlier instructions "that peaceable measures and circumspect conduct should be preserved, until their [Mi'kmaq] intentions are better known."[92] Nevertheless, at the same time as Cope was reemerging as a pain in his side, Hopson again had to face requests and petitions from the Acadians.

The oath issue kept surfacing. With the hardnosed Cornwallis returned to England, the Acadians presented Hopson with a memorial from which it was clear that they wanted to renegotiate the terms of their relationship with the Anglo-Americans. One could read the petition either as an acknowledgment on the Acadians' part that the British were the sovereigns of Nova Scotia or as a first step in trying to gain something more from the new administration. They asked whether their priests, who were subjects of the king of France, would be required to take an oath of allegiance. The Acadians pulled out the old red herring and threatened to emigrate from the colony if the British forced the clergy to take the oath. Hopson and the council astutely did not answer the question directly but agreed that the priests could remain in the colony provided that they registered with British authorities.[93]

A second memorial, this one from a group of Acadians who had fled from Beaubassin in 1751, then arrived before the council. The refugees wanted to return to their homes but needed Hopson's permission to do so. Of course, before they could receive the proper visas to settle on British lands, they would have to subscribe to an oath of allegiance. Yet, despite their refugee status, the Acadians dictated the terms to which they would take an oath. Using the earlier oaths offered by Ensign Wroth and Richard Philipps as their model, the refugee Acadians offered only a simple promise to be faithful to the British monarch: "Je promets et jure sincèrement que je serai fidèle à Sa Majestée le Roi George Second et a ses successeurs. Dieu me soit en aide." ("I promise and sincerely swear that I will be faithful to His Majesty George II and his successors. So help me God.") They could afford to offer no more than a lukewarm promise to "be faithful" because, they claimed, the Indians would allow them only that.[94]

Hopson and the council discussed the refugee Acadians' proposed oath. The Acadians were fortunate in that Hopson had never felt that the oath issue was worth fighting over; he believed that if the French could be removed from the colony, the oath would become moot, and more important, the oath by itself guaranteed nothing of Acadian obedience or allegiance. Thus, upon his recommendation, the council tried to meet the Acadians partway. The council proposed that if the Acadians promised "perfect loyalty," they could return to their lands. When the Acadians refused even that small (albeit significant) change in verbiage, they shattered any illusions that the Anglo-Americans possessed concerning the British hold over them.[95]

Other matters that demanded the government's attention soon distracted Hopson and the council again. Since 1749, the Board of Trade's agent in Europe, John Dick, had been recruiting "Foreign Protestants," mainly from Germany, Switzerland, and the Montbeliard region of France, to settle in Nova Scotia. All told, nearly five thousand settlers poured into Halifax within the first years of the town's founding, so many in fact that the camp quickly became overcrowded. The intention was for the foreign Protestants to settle other parts of the colony; the authorities inside Halifax thus understandably treated them as transients. Indeed, part of John Salusbury's critique of the treaty with Cope centered on giving the Indians provisions for the winter while the poor "Germans" inside Halifax lacked food and supplies. By January 1753 the destitute Germans had become almost unmanageable.[96] In May, Hopson assembled them and had them draw cards for the lots of land they would occupy in a new settlement about a day's sail from Halifax. The sea militia then transported them and a land force of ninety-two regulars and sixty-six militiamen under Colonel Lawrence to Mirligueche Bay.[97]

Under the protection of Lawrence's troops and the guns of the sea militia, the settlers staked out another town for the British. The council named it Lunenburg, reflecting its joint British-German provenance and in honor of King George II, who also happened to be the duke of Brunschweig-Lüneburg. The first order of business was defenses. Lawrence landed Joseph Gorham's Rangers to reconnoiter the area; then he put ashore prefabricated blockhouses that the soldiers and settlers assembled on the high ground that overlooked the beach. That seems to have been enough to deter any attacks, although Lawrence naturally remained "apprehensive of some mischief," especially after "the settlers growing very impatient to get on shore, have landed their wives & children without my knowledge, and seem so disposed to range about."[98] Fortunately for the overeager settlers, the Mi'kmaq of that area had recently agreed to peace, and there was an overwhelming Anglo-American force at the camp. By July, over 1,400 foreign Protestants had made the day's sail from Halifax to Lunenburg. The Germans spent the summer building the structures they would need to get them through the winter, as well as a large palisade that was to serve as the main barricade for the settlement. With most of their energies focused on construction projects, they could not give adequate attention to farming. Halifax would have to provision Lunenburg over the winter.

In early December, Lawrence (who was then in Halifax, having replaced Hopson, who had returned to England for medical care) heard rumblings that the hungry and overworked settlers were on the verge of rebelling. He dispatched Colonel Monckton on December 18 with orders to "use such Measures [as needed] to Reduce the Inhabitants to Obedience."[99] The show of force on the new governor's part quickly cut the legs out from under the rebellious Germans; it also suggested that Charles Lawrence was not a man to be trifled with.

Le Loutre's War, Phase Two

Governor Lawrence hardly could have been pleased with the state of the colony at the start of 1754. Most of the Indians were at peace, but that had come at the cost of ignoring several murders. Adding insult to injury, some Shubenacadie Mi'kmaq had abducted Michael

Francklin, with whom they supposedly had close and friendly trade relations.[100] The Acadians, although quiet since the bulk of the fighting had ended in 1751, still held the upper hand throughout most of the province, and the recent memorials about the oath showed that they had no intention of subscribing to any statement that would tie them too closely to the British monarchy. The French, meanwhile, had strengthened their hold on the borders of Nova Scotia. Louisbourg was firmly in their hands. Forts Beauséjour, Gaspereaux, and Menagoueche stood as rallying points for French interference in the colony. Last, the foreign Protestants were of questionable loyalty; many had fled to the Acadian and French settlements, while those who remained in Lunenburg and Halifax could rebel at any time.

In that maelstrom of challenges and threats, most Britons remained convinced that the Indians stood at the root of the troubles in Nova Scotia. The *Gentleman's Magazine* described the Mi'kmaq as "troublesome neighbors" and the settlements "incommoded by the Indians, who are in the *French* interest; for as they would not submit to us."[101] The Board of Trade similarly weighed in on its view of Indian affairs. The peace, the board informed Lawrence, "cannot be relied upon, unless the Indians are made sensible that every Infraction or Engagements on their part, whether from Native Treachery, or French Instigation . . . would not fail to draw upon them the dreadful and alarming Consequences."[102]

In that milieu, the French encouraged the Indians to recommence hostilities. New France's governor-general, Ange de Menneville, marquis Duquesne, wrote to Le Loutre,

> [T]he more I become acquainted with the project [the security of Canada], the more decided I am in thinking that we should never permit our Abenakis, Malecites, and Mickmacs to make peace with the English. I regard these savages as the mainstay of the Colony, and in order to keep alive this spirit of hatred and revenge, we must remove every occasion of allowing it to be bribed; and the present position of Canada demands that those nations which are strongly connected should strike without delay, provided the order shall not appear to come from me because I have precise instructions to remain on the defensive.[103]

The Abenakis, among the sauvages domiciles outside Quebec at least, seemed particularly eager to help the French. They could not miss the rattling of French sabers over the Ohio Country. In the spring of 1754, they presented themselves to the marquis and advised that they were willing to raise the hatchet. Duquesne sent messengers to Boishébert and Father Charles Germain, missionary to the Maliseets, to encourage them to join with the Abenakis, "with whom they are allies." He also sent orders to Louis Du Pont Duchambon de Vergor (commandant of Fort Beauséjour) and to Le Loutre to turn the Mi'kmaq loose "on the usurpations of the English." The pretext would be that the Yankees again had invaded Abenaki lands. As grease for the skids, Duquesne promised the Indians seven thousand pounds.[104]

Le Loutre needed an issue to encourage the Mi'kmaq. The British had not overstepped reasonable bounds in their reaction to Cope's actions, and they continued to supply the Maliseets with trade goods and provisions. Le Loutre's trump card would have to be Anglo-American land hunger. While in France, he had learned of the Anglo-French boundary commission to resolve the Acadian border dispute and had even gone so far as to write to La Galissonière, the lead French negotiator, to recommend that the French hold firm to the borders established at Utrecht in 1713.[105] In August 1754, back in America, he used the meeting of the boundary negotiators for his ends. He communicated to Lawrence that he and the Mi'kmaq were amenable to peace provided that the Indians and British establish permanent boundaries in Nova Scotia. The Mi'kmaq had never before worried about boundaries, although there was precedent for establishing a formal boundary between the Anglo-Americans and the Indians in the Wabenaki Confederacy's negotiations with the British over the Maine frontier. Thus, although the boundary issue was not inextricably tied to Le Loutre, he nonetheless seized it as a straw man that the British would have to tear down. He presented them with a proposal whereby the French and Indians would abandon Annapolis Royal and Minas Basin if the British would agree to a border between Acadia and Nova Scotia that ran from Cobequid to Canso. That, in effect, required the British to give up Chignecto and with it, Fort Lawrence.[106] Lawrence advised Captain John Hussey, the British officer at Fort Lawrence who had handled the exchange of letters with Le Loutre, that the priest's "articles are so extravagant and so much out of our power to comply with, that the Council don't think it consistent to make any answer to or take the least notice of them. The terms in which they are drawn up shews that he is not serious because he asks what he knows to be both insolent and absurd, but this is no more than a piece with the rest of his conduct."[107]

Le Loutre had his fig leaf to cover his actions. He exhorted his Mi'kmaq flock to raise the hatchet to protect their lands, and upon his promise to pay for scalps, he found that the Indians would do his bidding. Several Mi'kmaq quickly returned to camp and presented him with some war trophies they had taken. Le Loutre hurried the Indians to Quebec to show Governor-General Duquesne the fruits of his labors. He then directed his energies and impressive rhetorical skills toward the Acadians. From his pulpit inside Fort Beauséjour, he spewed vitriol on the Anglo-Americans. Thomas Pichon, a British spy within the French garrison, reported that Le Loutre "preached a most vehement sermon" and continually exhorted the Acadians to prepare for and expect war with the British.[108]

Le Loutre, however, had grossly miscalculated Anglo-American contingency plans should war come. Governors Shirley and Lawrence were ready when George Washington's fateful encounter in Jumonville's Glen in western Pennsylvania finally thrust Great Britain and France into war. The two governors previously had agreed that they would marshal their available forces for an attack on Chignecto. Shirley had plans in place for a Massachusetts attack up the Kennebec River and through Maine, and in what must have been music to his ears, Lawrence, whose colony was funded by Parliament and not through a colonial assembly, agreed to pay the costs of any campaign that originated in Nova Scotia. The two men then started working their contacts in the imperial channels.[109] Lawrence wrote to Lord Halifax to suggest that although a well-supplied army of New England provincials could take Fort Beauséjour, another regiment of British regulars would be useful in Halifax.[110] In April 1755 Shirley presented his and Lawrence's grand strategic plan at a meeting of the other governors in Alexandria, Virginia.

The British commander in chief of the army in North America, Major General Edward Braddock, had called the Alexandria conference to formulate the courses of action to defeat France in North America. The governors agreed that in addition to campaigns to thrust Anglo-American armies into the Ohio Country, into western

New York, and up Lake Champlain to Canada, an Anglo-American force should move against Fort Beauséjour. Colonel Monckton would command the five hundred regulars already in Nova Scotia and an additional two thousand Yankees in an oversized two-battalion provincial regiment. The British officers would offer oversight and general direction, while the Yankees, commanded by John Winslow (a half-pay captain in the Fortieth Regiment) and George Scott (a captain in the Fortieth and Robert Monckton's replacement as commandant of Fort Lawrence), would focus on the burdensome work of transport, siege support, and hard labor that came with an eighteenth-century campaign. As in Queen Anne's War and King George's War, the New Englanders would provide the overwhelming proportion of manpower and materiel for the Anglo-American operations in Nova Scotia. Few doubted that they would expect substantial rewards for their efforts.[111]

The Anglo-Americans' approach to Fort Beauséjour was uneventful.[112] On May 23 the invasion force in forty-one transports and three frigates under Rous's direction sailed from Boston to Annapolis Royal, where three additional ships from Halifax carrying artillery and engineers joined them. On June 1, the Anglo-American armada set out for Chignecto. At sunset on the first, it was inside the Bay of Chignecto, waiting for the tides to turn to make its landing. Commandant Vergor sounded the alarm for the Acadians to muster, but only around three hundred heeded the order. By nightfall on the second, the majority of the Anglo-American troops had landed on the British (southeast) side of the Missaquash River. They made their encampment under the protection of the cannon of Fort Lawrence and prepared for the push to Beauséjour. After resting his men for a day, Monckton broke camp on June 4 and moved toward Pont à la Buot (End Bridge), where he hoped to move the army across the Missaquash. Louis-Thomas Jacau de Fiedmont, Fort Beauséjour's chief engineer, believed that he could stop the invaders there. He ordered the bridge destroyed and four small swivel guns put in redoubt to rain fire on the Anglo-Americans as they crossed the river. In the first exchange of fire between French and British soldiers in Nova Scotia since King George's War, Monckton's artillerists opened up with counterbattery fire against the French guns and suppressing fire on the small group of French, Acadian, and Indian skirmishers. Anglo-American pioneers performed bravely under fire and made short work of constructing another bridge. The Anglo-Americans were across the river and on French territory. Before the Anglo-Americans could round up the enemy fighters from the firefight at the bridge, however, the Frenchmen had retreated to the fort, taking with them their swivel guns and whatever supplies they could carry. They also set the hamlet around the bridge to flames to deny the Anglo-Americans its use.

Monckton spent the next several days preparing for the siege of Fort Beauséjour. The regulars and provincials entrenched their camp at Butte à Roger and brought forward supplies from Fort Lawrence and Annapolis Royal. On June 8 the British artillery officers reconnoitered the French position and determined that the best position from which to start their siege lines was a small, undefended rise on the northeast side of the fort. On the tenth, the Yankees set to work clearing a road down which the heavy siege guns would move. At that point, Beausoleil and a party of Acadians infiltrated the Anglo-American lines. Before Scott's battalion could drive them off, they killed an engineer and private. The raid hardly slowed the Anglo-Americans, however. Yankee sappers continued to move earth, and by June 13 the Anglo-American lines had come within mortar range of the fort. Monckton opened the artillery phase of the siege with his bunker-busting thirteen-inch mortar, expecting that the French would respond with the proper protocols of the *siège en forme*.

The French officers, however, had little interest left in fighting—and the Acadians even less. Although Vergor lied to them that reinforcements would come to their rescue (his request for reinforcements already had been denied), most of the three hundred Acadians and the few regulars inside the fort could see that Beauséjour was doomed. More important, they already had pricked the Anglo-Americans' ire enough, and continued resistance would only anger the besiegers more. Meanwhile, Vergor, who had received the command of Beauséjour as a reward for his service to the intendant of New France, lacked the leadership traits needed to rally his men and the Acadians at that crucial moment. When a British mortar round penetrated a French casement and blew four men (including the unfortunate Ensign Hay, whom the French had captured on June 8) to smithereens, Vergor lost his nerve and sent Monckton word that he was ready to surrender.

Monckton granted Vergor the full honors of war, although the commandant had done little to earn them. He allowed the French soldiers to march out of the fort with their colors flying and drums beating and go on parole to France. As part of the surrender agreement, Monckton promised to neither plunder the fort nor take retribution against the Acadians whom he found inside it. That last promise proved empty. By the end of the summer, Anglo-Americans had begun the wholesale deportation, the first act of the grand dérangement, of the Acadians from Nova Scotia.

The story of the Acadians' removal has been told many times. Indeed, it is the best-known part of Nova Scotia's colonial history. Henry Wadsworth Longfellow immortalized it in poetry (*Evangeline*), and successive generations of historians have described and analyzed it in prose.[113] The roundup and deportation of the Acadians stands as a shockingly terrible act. The six thousand to seven thousand Acadians whom the Anglo-Americans banished from their homelands in 1755, and the thousands that followed in later years, signified the largest forced migration of Europeans in the history of North America.[114]

Most of those who have addressed the Acadian removal have assigned blame to one Anglo-American or another. Thus, Samuel Vetch, for his call for deportation in 1708, has been noted for starting the ball rolling. Naturally, Richard Philipps, because of his criticism of the Acadians, receives blame for contributing to the conditions that led to the diaspora. Even Paul Mascarene, who as a young officer wrote that the British would never control Nova Scotia until they brought the Acadians into line, has not escaped those looking to blame someone. The two main culprits, however, remain William Shirley and Charles Lawrence.[115] It is difficult to not see them as conspirators in making the nightmare of the Acadian removal a reality.[116]

But the "why" as opposed to the "who" questions surrounding the deportation of the Acadians emerge as more germane to this discussion. Why, for example, did Anglo-Americans resort to such a horrific act, and why did the operation against the French Fort Beauséjour creep into one focused on the Acadians? The answer lies in the nexus of the nature of war making on the North American frontier and Anglo-Americans' experiences in Nova Scotia following the conquest of 1710. Nova Scotia was a far-removed, distant, and wild place for Britons and Yankees in 1755. It was truly a marchland where the normal rules of behavior, especially in the chaos of war, did not necessarily apply.

Warfare on the North American frontier was especially brutal. For nearly 150 years, Anglo-Americans engaged Indians and other Europeans in a life-and-death struggle for the eastern half of the continent. In the many wars that wracked the frontier, Anglo-Americans unhesitatingly massacred men, women, and children. The first American way of war was one of unrestrained violence, shocking brutality, and devastating effectiveness. Extirpation of the enemy, whether through death or removal, remained the end state of American frontier war making well into the nineteenth century, when Americans displaced the Indians of the East to the lands west of the Mississippi River. It was that tradition of warfare that Yankees such as John Gorham and John Winslow, and Britons long experienced in North America such as William Shirley, brought to Nova Scotia. The British as well had a history of deporting troublesome and rebellious subjects. Their most recent experience in forced deportation had been the banishment to the colonies of nearly a thousand Highlanders following the Jacobite Rebellion of 1745. Still, there was something more to account for the scope and scale of the operation in 1755.

More often than not, the root cause of the extreme violence on the frontier was Anglo-Americans' insatiable hunger for land. Few in either New or Old England doubted that if Anglo-Americans could extirpate the Indians—or in the case of Nova Scotia, the Indians and Acadians—settlers would fill those lands and prosper. Aspiration for Acadian lands was never far from the center of Anglo-Americans' grand strategic thinking. Vetch, for instance, proposed removing the Acadians because he wanted to expropriate their lands. Perhaps in his private moments, he saw himself becoming baron or, better yet, viscount of Nova Scotia. Gorham no doubt had smaller visions of grandeur; as one who had fought and bled against the Acadians, he knew how difficult removing them by force would be. It is ironic that the fearsome ranger captain preferred the more subtle tactic of having the government impose oppressive quit rents on the Acadians to drive them out of the colony.[117] By 1755 Yankee and British soldiers had replaced rents as the tool they would use to get the Acadians to leave. We may safely assume that some of the New England soldiers who joined Monckton's army believed that the Acadians' lands would be a bonus to the conquest of Fort Beauséjour.

Part and parcel with Anglo-Americans' patterns of war making and land hunger was the Yankees' identity as faithful and loyal, and therefore deserving, subjects. In that sense, they were the antithesis of the Acadians. John Winslow, for instance, tellingly wrote, "Although it is a Disagreeable Part of Duty we are Put Upon, I am Sensible it is a Necessary One."[118] While his men arrested Acadians *igni ferroque,* he fretted that the British might not give the Yankees their proper due, their fair share in the spoils of victory. The possibility that the British might again abandon the Yankees—all of New England remembered what had happened at the end of King George's War, when leaders in Britain returned Louisbourg to France—offered reason enough for the British to be concerned about the Americans' continued military service in the new war for empire. "If the troops now here," Winslow warned Monckton, "who are known and respected in their own country, are slighted, it will be impossible to get assistance from the same source on a future occasion. The great principle with the people of the colonies is honourable and good usage."[119] Nothing, of course, would show the Britons' honorable and good usage of the Yankees more than to give them the Acadians' lands.

Those factors alone, however, do not completely explain the deportation. By 1755 Anglo-Americans had come to believe that Acadians deserved whatever fate befell them. Since 1710, the Acadians had refused the oath. The last decade had seen them, at least in the eyes of most Anglo-Americans, aid the French and Indian enemies who perpetrated outrages and murders across not only Nova Scotia but also the New England and New York frontiers. Of course, the hardening of attitudes toward the Acadians took time. Commodore Charles Knowles in 1746, for instance, expressed his opinion to Newcastle "that it will be necessary to drive all the Acadians out of Acadia" if the British wanted a lasting peace in the colony. At that time, Knowles qualified his recommendation with doubts about the feasibility, practicality, and morality of such an act. "It may be doubted," Knowles wrote, "whether under the circumstances of these people it would clearly appear to be a just usage of them."[120] But by July 1755 the winds of King George's and Father Le Loutre's Wars had blown away the concerns about "just usage" of the Acadians. Then, in August, Joseph Gorham brought news of the French victory over Major General Braddock at the battle of the Monongahela.[121] It was in that context that Jonathan Belcher, whom the Board of Trade had directed to supply a legal opinion on a possible deportation, advised that the removal had become "necessary."[122] Lieutenant Governor Spencer

Phips of Massachusetts also supported pulling off the kid gloves with the Acadians. In August, he wrote to Monckton that the "best precaution" for the safety of Nova Scotia would be removal.[123] Thus, removal of the Acadians had less to do with their religious and cultural identity as Acadians and more to do with the perceived military necessity of securing the colony, the very task that the army had been sent to Nova Scotia to accomplish.

The Acadians had overplayed their hand. As Naomi E. S. Griffiths observes, of the six men who sat through the discussions on the refugee oath in 1753, four of them (not the least of whom was Charles Lawrence) were present for the discussions of 1755.[124] There was no one left in the Anglo-American camp whose offers of compromise the Acadians had not rejected. It therefore is not difficult to see how Lawrence and his advisors would be inclined to see any discussions over the oath as pointless, and asking the Acadians—who, after all, were the ruled, not the rulers—to compromise was akin to asking for a slap in the face.

Yet wrapped within past history, anger, and pride, the most obvious reason for the Anglo-Americans' choosing to deport the Acadians in 1755 was that they could. For the first time since the British conquest, a British governor was in a position to make real the threat to punish the Acadians if they did not comply with his instructions. Governors Nicholson, Vetch, Caulfield, Doucett, Armstrong, Mascarene, Cornwallis, and Hopson, to one degree or another, had all blustered and fumed for decades but always lacked the manpower to make real their threats. Such was not the case for Charles Lawrence in 1755. Hundreds of Anglo-American soldiers, both British regulars and Yankee provincials, were camped in the middle of the Acadian heartland. Lawrence had a free hand to do as he wished with the Acadians.

The die was cast when the British demanded that the Acadians take an unqualified oath of allegiance to King George II on July 3, 1755. As had so often been the case, the Acadians equivocated and then refused. Lawrence then issued deportation orders to Monkton on Chignecto, Winslow at Minas Basin, and Handfield in Annapolis Royal. Charles Morris's 1746 survey of the colony, which Shirley had commissioned to learn where the best and most prosperous Acadians lands sat for future New England settlements, made the task surprisingly easy. Although Morris advised that "it would be difficult to apprehend them [the Acadians], but by some stratagem," Anglo-American troops met little resistance initially.[125] Because the plan was to ensure that the Acadians were "rooted out" of the province, the Yankees systematically destroyed the settlements, torched the fields, and destroyed the dykes that held back the sea. They erased a century and a half of work. Even though the Acadians then subscribed to the unqualified oath, it was too little, too late. History had overtaken them, and the oath, the very point of contention for so long, had become worthless.

For nearly forty-five years, individuals had had relatively free rein to set the course that the empire would take in Nova Scotia. But by 1755, the legacies of an immediate past war, conflict, and suffering (as well as the Acadians' own actions) had produced an uncontrollable momentum of Anglo-American hostility that overwhelmed the Acadians. The individuals who made the decision to deport the Acadians and then executed it were not particularly evil men. Rather, they were the products of their time whose experiences had shown that Acadians, Indians, and Frenchmen consistently had proven themselves intractable enemies and barriers to both the security of the empire and the path to the Anglo-Americans' personal prosperity. The deportation, despite all the suffering it caused, made perfect sense to them. In instances where people find themselves confronting forces larger than themselves that they cannot control, tragedy usually follows. Such was the case for the Acadians in the autumn of 1755.

6

The Guerrilla War, 1755–1760

Crushing the last remnants of Acadian, Indian, and French resistance in Nova Scotia took nearly five years following the Acadian proscription of 1755. While the Seven Years' War moved toward the climactic battles between the British and French armies on the Plains of Abraham and at Saint-Foy, Anglo-Americans squared off against Acadians and Indians desperate to regain their homes and win back their independence. If "guerrilla warfare" as a military term best describes operations that paramilitary and indigenous forces conduct in hostile-held territory within the milieu of an insurgency—a movement that seeks to overthrow a government through armed conflict—Acadian and Indian resistance after 1755 stands as one of the eighteenth century's foremost guerrilla wars.[1] Of course, Acadian, Indian, and French participants did not call their struggle a guerrilla conflict, any more than Anglo-Americans at the time would have termed their efforts as counterinsurgency. Nonetheless, to the modern student of war, the violence that engulfed Nova Scotia between 1755 and 1760 is most properly understood as guerrilla and counterinsurgency warfare.

Western professional soldiers and military thinkers have struggled for decades with the riddle of how to defeat guerrillas. The French,

Britons, and Americans all have developed overarching schemes to combat them, most often in the form of counterinsurgency theory. From those who sought to physically and politically isolate the guerrillas from local civilian populations, usually done with "concentration camps" or "strategic hamlets" (ironically, seen as the foundation of "winning hearts and minds"), to those who chose to terrorize into submission the guerrilla and his base of popular support, soldiers tasked with defeating insurgents have generally focused on a guerrilla's operating environment. Americans have preferred to play to their strengths and therefore have sought ways to force guerrillas to fight on terms most favorable to the U.S. military's overwhelming conventional might. Others (most notably the French and to some extent the British) have thought that the best way to defeat an insurgency was to "out-guerrilla the guerrilla." The most creative leaders have naturally looked to combine all the elements of antiguerrilla operations into a coherent whole.[2] Yet in the end, in the best known of the post-1945 guerrilla wars—the French in the First Indochina War (1945–54) and the Algerian War (1952–64), the British in the Malaysian Emergency (1948–60), and the United States in the Second Indochina War (1954–73)—Western armies have a record of only limited success in antiguerrilla, or counterinsurgency, warfare.

Anglo-Americans, however, defeated their guerrilla enemy in Nova Scotia. Isolated on the far reaches of the empire and away from the center of the "regular" or "conventional" war, Anglo-Americans crushed a capable and desperate guerrilla adversary. The details of the British army's eradication of guerrilla resistance on the Nova Scotia frontier between 1755 and 1760 illuminates both the brutality of that conflict and the harsh, albeit effective, methods of mid-eighteenth-century Anglo-American counterinsurgency warfare.

The Acadians and Indians resorted to guerrilla warfare in the late summer of 1755 because they had no other choice. The best-known theory of warfare that fully encompasses guerrilla warfare—Mao Tse-tung's ideas of "protracted war"—stresses that guerrilla operations are a precursor to a point in time when revolutionaries' conventional forces can meet and defeat the regular forces of the enemy.[3] For the Acadians and Indians of Nova Scotia, however, there was little hope that a French army would come to their rescue. Instead, the Acadians had to fight virtually on their own—and in their own ways—if they wanted to drive the Anglo-Americans from their homelands.

The Acadian Guerrillas

The guerrilla war began almost immediately following the surrender of Forts Beauséjour and Gaspereaux in mid-June. Entire Acadian families fled into the woods of present-day New Brunswick rather than surrender to the Yankees. Father Jean Manach led his flock of Acadians, métis, and Mi'kmaq to an Indian village near the mouth of the Miramichi River. That refugee camp served as an Acadian-guerrilla sanctuary until 1760. Fort Menagoueche on rivière Saint-Jean became untenable when one hundred Maliseets passively stood on the shore and watched the Anglo-American sea militia attack.[4] Charles des Champs de Boishébert razed the fort and with a handful of *troupes de la marine* and Acadians escaped into the forest. Father Jean-Louis Le Loutre likewise torched his church on Chignecto before fleeing.[5]

Anglo-Americans needed to pacify the Missaquash Valley before they could give chase to the Acadians and Mi'kmaq. In late July, in an ominous precursor to what would come, one of Silvanus Cobb's men was shot from his horse and killed in an ambush outside Fort Monckton (the rechristened Fort Gaspereaux). Cobb assembled a troop of one hundred men, though the Yankees were too slow in mustering to catch the killers. Captain Abijah Willard, another of the company commanders in George Scott's battalion, criticized their lack of expediency: "He [Cobb] lett the Indians [assuming the killer was an Indian and not an Acadian] get fur a nuff before he up on persute of them." Colonel Robert Monckton, from Fort Lawrence, dispatched two hundred men to "Inquire into ye Affair," but the large column failed to find any Indians or Acadians.[6]

As the rounding up of the Acadians progressed and other Acadians learned of their neighbors' fate, many more chose to flee rather than come in peacefully to be exiled from their homes. In August, Cobb, in the *York and Halifax,* reconnoitered the settlement of Chipoudy (present-day Shepody, New Brunswick) and learned that a large party of Acadians had congregated both there and along the Petitcodiac River. With the deportation in full swing, those Acadians needed to be rooted out and taken into custody, especially in light of the Anglo-American high command's concern that "an Insurrection may follow from Despair." Charles Lawrence stressed to Monckton the imperative "to drive the deserted French Inhabitants, at all Events out of the Country."[7] Monckton thereupon directed Major Joseph Frye to take two hundred of his Massachusetts provincials and carry the proscription into New Brunswick.[8]

Frye was unaware that a substantial force of Acadians, Indians, and Frenchmen were waiting for him at Chipoudy. As an officer in the troupes de la marine, Boishébert was well schooled in the tactics of petite guerre. Upon learning that the British were deporting the Acadians, he had moved to Chipoudy with 120 fighters to defend that settlement, one of the last standing.[9]

The Yankees arrived at Chipoudy on September 1 and set about systematically destroying the village and rounding up Acadian women and children. Near the end of the operation, when Lieutenant John Indicot had only fifty men ashore to herd the prisoners to the transports, Boishébert attacked. The guerrillas—in the confusion of the fight, the Yankees thought there were three hundred men attacking them—quickly drove Indicot and his men behind a dyke. Frye landed with reinforcements and rallied Indicot's now-disorganized and frightened provincials. As soon as they had hit, however, the enemy dispersed. All told, Frye lost twenty-two men—not the eighty that the French would later claim—of his command killed or captured and another six wounded. Among the dead were the battalion surgeon's mate, named Jacob March, and a subaltern, a Lieutenant Billings. Boishébert's losses were only one dead and several wounded, which his forces took off the battlefield, leaving the Yankees to wonder whether they had harmed the guerrillas in any way.[10]

The fight at Chipoudy proved a rude awakening for the provincials. Unlike their officers, most of the Yankee privates were little more than raw recruits. The Yankees had won at Fort Beauséjour, to be sure, but that was hardly an event that tested their battle hardness. They simply overwhelmed the French, who put up only feeble resistance anyway, with men and materiel. Indeed, Fred Anderson notes, "It is unlikely that the majority of provincial soldiers in any unit that served during the war had a concrete idea of what lay ahead when they went into action." Their first experience with combat—a firefight in which 50 percent of those who had participated had become causalities—understandably would have led many rank-and-file soldiers to wonder what they had gotten themselves into.[11] News of the defeat quickly spread throughout the Yankee camp. Captain Alexander Murray of the regulars could see that morale was low and trepidation high around the Yankee campfires. He tried to prop up the men's spirits. He reminded Lieutenant Colonel Winslow that death "is the Fortune of War" but predicted "the Lads will Stand Fire better another time and I hope will Soon wipe off their Scores at next Meeting."[12] Most of the New England provincials probably found little solace that there would be more meetings between them and the guerrillas.

Chipoudy was the first bright spot in what had been a difficult couple of months for the Acadians. Boishébert rescued thirty Acadian families and brought off several fields' worth of crops and supplies. The Acadians could not afford to waste anything. New France's native-born governor-general, Pierre de Rigaud de Vaudreuil de Cavagnial, marquis de Vaudreuil—son of the earlier governor-general Vaudreuil—directed that Boishébert and the Acadians remain in place and forbade them to come to Quebec. Vaudreuil wanted to concentrate as many Indians and Acadians as possible on the eastern front to harass and keep the British off guard. He also was concerned that if the Nova Scotia Acadians fled, the Acadians on Île Royale and Île Saint-Jean also would lose heart and give the Anglo-Americans those places without a fight.[13]

With an insurgency apparently in full gear, Lawrence and Monckton could not afford to release their troops for service elsewhere. That was a serious problem for William Shirley. Even before the Beauséjour operation had begun, all other recruiting efforts in New England were put on hold as the colonies tried to fill the rolls of the provincial regiments.[14] Shirley had burned the candle at both ends when he presented the Nova Scotia campaign as one that the provincials could handle with only minimal support from the regulars. Traditionally, the colonies' militia had been the recruiting—in some cases, drafting—pools for the provincial forces, and the provincials in turn helped fill the ranks of the regular regiments. The high command had agreed to the Nova Scotia diversion primarily on Shirley's claim that it was feasible and then, in "a madly ambitious plan approved by men studying maps in London unaware that their ignorance of American geography, politics, and military capacities had foredoomed it to failure," directed Shirley to reactivate the Fiftieth and Fifty-first Regiments and lead them against the French at Niagara.[15] Those two "American" regiments had been activated for King George's War but had been disbanded when the fighting ended in 1748. Shirley thus faced

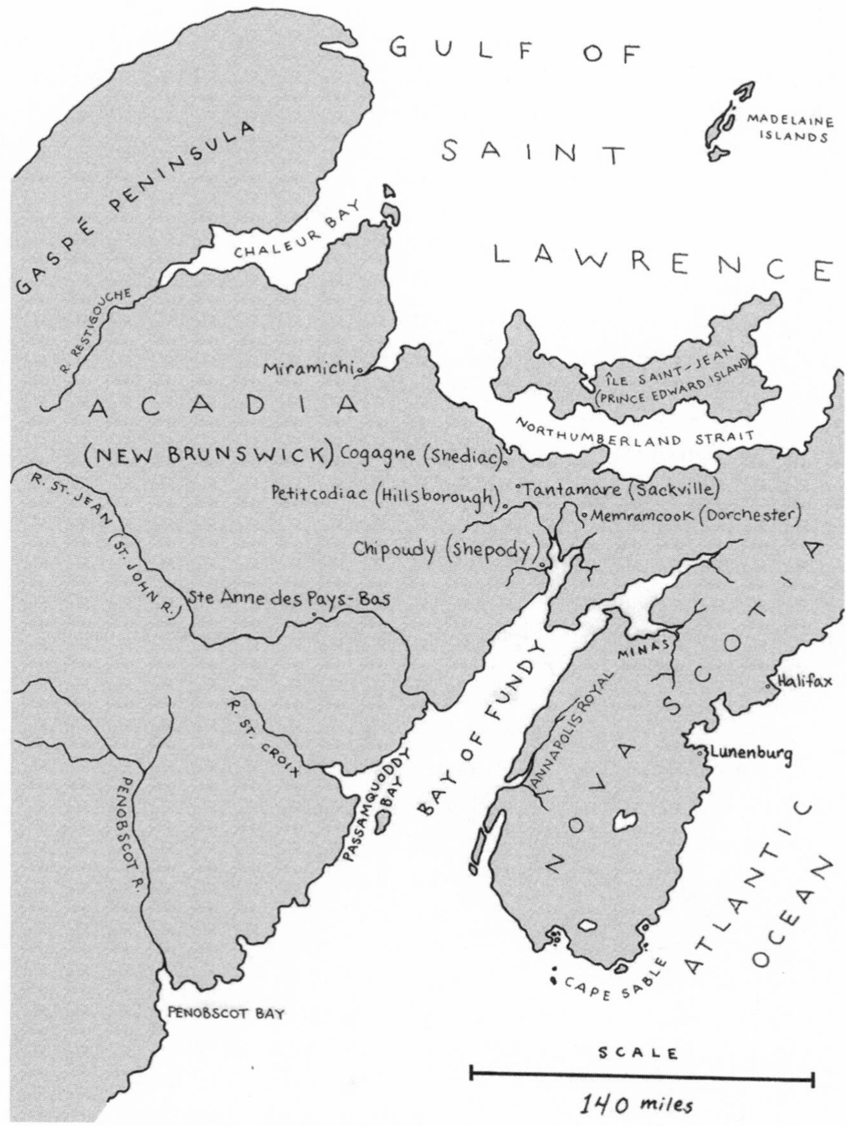

Area of operations in the guerrilla war.

the unenviable task, albeit one of his own creation, of filling out two new regular regiments when the town of Boston alone had already sent 433 men to join the provincial regiments and another 200 for the regulars.[16] The Yankees in Nova Scotia thus would have to make do with the resources they had on hand.

The provincials, of course, had more to worry about than whether or not Shirley could keep his promises to his patrons in London. As Anglo-Americans tentatively ventured from Forts Cumberland (their name for what had been Fort Beauséjour) and Lawrence (formerly Beaubassin) to complete the work of the Acadian proscription, they had to remain vigilant against guerrilla attacks. As regular forces are inclined to do, they assumed that if they sent large parties into the field, the guerrillas would not dare attack these troops. They were right. The trade-off, of course, was that their patrols became large, ponderous columns that stood little chance of catching fleeing Acadians or engaging and killing enemy fighters. On September 15, for example, Majors Jedediah Preble and Benjamin Goldthwait took four hundred men to destroy an Acadian village a short distance outside Fort Monckton. The task of burning two hundred buildings, which should have taken no more than a company, required an entire battalion.

Guerrilla hit-and-run raids became more common in the autumn. On October 23, for instance, a Lieutenant Curtis took a company from Fort Cumberland to herd cattle, sheep, and horses for the garrison. Suddenly, the provincials came under fire from nearby woods. Curtis "ordered his party to Pursue them: which they Did very vigoreously Keeping a Constant Fireing." The Yankees then realized that they had fallen into an ambush and faced what they believed to be a hundred guerrillas (probably a gross overestimate driven by confusion and fear). The provincials retreated but found themselves being pursued. They avoided a total rout by regrouping behind a dyke. After their return to Fort Cumberland, a reinforced party sought to make contact with the guerrillas. They failed, of course; the guerrillas by that time were long gone. Although the Yankees considered the day a success since "No Great Damage" was done to them, nothing was said of the fate of the cattle, sheep, and horses. Most likely, they ended up in the guerrillas' hands and stomachs.[17]

The Yankees lacked a coordinated concept of operations by which to deal with the guerrillas. They defaulted to sending patrols willy-nilly into the field in hopes that these would search out and destroy the enemy. John Thomas described one such mission. On the night of October 29, Thomas and his colleagues were sent to destroy a small village about three miles from Pont à la Buot. Upon arriving at the settlement, they saw that smoke was coming from the chimney of one of the buildings. Thomas and his comrades "surrounded the House and Rushed on it[,] upon which we received a discharge of three Guns." They quickly realized that Curtis's company had secured the house as their bivouac and were aggressively engaging what they thought were guerrillas. After everyone settled down and avoided any more unintended attempts at fratricide, Thomas and his mates returned to Fort Cumberland. He complained in his journal that the snow began falling around one o'clock A.M., which made for a cold and miserable night march.[18]

The unpleasant business of patrolling continued through the late autumn. On November 13 Thomas's company was again in the field. They marched in "very Cold" weather "but Discovered no Enemy." The next day, they encountered three guerrillas and discharged their weapons at the enemy but did not know whether they had wounded or killed anyone. Thomas's party reached Tantamar (Sackville) at around eleven o'clock A.M. and proceeded to kill livestock. Several guerrillas harassed them as they went about their pillaging, but as usual the Yankees did not capture or kill any of the guerrillas. On November 15, the Yankees burned the church and ninety-seven other buildings at Tantamar, then marched twelve miles to Memramcook. There they linked up with seven hundred men under George Scott, including his new "light infantry" company of regulars.[19] At dawn on the seventeenth, they attacked the twenty houses in the village. All were deserted except for one that contained nine women and children. They arrested these Acadians and killed two hundred head of livestock.[20]

The Yankees then withdrew from Chignecto and Minas Basin. They had destroyed nearly everything of value in the Acadian homelands, and it was highly unlikely that the French would launch a large-scale winter expedition against Forts Cumberland, Lawrence, or Edward (in Minas). Furthermore, the Massachusetts Assembly had complained that the Bay Colony's troops in Nova Scotia had been treated "poorly." The Yankees expected both their local representatives and the British army to abide closely to the contract under which they had enlisted. The grumbling began when the troops realized that they might have to spend the winter billeted in tents outside the forts. If the prospect of passing a Nova Scotia winter with only minimal shelter was not enough to concern them, there were rumors floating about that the British army might extend the New Englanders' enlistments past the twelve months for which they had volunteered.[21] William Shirley warned Henry Fox (the secretary of state for the Southern Department) that the scheme for "enlisting such of the Soldiers of it [the Massachusetts provincial regiment] into the King's Regiment, as could be got to do it . . . was communicated to the Massachusetts Assembly in so unfavorable a light . . . that it inflamed the whole Province."[22] The Yankees decided that Halifax offered a more luxurious posting for the winter.

While the regulars watched, no doubt with some sense of envy if not disgust, the provincials broke camp and headed east. George Scott, holder of a captaincy in the British army, chose to remain behind with his light infantrymen and transferred command of his provincial battalion to Jedediah Preble. The men of the Fortieth, Forty-fifth, and Forty-seventh Regiments—just over two thousand, all told—would have to garrison the Chignecto forts. Although Lawrence and Monckton had more regulars to work with than at any other time in the colony's history, those forces had much more to do. In addition to Chignecto, they would have to provide detachments for the protection of Halifax, Fort Sackville, Dartmouth, Annapolis Royal, Fort Edward, and Lunenburg.[23] Monckton, however, seemed not overly worried that his men might need him at the front. Perhaps he was of the same mind as the Yankees when he left for Halifax and made Scott the senior British officer on Chignecto.[24]

The French also settled in for the winter. Boishébert led his guerrilla band to Cogagne (Shediac) and joined the 600 Acadian refugees who had made their camp there. The Mi'kmaq, on their way to their winter hunting grounds, presented these allies and friends with cattle to help feed them.[25] Another 1,000 Acadians under the spiritual guidance of Jesuit Father Charles Germain had joined with Manach and established Le Camp d'Esperance (Camp Hope) near Baie de Miramichi. Some reports claimed that there were upwards of 3,500 Acadians at Camp d'Esperance.[26] Regardless, a substantial body of Acadians stood opposite the Anglo-American forces on Chignecto. If the French could have mustered the manpower and supplies, including some cannon, they perhaps could have given the British a run for their money on the isthmus. As late as autumn of 1756, Louis-Joseph de Montcalm, marquis de Montcalm, commander of the French armies in North America, asked the Ministry of Marine for reinforcements to take the war to what he believed were vulnerable Anglo-American positions in Acadia.[27]

No large-scale French campaign against Chignecto was forthcoming, however. The Acadians, Indians, and Boishébert would have to depend on petite guerre to make life difficult for the British. They were certainly encouraged in early January 1756 when 226 banlieu Acadians seized the *Pembroke* that was transporting them to North Carolina.[28] The mutineers turned the ship around and somehow managed to avoid the Anglo-American ships plying the waters off New England and Nova Scotia. They sailed the *Pembroke* as far as they could up rivière Saint-Jean, burned it, and then wandered the woods until they linked up with Boishébert's partisans. It was no small feat; there were twelve portages between the Saint-Jean and Miramichi rivers alone, but the mutineers were clearly desperate people inured to hardship. Although they presented him with more mouths to feed, they also gave Boishébert a much-needed infusion of 33 men of fighting age.[29]

Boishébert then began harassing Forts Lawrence and Monckton. Garrisons of regulars were stretched out across Chignecto at Forts Cumberland (1,000), Lawrence (150), and Monckton (150), isolated from one another and dependent on supplies from Halifax. Although none of the forts (especially the heavily garrisoned Fort Cumberland) was likely to have fallen to the guerrillas, having to guard and remain vigilant against raids would make for a long winter for the troops inside them. On January 20, 1756, Boishébert sent François Boucher de Niverville to Baie Verte to burn a British schooner that had taken a French privateer into the bay. Niverville took the sailors completely by surprise, killed 7 of them, took 1 prisoner, and burned the ships. At the same time, Boishébert led 120 guerrillas against Fort Cumberland. His plan was to reconnoiter the British position and perhaps take some prisoners.[30]

The raid on Fort Cumberland contributed to Boishébert's reputation as the "white ghost." Clad in the white uniform of an officer in the troupes de la marine, Boishébert managed to stay one step ahead of the parties sent to apprehend or kill him. He already had escaped from Fort Menagoueche, bested Major Frye at Chipoudy, and ambushed Lieutenant Curtis. He proved just as elusive to George Scott. A certain Daniel—a "snake" that the French had thought they had killed—deserted the French camp and warned Scott that Boishébert was on his way to Fort Cumberland.[31] Scott carefully arrayed four hundred British troops in an ambush. If he could decapitate the guerrilla leadership, perhaps he could put the insurgency to an end. Yet just when it looked as if Boishébert would fall into Scott's trap, the wily partisan suspected something was not right and retreated into the woods. An entire battalion of regulars, as a result, spent several days concealed in the cold woods to no effect. Events on Chignecto then entered a lull, as both the guerrillas and the British regulars passed the winter days without causing each other problems. Still, that did not mean that the regulars could drop their guard while they spent most of early 1756 battling the winter weather, tedium, and drudgery.

Both the British and the French high command focused on the Ohio Valley in the spring of 1756. Montcalm marched against the Anglo-American garrison that had occupied Oswego over the winter, and the British tried to both reinforce that garrison and push northward along the Hudson River–Lake Champlain invasion route into Canada. Neither side, therefore, spared resources for Nova Scotia.

Because their twelve-month enlistments were due to expire in the spring at the one-year anniversary of the Beauséjour operation, the provincials sailed from Halifax for Boston in April. All that remained of Anglo-American arms in Nova Scotia were the Yankee rangers—and many of the best of them, such as Captain Thomas Speakman, had left Nova Scotia to join Robert Rogers's larger ranger force in New York[32]—and the Fortieth, Forty-fifth, and Forty-seventh Regiments. Governor Lawrence, Shirley reported, complained that his number of troops was "barely sufficient to do the Duty requisite at the Several Posts within that Province."[33]

Despite the vulnerabilities of Anglo-American forces in Nova Scotia, Boishébert could do little against them. Recognizing "the impossibility of resisting an infinitely superior force, he prudently retired" to Miramichi. Conditions at Camp d'Esperance were horrendous; in January, Boishébert had to reduce the daily food ration to half a pound of bread. When the bread ran out, the Acadians ate the hides off dead cattle and then even the leather from their boots. Discipline and order began to crumble in the camp. Boishébert had to put down a riot when several Acadians took up arms to force others to give them their provisions. He eventually resorted to offering fifty-pound bounties to any Acadian who told him of trouble brewing in the camp. "The vigilance which was required for the maintenance of the Acadian families & the migration of part of them," he wrote in his third-person postwar memorial, "did not allow of harassing the enemy as often as the young commandant would have wished."[34] It took most of the next year to recover from the hardships of the winter.

Still, the British could not afford to look past the threat of Indian or Acadian attacks. The simplest day-to-day tasks became fraught with perceived dangers. In the autumn of 1756, for instance, fifty armed Lunenburg men left for Minas Basin to collect free-ranging cattle and horses. With the basin cleared of Acadian farmers, it had become an open range for stock and draft animals. The Lunenburg men collected 120 animals and began their cattle drive home. That the herders left much to be desired as cowboys—they were able to bring in only half the animals they rounded up—is understandable. The antiquarian historian Mather Desbrisay described their trek as "a truly hazardous journey made through an enemy's country, an enemy, who, though uncivilized, was not wholly ignorant of some of those resources by which successful Generals have been largely aided, on modern fields of warfare."[35]

The only fighting, if one can call a strategic retreat "fighting," in 1756 took place outside Fort Monckton. The Mi'kmaq who had camped in the woods surrounding Baie Verte effectively had pinned the small garrison of regulars inside the fort. Because of the threat of ambushes, it was practically impossible for the Anglo-Americans to supply the fort from land. Niverville's raid in the summer of 1755 had shown that the port side was vulnerable as well. Boishébert similarly recognized that Fort Monckton was the most vulnerable British position on the isthmus, and in early autumn he prepared to attack the fort. In October, he had enough men and materiel in place to move against it. Suspecting that the guerrillas were on their way, the regulars inside Fort Monckton abandoned it for Fort Cumberland and burned it to the ground.[36] The British presence on Chignecto thus consisted of only Forts Cumberland and Lawrence. By the end of 1756, the French certainly had not won the guerrilla war in Nova Scotia, but neither had the Anglo-Americans. If they hoped to make

Nova Scotia safe for settlement, Anglo-Americans would have to find some way to pacify the countryside.

Guerrilla Raids and Anglo-American Impotence

In late 1756 and early 1757, the next campaigning season was shaping up to be the climactic one for the war in Nova Scotia. The coalition government of William Pitt and the duke of Newcastle, after the poor showing of British forces on the Continent and in the colonies, shifted gears and supported an all-out war in North America. John Campbell, Fourth Earl of Loudoun, had arrived in New York in July 1756 and energetically set to reorganizing the army's logistic network and weaning it off its dependence on American contractors. By the spring of 1757, he had made tremendous strides in improving the morale and supply system of the army. The time seemed right for a campaign against Louisbourg. Pitt therefore sent six thousand regulars from Cork, Ireland, to Nova Scotia, where they would link up with most of Loudoun's North American army and reduce the "Dunkirk of America."[37]

The largest army that Great Britain ever had sent to North America assembled at Halifax in June and July 1757. On paper, Loudoun's force was more than enough to take Louisbourg. Similarly, the availability of the piers, docks, and provisioning areas at Halifax justified the Board of Trade and Admiralty's foresight in establishing a settlement there six years earlier. Over twenty thousand Anglo-American soldiers and sailors milled about the town and port. Indeed, Loudoun would have been justified in expecting to have a relatively easy go of it.

Yet, nothing came of the British efforts. Fever soon broke out among the troops, and Loudoun believed that it "was so serious among the seamen and troops in Halifax that it would have been unwise to attempt an attack on Louisbourg." By July more than a thousand of them had been hospitalized.[38] John Rous's sea militia reconnoitered Louisbourg and reported that a French fleet was in the harbor. The ships of the Royal Navy confirmed Rous's report.[39] Then, in the midst of watching the days pass and hoping that he could move against Louisbourg before his army withered from sickness, the worst of news reached Loudoun's headquarters. Montcalm had assembled over eight thousand French regulars recently arrived from the mother country, troupes de la marine, Canadian militia, and Native American allies and had besieged Fort William Henry—the main Anglo-American post guarding the upper Hudson Valley—on August 3. With a French army on the loose in New York, the capture of Louisbourg suddenly seemed of secondary importance. Fearing the "entire loss of my Master's Army, which might probably have been attended, with the loss of part of his Dominions in this part of the world," the earl ordered the armada to sail for New York on August 6.[40] For several days, it looked as if Loudoun might not reach New York in time. On August 9, Fort William Henry fell, and "nothing seemingly prevented him [Montcalm] from following the road that pointed toward the next logical objective [Fort Edward, then Albany, and then onward from there.]" Fortunately for Loudoun's damaged reputation, Montcalm had little interest in moving south. New France faced famine conditions, and the men of his army were needed in the Saint Lawrence Valley for the harvest. Ironically, the New England militia whom the regulars disdained mustered more than seven thousand soldiers and rushed four thousand of them to Fort Edward to block the road to Albany. Taken together, the affairs at Fort William Henry and Halifax showed that even the best-organized armies must have commanders with fighting spirit if they are to be of any use.[41]

Nonetheless, at least one positive for Anglo-American arms came out of Loudoun's Halifax sojourn. His decision to leave the First, Twenty-eighth, and Forty-third Regiments in Halifax gave Governor Lawrence badly needed manpower. The Forty-third Regiment took up residence at Annapolis Royal, while the Twenty-eighth moved out for Fort Cumberland and the First remained in Halifax.[42]

Even with rangers out "every day to scour the country" and thousands of regulars in the forts and on transports, the province had remained a dangerous place.[43] On July 20 Indians captured two of Gorham's rangers outside Fort Cumberland. Another party of Indians captured John Witherspoon near Fort Anne. On July 29 four soldiers of the Forty-third Regiment went missing from Halifax. The British found two of them dead and scalped. The other two were nowhere to be found. Although the one- and two-at-a-time losses were not significant from a manpower perspective, they showed that the Indians and Acadians could act with impunity throughout the colony. The only way to solve that problem was to root them out of their sanctuaries and destroy them. On August 6 Lawrence therefore ordered the Forty-third Regiment to "hold themselves in readiness to sail at a moment's warning" for an expedition up the Saint John River.[44]

The threat of guerrilla raids behind the British lines in Nova Scotia, however, compelled Lawrence to call off the attack. As he and Monckton worked out the details of the Saint John expedition, they received intelligence that Boishébert had been at Louisbourg with a reported eight hundred Acadians, Indians, and troupes de la marine.[45] With the bulk of the Anglo-American force returned to New York, they rightly worried that Boishébert might be so bold as to move against Fort Cumberland or perhaps even Fort Anne. On August 17 they therefore suspended the expedition up the Saint John and ordered the Forty-third Regiment to march posthaste to Fort Cumberland. Eleven days later, a French deserter told the British that a large force from Île Royale was preparing to descend on Nova Scotia, and two days later, guerrillas assumed to be scouts were seen outside Dartmouth. Clearly, Boishébert and the French intended some kind of raid, if not outright attack, on the Anglo-American positions in Nova Scotia.

Just before the Forty-third arrived at Fort Cumberland, guerrillas took sixty head of cattle and some horses right outside the fort's gate. Something had to be done to stop the guerrillas' forays. Monckton therefore directed Lieutenant Colonel Hunt Walsh to take the Twenty-eighth Regiment and a company of rangers to Baie Verte and level it. On September 6 the party sallied forth and burned what was left of Baie Verte, destroyed several canoes and boats, and tore down eleven bridges between the port and their post. They met neither humans nor cattle and could "not discover any human tracks in any part of the country where they have been." They returned on the seventh, and three days later, Captain John Knox of the Forty-third Regiment was told that his company would be part of an 800-man joint force of rangers and regulars that would march against Chipoudy, which seemed to be the originating point for the guerrilla raids. The plan was to "bring off their cattle, burn their corn and settlements, and [in] other ways distress them as much as possible."[46] Monckton clearly had decided that if his forces could not use the infrastructure of Chignecto, then neither would the guerrillas. Hindsight proved it to be an effective tactic. Boishébert in fact had moved a force of 80 regulars, 250 Acadians, and 300 Mi'kmaq as far forward as the Tantamare River but could remain there only for a week "on account of a lack of provisions."[47]

Guerrillas then attacked on the outskirts of Fort Anne. Reports came in that the Indians raided the faubourg for cattle and supplies and burned what they could not take with them. Rather than seizing the opportunity to engage the elusive enemy, however, the troops inside Fort Anne let them accomplish their deeds with no interference. The garrison was "too weak," Knox wrote, to venture out and challenge the raiders.[48] It was another poor showing for the regulars.

The anxiety over guerrilla attacks added to the oppressive boredom of garrison duty. Most of the regulars' duties involved standing watch waiting for something to happen. On the night of September 21, the garrison of Fort Cumberland thought that it might have a fight on its hands the next morning; sounds of several shots in the swamp near the fort convinced Monckton to order the troops to stand at arms all night. The shooting came from rangers who were waterfowl hunting. The same night, a sentry killed another British soldier when the latter approached the fort with a blanket wrapped around his shoulders in Indian fashion. The next day, two regulars deserted the fort. Upon seeing some Indians near what had been Baie Verte, one of them fled back to the fort, where he preferred to take his chances with British discipline rather than face the Mi'kmaq.[49]

Elements of the Forty-third Regiment got their first taste of combat with the Indians in October. It must have been a wholly unsatisfactory experience for them. The white ghost appeared standing on the shore near Fort Cumberland, so Monckton ordered several patrols out to see what they could find. After spending most the day rooting around, one party came upon what looked like an abandoned Indian camp. Fearing a march in the dark back to Fort Cumberland, the regulars decided to occupy the camp for the night. In the darkness, the Indians attacked. The panicked regulars "fired so furiously, some one way, and some another, that it was with difficulty that their Officers could retrain them."[50] No one knew whether they had hit any of their intended victims, but that really would not have mattered as far as the regulars were concerned, since all of them returned safely to Fort Cumberland.

With the major campaigning season coming to a close, both sides again moved to winter quarters. The Forty-third Regiment sailed from Fort Cumberland to Fort Anne and left the Twenty-eighth and rangers behind. Boishébert again made his camp near the Miramichi River, where he hoped to receive supplies from New France. Governor Lawrence, while conducting an inspection of Fort Cumberland in late October, saw several fires outside the fort that he supposed were Boishébert and his men, but in reality they could have been any Acadians or Indians.

Small raids continued throughout the winter. On October 28 several Indians tried to capture some teamsters outside Fort Anne but were unsuccessful.[51] Fear of Indian ambushes forced Captain John Knox to use his company for the less-than-glorious task of escorting the garrison's apple pickers. Knox and his fellow officers decided to remain in the field after they had safely returned their charges to Fort Anne, and they promptly got lost in the woods. They found no Indians. News reached Annapolis Royal that Indians, meanwhile, had raided Fort Cumberland and stolen a sloop, which they burned when pursued by Gorham's Rangers.[52]

That cat-and-mouse game outside Fort Anne intensified in late November and early December. On November 29 the garrison witnessed several fires burning on the north side of the Annapolis River. The next morning, patrols went forth to investigate, and on December 1, Knox's company found several moccasin tracks. They carefully followed the tracks to a building where they "caught some of the river vermin [Acadians] in their own trap" and arrested them. Knox's men also found a building filled with supplies. The regulars filled their haversacks with loot, then torched the storehouse. Further patrolling revealed an Acadian camp a mere three miles from the fort. During the operation, the regulars captured forty-eight Acadians. Knox was perplexed; he had assumed that the "greatest part of them, had been seized and sent out of the province."

Yet there remained significant numbers of Acadians in the woods surrounding Fort Anne. In early December, Acadians attacked a woodcutting party; they killed a British grenadier and captured 3 regulars and 6 rangers. Upon hearing the ruckus, 2 officers and 13 regulars gave chase and tracked a blood trail for two miles but in the end returned to Fort Anne with only the grenadier's body, "not scalped, but stripped of clothing except for breeches." That night, the Acadians returned to the woods outside the fort and made a *feu de joie* to celebrate their victory and taunt the Anglo-Americans. The British sent 130 men to catch the revelers but made no contact. The next morning, the British patrol cautiously approached a mill where they assumed Acadians were waiting in ambush. After that brief but tense moment, "We continued our route through very difficult and disagreeable forests," Knox wrote, "some rough, others swampy." Around noon, the patrol crossed a path that took them to what had been Pierre Godet's homestead, about twenty-two miles from the fort. The officers determined to cross to the opposite side of the Annapolis River and double back on the fort and possibly catch the guerrillas from the rear.

The officers, concerned that the guerrillas might find them first, began the patrol early the next morning. They had spent the night sleeping armed, relieved their sentries every hour, and had their subalterns check the troops every fifteen minutes. The regulars began by marching six more miles up the river in search of a passable ford. They turned around and marched to within eighteen miles of Fort Anne to the ford at Renne Forêt River. Acadian William Johnston had fifty-six men waiting in ambush. As the regulars crossed the river, they "were suddenly attacked by as horrid a yell as ever I [John Knox] heard." One British officer was killed on the spot. Knox and the other officers rallied the men and returned fire. During the brief but brisk exchange, the British lost twenty-four men killed (the captain, a sergeant, and twenty-two privates). Knox estimated that of the forty or so Acadians who ambushed the patrol, about a dozen were killed or wounded. In fact, seven Acadians were killed, four suffered minor wounds, and five had serious injuries.[53] Johnston carried his dead and wounded into the woods, and Knox's party made it back to Fort Anne without further incident.

After the Renne Forêt River ambush, the regulars hunkered down in Fort Anne and showed little interest in leaving. On January 17, 1758, Knox noted in his journal that the weather had been brutally cold for the previous fifteen days, which certainly contributed to the regulars' preference for staying indoors. "Notwithstanding the rigour of the season," he also noted, "the *Gens de Bois* are almost every day hunting and shooting on the opposite side of the river, even within range of our guns; which sometimes provokes us to give them a shot." Knox soon developed a grudging respect for the Acadians. "The skulking wretches are so amazingly hardy, that they scarce pass one day with scouring the environs of this fortress."[54]

For the Acadians, the winter must have been almost unbearable without provisions and adequate shelter and facing the constant threat of ranger raids. On March 20, 1758, several of them approached Fort Anne under a flag of truce. They wanted to ransom a Mr. Eason, whom they had captured December 6, for food. Knox described the guerrillas as "a raw, hardy, active, yet mean set of fellows, and as meanly clothed." He also observed with a pang of anger that an Acadian carried a British musket and cartridge box with the Forty-third Regiment's emblem on it, while another wore a bowling hat common among the soldiers.[55] On April 1, several other Acadians and Indians approached Fort Anne for another prisoner exchange. In October of the previous year, when it left for Halifax, the Fortieth Regiment had taken two métis, Clare and Anselm Thomas, as hostages.[56] The Acadians and Indians said that they would return four British prisoners they had taken on December 6 for Clare and Anselm. Upon learning that the métis were not in Annapolis Royal and that Anselm had died of smallpox in Halifax, the Acadians and Indians departed. A second party led by a "Frenchman (or rather Canadian, which, by multiplicity of buttons and his leather cue in his hair)" appeared to exchange furs for rum and tobacco. The commanding officer at Fort Anne rebuked their offer and told them that he would only exchange prisoners.[57]

Monckton certainly misjudged the capabilities and intentions of the Mi'kmaq and Acadians when he wrote on March 22 that all remained "in a perfect state of tranquility within the Province."[58] A week later, forty guerrillas attacked a schooner at Fort Cumberland and killed its master and two sailors. The previous day, a platoon of Gorham's Rangers had raided Chipoudy and found only women and children; the men had left for Fort Cumberland, where they attacked the schooner. Beyond missing the guerrillas on their march, the rangers were shocked to again see a large settlement at Chipoudy. Despite the Yankees' burning and pillaging of the previous years, "the Officers were in raptures with that part of the country where they had been, and are of opinion, of appearance of the enemies settlements, that they are very numerous, and live more comfortably, than they could possibly be supposed to do, in their precarious situation."[59]

The Acadians remained elusive foes who had grasped the fundamental tactics of guerrilla warfare. Rarely would they stand and fight, and they engaged the Anglo-Americans only when they were confident of success. A detachment of the Forty-third Regiment realized this on a march to Fort Edward. They came upon several Acadians who, much to the frustration of the regulars, immediately fled. Of course, the goal of most guerrillas was to kill and capture Anglo-Americans. On May 12 a dozen Acadians ambushed an engineering party outside Halifax and killed two regulars. At their head was an officer bedecked in a white waistcoat and laced hat.[60]

Knox correctly observed that the guerrilla leader in the French officer's uniform probably was not Boishébert; he was busy with the defense of Louisbourg.[61] It was clear to everyone on the French side, whether in Paris, Quebec, or Miramichi, that the Anglo-Americans would again move on Louisbourg. With British arms stalled in Europe—the duke of Cumberland surrendered an entire field army to the French in 1757—Pitt had focused the British war effort in North America. Henceforth, the British would go on the strategic defensive in Europe and the offensive in North America, where Pitt perceived the French to be weaker. He appointed a new group of young, capable, and ambitious officers—most notably Jeffery Amherst and James Wolfe—to lead the North American armies. Because he also would need the help of the provincials, Pitt reformed the basis of provincial-regular relations. All told, over twenty-three thousand provincials answered his call to service for campaigns against Fort Carillon (Ticonderoga) and Louisbourg.[62] Knox peevishly wrote in his journal that while the provincials were being recruited, "the regulars remain in the different forts and garrisons, to hew wood and dig sand, &c. then the French will be finely humbled in America."[63] When orders arrived that the Forty-third Regiment would replace the Twenty-eighth Regiment, which would leave Fort Cumberland to join the armada against Louisbourg, Knox whined that he was "thus doomed to an unsoldierlike and inactive banishment."[64] The orders to take a detachment of men and "scour this province" and then establish a blocking position at Canso to kill or capture any Acadians who tried to cross into Nova Scotia proved of little consolation to him.[65]

Boishébert suffered his own disappointments during the 1758 Louisbourg campaign. First, the Maliseets refused to accompany him to Louisbourg.[66] All told, he would have only 100 Acadians (some from Port Toulouse) and 230 Mi'kmaq under Abbé Pierre Maillard to conduct his petite guerre behind Jeffery Amherst's lines. Boishébert first tried to disrupt the Anglo-American operations by skirmishing with a landing party at Gabarus Bay, the Yankees' landing zone in 1745 that had allowed them unimpeded access to the rear of the fort. But in a repeat of the events of thirteen years earlier, the Mi'kmaq had no interest in fighting an open-field engagement with the Anglo-Americans. Still, Boishébert soldiered on, killed a British soldier, took a prisoner, and burned a blockhouse. He had to flee when Colonel Scott's light infantry company appeared and gave chase.[67] With his allies not cooperating, and with Gorham's Rangers scouring the countryside, Boishébert retreated to a position near Mira Bay north of the fortress.[68] The Indians grew discontented with Boishébert's leadership. They fit well into a scheme of a guerrilla war on isolated outposts, but they were of less value against the overwhelming numbers of Anglo-American troops on Île Royale.

Despite the Indians' willingness to raid the British supply and communication lines, Boishébert correctly preferred not to disperse and weaken his force at that critical moment. The Mi'kmaq, Father Maillard observed, became "disgusted with the idea of remaining in camp in which nothing was done but sleeping, and eating the livestock of the inhabitants. There was a failure in discipline and all decided to retreat."[69] Soon after the Indians left, the Île Royale Acadians followed. When it became clear that the French inside the fort could not hold out for long (on July 26, 1758, they surrendered), and he could do nothing to help, Boishébert returned to Nova Scotia.[70] Likewise, hundreds of Île Royale Acadians fled to refugee camps south of Baie des Chaleurs, thereby avoiding the ambush at Canso.[71]

The fighting continued in Nova Scotia during Boishébert's absence. In April two regulars were scalped outside Lunenburg.[72] On June 28 guerrillas took several captives from Fort Cumberland, and a French privateer took two small ships.[73] A Lieutenant Meech of Benoni Danks's Rangers—Danks's company had served alongside Joseph Gorham's Rangers as an independent unit since 1756—and fifty-five men advanced up the Petitcodiac River, suspecting that was where the raiders originated. They soon made contact with forty Acadians but as usual were unable to catch them. While returning to Fort Cumberland, Meech's patrol bumped into the rest of the company under Captain Danks. Danks, who had experienced his share of frustration in fighting the guerrillas, did not want to let an opportunity to kill and capture the enemy pass. He ordered Meech to join him in pursuit. On July 1 the Anglo-Americans finally sprung an ambush on the guerrillas instead of vice versa. Danks's Rangers engaged about thirty Acadians, killed and scalped three of them, and captured others.

Danks's was the first "victory" that the Anglo-Americans could claim over the Chignecto Acadians since 1755. Nonetheless, it became engulfed in the subsequent historical controversy over the Yankees' treatment of the Acadians. In 1791, for instance, Hugh Graham, one of Nova Scotia's first Presbyterian ministers, related how Danks in fact had murdered four peaceful Acadians and then presented them to Colonel Montague Wilmot (later Nova Scotia's governor) as Mi'kmaq to collect the long-standing bounty on Indian scalps. Despite the protestations of Fort Cumberland's paymaster, Wilmot rewarded Danks with fifty pounds. Danks thereafter went down in local lore as "one of the most reckless and brutal" of the rangers.[74] Years after the fact, many in Nova Scotia had forgotten, or wanted to forget, the brutality that the conquest of the colony had entailed.

The Climactic Anglo-American Offensive

The level of the Acadians' suffering greatly increased in the late summer when the British launched a three-pronged offensive to sweep the colony clear of guerrillas and their supporters. The first target was the Acadian refugees who had hid out on Cape Sable. The Cape Sable Acadians had made occasional forays against Lunenburg and, much to the frustration of the British, remained unmolested in their distant sanctuary. Major Henry Fletcher led the Thirty-fifth Regiment and a company of Gorham's Rangers into the heart of Cape Sable. Using two sloops of the navy to prevent "the vermin from getting off in their canoes," Fletcher's party first cordoned off the cape and then swarmed over it. More than 100 Acadians and the superannuated Father Jean-Baptiste de Gay Desenclaves surrendered. Around twenty-one Acadian families totaling about 130 souls, and 6 or 7 Indians, avoided capture.[75] Fletcher transported the captives to Halifax, where the British incarcerated them in preparation for deportation to France. Although there were rumors in October that the Acadian prisoners were conspiring with discontented settlers at Lunenburg to commit arson in Halifax, the truth of the matter was that the Acadian captives were vanquished people who had come to passively await their fate. Father Desenclaves assured the British that the holdouts on Cape Sable had had enough fighting and would come in peacefully.[76]

The next focus would be the Acadian refugee camps in the Saint John River valley. Jeffery Amherst ordered Monckton to prepare for a major expedition. With Louisbourg in hand, Amherst wanted to remove all pockets of resistance that might sit in the army's rear when it moved up the Saint Lawrence toward Quebec. Amherst was more than generous in giving Monckton the resources he would need; the strike group would include the entire Thirty-fifth Regiment and the Second Battalion of the Sixtieth (Royal American) Regiment, for a total of over nine hundred combat-effective regulars. In addition, Monckton would have the service of a fifty-man detachment of royal artillery and their battery as well as two hundred irregulars (Gorham's, Danks's, and Scott's companies).[77]

Monckton proved the right officer for the assignment. He sailed from Halifax with his army on September 13 and sent Cobb to Chignecto to pick up Danks's Rangers and whaleboats. All arrived off the site of the abandoned Fort Menagoueche a week later, whereupon Scott's light infantry secured the landing zone and made a reconnaissance of the area. They found no Acadians but discovered tracks leading into the woods. Monckton's turncoat Acadian guide explained that Acadians preferred to travel by canoe. The guide also claimed that a large French camp sat fifteen leagues upstream and past some falls in the river where only shallow draft vessels could travel. Monckton detailed three hundred men to establish a base camp and requisitioned all the available small crafts from Chignecto and Annapolis Royal.

By October 1 Monckton had moved his boats, regulars, and rangers above the falls. On October 3 the Anglo-Americans reached the Acadian settlement of Grimrose. Forty to fifty Acadian families from Chignecto had settled there in 1755 and built a small village. Anglo-Americans again forced them to abandon their homes. Monckton's troops burned every building in the village, torched the fields, and killed all the livestock. Two days later, Monckton reached the Island of Métis in the river. The Acadian guide would go no farther, claiming that the river at that point was too shallow for the Anglo-American vessels. Monckton nevertheless pushed his men forward. Captain McCurdy of the rangers struck the hamlet of Jemseg and burned it to the ground. His appetite for destruction satiated, Monckton then returned to the mouth of the river.[78]

Monckton's campaign cleared the Saint John Valley of resistance. An Acadian prisoner related that the other Acadians were fleeing west to Canada. "As for the Indians," Monckton cheerfully reported, "they were disposed to get terms from the English." The three hundred troops that he had left at the mouth of the river, meanwhile, had built Fort Frederick. The presence of the Anglo-American fort proved the final nail in the coffin of any potential Maliseet support for the French. The Indians could see that the blockhouse could just as easily become a trade house, and opposition to the Anglo-Americans guaranteed that their "fishing and hunting would be cut off."[79] When Jedediah Preble led a provincial force from Massachusetts against the Penobscots in May of the next year, he faced almost no Indian resistance. Governor Thomas Pownall met with leaders of the Penobscots and Passamquoddies, who assured him that they and the Maliseets were "one nation" committed to peace. Indeed, the Indians seem to have understood that since the Acadians and French were suffering their death rattles, a new relationship needed to be forged with the Anglo-Americans. They told Pownall that they were "Brethren of King George" and because "their Old Men were Dead, and the Treaties buried and lost," they would like to open a new round of negotiations.[80]

The Petitcodiac settlements were the final target. Monckton parceled out five companies to Fort Frederick, five to Fort Anne, and two to Fort Edward and placed all the irregulars under Scott's command. On November 12 Lieutenant Meech's platoon of Danks's Rangers sailed up the river and returned the next day with four men and twelve women and children as prisoners. The captives told the rangers where they could find more Acadians, that the refugees did not know that the Anglo-Americans were in the area, and most important, where Beausoleil's house sat. Scott enthusiastically directed his entire force without pause to "rout and destroy several places at the same time." The different ranger companies spread out all along the river while Danks's company, in Cobb's sloops, sailed for Beausoleil's. They returned later in the day bearing the disappointing news that they had found the residence empty. Nevertheless, they had burned it to the ground and killed all the livestock.[81]

The rangers and light infantry spent several days laying waste to the Petitcodiac Valley. One party of Acadians halfheartedly tried to resist them early on the morning of the fourteenth, until Scott's reinforcement of a platoon of rangers drove them into the woods. The rangers then took a dozen Acadian women and children hostage. Two of the rangers went missing in action, but their officers were not worried; they blithely assumed the men had "suppos'd after Plunder." Meanwhile, Cobb ferried the rangers up and down the river "to destroy the houses & grain from the head of the River." The Yankees pillaged and plundered through the night. Gorham reported back to Scott late on the afternoon of the thirteenth that his men had "burnt all the Houses with a Vast quantity of Grain and kill'd all the Cattle as far down River as Old Beausoleils where he left the remainder of his party burning and destroying the Enemys substance." At ten o'clock P.M., Gorham returned up the river with more rangers for a second night of burning. Both Danks and Gorham returned to camp the next afternoon; Gorham said that he had destroyed over a hundred homes, and Danks claimed credit for destroying twenty-three buildings as well as fields and livestock. Danks also informed Scott that he had sent one of his male Acadian captives—he kept the man's wife and children hostage—"with a threatening message to the Inhabitants letting them know if they did not come all in and surrender themselves to me they must expect no mercy if they fall into my hands." Around midnight, the Acadian returned to Danks and reported that "the Inhabitants were all making off as fast as they could." With many of the buildings still smoldering, Scott and the rangers left for Fort Frederick with their prisoners in tow.[82]

In land always better suited to trapping fur than hunting or agriculture, the Acadians faced starvation and had few places left to flee in the wake of the British offensive. Following the capture of Louisbourg the previous summer, James Wolfe took three entire regiments (the Fifteenth, Twenty-eighth, and Fifty-seven) and seven ships of the line to destroy Acadian fields and settlements on the coasts of the Gaspé Peninsula. Another party of regulars under Lieutenant Colonel Andrew Rollo arrested and deported nearly 2,200 Acadians from Île Saint-Jean and built Fort Amherst on the ruins of what had been Port-La-Joie.[83] The rangers, meanwhile, returned to Chignecto. Unlike regulars in winter quarters, the rangers would seek to strike at Acadians no matter the weather. The refugees therefore could not afford to return to the Memramcook or Petitcodiac valleys. Indeed, on

Christmas Day, 1758, Amherst wrote to Monckton that Nova Scotia finally appeared to have been cleared of Acadians and Indians and that the only potential safe haven for the enemy was along the Penobscot River, a region that Preble and Pownall were prepared to sweep in early 1759.[84] Affairs in Nova Scotia seemed so settled that Amherst ordered Monckton to send Gorham's and Danks's Rangers to Wolfe at Louisbourg.[85]

Early 1759 passed with only little fighting in Nova Scotia. In January, four rangers went missing from a woodcutting and cording party out of Fort Cumberland. The relief party that was sent to look for them first found the corpse of a scalped grenadier on the road between the fort and Baie Verte. The next day, they found the rangers' scalped bodies, suggesting that Indians had done the killing. But the snow had become so deep that the rangers had to carry the bloodhounds that they had taken to track Acadians and Indians. Convinced that there was no way they could find the killers in those conditions, they returned to camp.[86] Near the same time, another ranger party advanced up the Saint John River to lay waste to the Acadian village of Saint-Anne des Pays-Bas (near present-day Fredericton). Monckton, convinced by impassable woods and low water levels in the river that he could not reach it, had spared Sainte-Anne the previous fall. In late January, a company of rangers used the frozen river as a highway to reach the hamlet. On February 18 the rangers burned 147 houses, a church, and all the barns, stables, and granaries. They killed and scalped six men but spared four men, two women, and three children, whom they brought to Fort Frederick.[87] The Saint-Anne raid closed out the fighting for the near term. In the late winter of 1758 and the spring of 1759, the Anglo-Americans had a larger goal on which to focus: Quebec.

James Wolfe, whom Amherst had given command of the eastern wing of the army, used the lull in the fighting to reapportion the Anglo-American troops in Nova Scotia. Wolfe had a very low opinion of provincials and used them only for garrison duty. He depended on British regulars trained as rangers, such as Scott's light infantry, for combat operations in Nova Scotia.[88] In that respect, he was something of a visionary, even if his orders at times seem disjointed. "Our troops," Wolfe wrote, "[m]ust be employed in a very different manner from what has been the Practice hitherto—they must learn to live in the Woods as the Indians do—to keep 'em in continual apprehension of being attack'd . . . instead of shutting themselves up in Fort & Block House—& abandoning the Settlers to the rage of these sanguinary Monsters—From Cape Sable to Cape Canso, there cannot be sixty fighting men, of the Mick-Mack Tribe—& by our amazing indolence and ignorance, they have harrass'd every Corner of the Colony with almost impunity." Wolfe ordered additional reforms.

> Regiments that are Commanded by old men—& have old Infirm Officers, are by no means fit for the protection of this Colony, & for the never ceasing War that should be made upon the Indians, till they are totally exterminated or driven to a distance, Young officers, arm'd & dress'd for the particular service of the Woods, would spread Terror, amongst them, & even root 'em out. The American Rangers are for the most part, Lazy cowardly People—the best men they get upon the Continent for that Service, are Irish Vagabonds, & Convicts, the Inhabitants are a poor Spirited Race; but a Regt. of Foot can furnish Officers & men of a right stamp for the laborious business.[89]

Wolfe's assessment of the means by which the British army should conduct operations in Nova Scotia was essentially correct, even if his view of the rangers was grossly unfair. Wolfe rarely spared anyone criticism; he was arrogant, surly, and perhaps a manic-depressive. But it should be noted that his disdain for Americans did not preclude him from drafting both Gorham's and Danks's Rangers for the Quebec campaign. They more than adequately accomplished the dirty work of terrorizing into submission the *habitants* of New France. Gorham's and Danks's Rangers proved as effective in Canada as they had in Nova Scotia. In August, they burned fifty houses on one patrol, and on another they destroyed all the settlements in the Bay of Saint Paul. Wolfe certainly appreciated their skills. On August 6, he ordered Monckton to use the rangers "to destroy every building except the churches between the Chaudiere and the Etchemin [rivers] and from Monckton's Camp down to the Church at Beaumont"—essentially the south bank of the Saint Lawrence River for over ninety miles![90]

While Gorham's and Danks's rangers burned, killed, and pillaged all they could reach in the Saint Lawrence Valley, New England's provincials sat in Nova Scotia. John Knox was greatly relieved to learn in April that the Forty-third Regiment would be part of the

Quebec invasion force and happily had passed off responsibility for garrisoning Fort Cumberland to the provincials under the command of Joseph Frye. The Yankees did not strike Knox as particularly soldierly; he described the privates as "a poor, mean, ragged set of men of all sizes and ages; their Officers are sober, modest . . . but their ideas, like those who have not been out of their own country, or conversed much with Europeans, are naturally confined."[91] That did not matter. All that was expected of them in Wolfe's scheme was to occupy the forts, and Knox was relieved to be finally freed from what to him seemed a prison sentence in Nova Scotia. The regiment under John Thomas—not to be confused with the John Thomas who recorded the series of patrols earlier in the war—replaced the regulars elsewhere throughout the colony. Jotham Gay's company of Thomas's regiment took over Fort Edward on May 10, and other companies garrisoned Lunenburg, Halifax, and Fort Anne.[92]

There was little for the Yankees to do while the Quebec operation moved forward. Boishébert was outside Quebec where Governor-General Vaudreuil had ordered him to retreat with as many Indians as would join him.[93] Of course, the Yankee officers fretted that guerrillas might still be around and therefore forbade their men to leave the fort without their permission. The most aggressive enemy the Yankees faced, however, were the hogs that kept rooting up and eating the gardens. A small bit of excitement came the way of Jotham Gay's company when a ranger whom Danks had left at Fort Edward assaulted another soldier. The entire company mustered to watch the ranger receive fifty lashes. When not herding swine and meting out punishments, the provincials drilled and occasionally practiced their procedures should the enemy attack.[94] In September, Thomas's provincials at Annapolis Royal tried their hand at firing their weapons at live targets. They stumbled upon some Acadians who were driving cattle through the woods. They opened fire, and the Acadians "immediately ran off & left as much booty [cattle] with our Party." Despite the death of a Lieutenant Armstrong outside Fort Cumberland on September 29, essentially, the fighting was over in Nova Scotia.[95]

The Yankees at Fort Cumberland received the news of Quebec's surrender on October 20, and the Acadians were not far behind in surrendering. On October 26, Father Manach flagged down Captain Alexander Schomberg in the *Diana*.[96] Schomberg had taken up station in Baie de Miramichi and must have been pleased if not surprised to find the French priest offering to surrender. On November 13 several Acadians appeared outside the walls of Fort Cumberland. They, too, had had enough of fighting and privation. Five days later, another Acadian arrived and claimed that he represented 120 Acadians at Miramichi who wanted "to come in for they hant much Provision to carry them through the winter." Joseph Frye noted a "great many more coming in" over the following days.[97] Father Maillard gave himself up to Schomberg and the crew of the *Diana* on November 26.

The Mi'kmaq, who already had broken into their winter hunting bands, did not come in until January. Three Indians arrived at Fort Cumberland to surrender on the eleventh. Frye fed them and directed them to return to their families and friends to tell them that the Yankees would not harm them. Thereafter, "French [Acadians] and Indians keep coming in more or less every day." The Yankees were true to their word not to exact retribution and instead gave food and clothing to those who surrendered. On January 29 Father Manach and two Mi'kmaq, Paul Laurence and Augustine Michael, came to Fort Cumberland to confer with Frye. The Indians agreed to lay down their arms, then formalized the "Treaty of Peace and Friendship" with Lawrence on March 10, 1760. Frye hoped that he would have "no more treaties to make with savages." It would not be that easy. Manach gave the colonel a list of fourteen other "chiefs" with whom the Anglo-Americans would have to meet.[98]

To reach all the Mi'kmaq leaders on Manach's list took him over a year. Nonetheless, if he was anything like his men, for whom providentialism defined the experience of war, Joseph Frye probably felt favored by divine justice when he accepted the surrender of the Acadians and Mi'kmaq.[99] Frye had a long history of suffering at the enemy's hands. He first had come to the colony as a provincial officer in 1755, only to have Boishébert's guerrillas defeat him at Chipoudy. When most of the Yankee provincials left Nova Scotia in 1756, Frye naturally went with them. He then commanded a regiment at Fort William Henry in 1757. It was there that he watched as the regulars and provincials surrendered to Montcalm's troupes de la marine and Indian allies.[100] He saw his men "Rent to Pieces" in the massacre that followed.[101] Yet, to his credit, he showed no interest in meting out punishment on the Acadians and Indians. The previous five years had seen enough killing and suffering. More important, his side had won. Anglo-Americans had cleansed Nova Scotia of Acadians, had chastised the Mi'kmaq, had shown the Maliseets that there was no future in siding with the French, and stood on the verge of delivering the coup de grace to New France. In early 1760, after five years of struggle for Joseph Frye and fifty years for the empire, it finally looked as if Anglo-Americans had a tabula rasa on which to draw Nova Scotia in their image.

Epilogue: Nova Scotia, 1760–1768

The years following the end of the guerrilla war were surprisingly easy from a military perspective for Anglo-Americans. As the last act of the fifty years' war for Nova Scotia, the previous half decade of fighting had seen Anglo-Americans crush virtually all opposition to their rule. As a result, Anglo-Americans had carte blanche to do with Nova Scotia as they wished.[1] In the immediate aftermath of the war, Yankees and Britons settled the colony with thousands of loyal Protestant subjects, drove the Maliseets and Mi'kmaq to poverty and despair, conceded a small place for the Acadians, and limited all remnants of French influence in the province. Indeed, by 1768, as the imperial crisis that eventuated in the American Revolution gained support in the other colonies, Nova Scotia had become the most British of the British colonies in North America.

By the autumn of 1758 the proscription and removal of the Acadians appeared complete and the Acadian-Indian insurgency seemed on its last legs, thereby making Nova Scotia safe for settlement. Many New Englanders naturally turned their attention to Nova Scotia and clamored for information about the colony. They wanted to know what particular encouragements they would receive for settling there, how much land they could take and at what tax rate, whether a representative government in which they could participate had been formed, and what the colony's position was on religious freedom.

Charles Lawrence, of course, presented Nova Scotia as a new utopia. He gave the land-hungry Yankees every encouragement.[2] The Crown, he observed, had set aside thousand-acre parcels for townships. Each family head who came to Nova Scotia would receive one hundred acres in his name and another fifty acres for each head right. Quit rents had been set at an annual rate of only one shilling for each fifty acres. All told, an individual could hold title to up to one thousand acres in his name, and the land would be his and his family's in perpetuity, provided they improved one-third of it within ten years, the second third within twenty years, and the final third within thirty years. The townships had been laid out near the major forts and garrisons, which not only offered the protection of the king's troops but also promised prospects for trade and exchange. Meanwhile, the Crown had yet to levy any taxes on Nova Scotia, and all "except for papists" would have full citizenship. As icing on the cake, each township also would receive two representatives for each fifty families in a colony-wide assembly.[3]

Land agents and then settlers began arriving in Nova Scotia in early 1759. Thus began Nova Scotia's Planter era, which lasted through the American War of Independence to the end of the eighteenth century.[4] In April, agents from Connecticut and Rhode Island filed claims to the newly organized townships of Minas Basin in the "empty" Acadian lands. In May, settlers from Connecticut received grants to the townships of Minas and Rivière-aux-Canards, which they renamed Horton and Cornwallis, respectively. The area of Pisiquid became Avon Township, and the village on the east bank of the river became Newport once emigrants from Rhode Island settled there. Other Yankees took up residence on Cape Sable, where they formed the township of Barrington. Fishermen from Cape Cod built Liverpool on the site of the Acadian fishing village at Port Rossignol. Other settlers poured into Halifax.[5]

Yankees spread over Chignecto as well as present-day New Brunswick, which would not become a separate colony until 1784.[6] Captain Benoni Danks established a homestead outside Fort Cumberland. He had to wait several years to take up full-time residency there, however, because the rangers were needed for the campaigns in Cuba in 1762. Settlers from Rhode Island built Sackville and welcomed a party of Baptist settlers from Swansea, Massachusetts, several years later. Along the Saint John River, Yankees established the towns Fredericton, Maugerville, and Sheffield. In 1765, the "Committee for the Nova Scotia Grant," also known as the Saint John River Society, received a sixty-thousand-acre grant on behalf of its sixty proprietors. The society began as a collection of officers from the Forty-fourth and Sixtieth Regiments on garrison duty in Montreal. It quickly grew to include leading figures of the imperial bureaucracy such as General Thomas Gage (later commander of royal forces in North America) and Thomas Hutchinson (governor of Massachusetts). Beamsley Glazier, a Yankee who had served as an officer in the provincial and regular armies, acted as the primary land scout. He gushed that "as to the goodness of the land on St. John's River[,] you never saw any like it but on the Mohawk."[7]

The New England immigration to Nova Scotia continued throughout the 1760s. The removal of the Acadians had for all intents and purposes resulted in an "econocide" that retarded the development of the colony for a generation. Still, in August 1764, the Anglo-American population of Nova Scotia was estimated at 10,000–13,000 people (including 1,200 troops), well on its way to reaching the 1755 population of 18,000. The key difference between the mid-1750s population figures and those a decade later was the relative proportion of Anglo-Americans in the latter. The 1767 census of Halifax showed that fully half the town's inhabitants were American-born.[8] In the late 1760s, the population of Yankee immigrants reached a plateau of around 14,000 that lasted to 1781, only to see a huge spike following the American War of Independence. Perhaps as many as 30,000 Loyalists fled to Nova Scotia in the immediate aftermath of the war.[9]

The Maliseets and Mi'kmaq stood by as the Yankees overwhelmed them. Abandoned by their French allies and clearly no match for the military power that Anglo-Americans could project against them, each of the Mi'kmaq bands made peace with the Anglo-Americans through the summer of 1760 and into 1761. The treaties of 1760 and 1761 were far harsher for the Mi'kmaq than the previous British-Indian agreements—Mascarene's Treaty, the Articles of 1749, and Cope's Treaty in 1752. In 1760, Anglo-Americans had no reason or desire to compromise with the Indians. Thus, they insisted that the Mi'kmaq "acknowledge the jurisdiction and Dominion of His Majesty George the Second over the Territories of Nova Scotia or Acadia and . . . make submission to His Majesty in the most perfect, ample and solemn manner." Furthermore, the Mi'kmaq had to provide hostages to guarantee their future good behavior and could trade only at Crown-approved truck houses.[10]

The treaties confirmed what both Yankees and Mi'kmaq must have suspected for some time: there was no place for the Mi'kmaq in an Anglo-American Nova Scotia. Although Nova Scotia's governor, Jonathan Belcher, issued warnings in 1762 that the Crown would protect lands claimed by Indians, and several areas (based, ironically, on some of the boundaries that Le Loutre had first proposed in 1754) were set aside for the Mi'kmaq, incoming settlers simply ignored the proclamation.[11] Yet throughout the period, the British continually sent mixed messages to Indians and would-be settlers alike. In 1763, on the heels of Belcher's proclamation, Cape Breton Island (Île Royale) and Prince Edward Island (Île Saint-Jean), two possible refuges for the Indians, were annexed to Nova Scotia. The news was not that much better for would-be Yankee settlers; within four years, the entire surface of Prince Edward Island—1,400,000 acres—except for plots for town sites had been auctioned to absentee British proprietors.[12] Although the Crown had issued the royal proclamation as the first step in an orderly expansion of the North American colonies and directed that the Indians "should not be molested or disturbed in the Possession" of their hunting grounds and forbade the purchase of Indian lands by parties other than the government,[13] Yankees in Nova Scotia ignored it. In August 1763, for instance, Charles Morris, the surveyor who had developed the operational plan for the Acadian removal and who then was a member of the Saint John River Society, directed that the New England squatters, many of whom were veterans of the provincial regiments, should be allowed to remain in the Saint John Valley. "They will be of great use," Morris wrote from Halifax to the colony's agent in London, "and their removal would cause their total ruin."[14] Of course, the potential ruin of the Maliseets and Mi'kmaq was not a concern. When the British sought to organize Indian diplomacy and trade in 1765 by creating northern and southern departments for Indian affairs, none other than Lieutenant Colonel Joseph Gorham became the Crown's agent in Nova Scotia.[15] The Indians essentially had become landless peoples with no one to protect them under the law.

Few Mi'kmaq were to be found in Nova Scotia after signing the treaties. Two contemporary documents, albeit biased in that they focused on only Anglo-Americans, suggest as much. The census of 1764 listed only 70 adult Mi'kmaq males in the entire colony.[16] Three years later, Indians were not considered important enough to be included among the five "race stocks"—Acadian, English, German, New England Puritan, and Scots-Irish—in the colony's population survey. While some Mi'kmaq might have continued to live in the woods, they were few and far between in the Anglo-American settlements. Between Barrington, Cornwallis, Hopewell, and Liverpool townships, for instance, there resided only 11 Mi'kmaw men, 7 boys, 6 women, and 4 girls. In the same communities, there were 36 black men, 19 boys, 30 women, and 19 girls. Anglo-Americans had pushed the Mi'kmaq to the extreme margins of Planter Nova Scotia.[17]

The Mi'kmaq who remained in Nova Scotia, reformer Walter Bromley noted in the 1810s, were "reduced to the most awful[,] the most horrible fate of human wretchedness." Anglo-American traders took advantage of the Mi'kmaq, supplied them with the alcohol that destroyed both their bodies and their spirits, and drove them to extreme penury. Poverty in turn fed Anglo-Americans' disdain for Indians. Eventually, Bromley lamented, it became "no greater sin to shoot an Indian, than a Bear or Carraboo."[18]

The Acadians were no better off than the Indians. Several thousand Acadians were incarcerated in camps outside Halifax and at Fort Edward.[19] The Nova Scotia Council estimated that about 1,500 Acadians remained at large in New Brunswick. Governor Belcher fretted that with the fighting continuing in Quebec, the Acadians as much as the Indians posed a threat and he was therefore not inclined to offer them any kind of amnesty. Although the Royal Navy had defeated the last remnants of the French navy in North American waters at the battle of Restigouche Bay in 1760, Acadians on the Gaspé and at Restigouche continued to equip and crew privateers that prowled Chaleur Bay and the Gulf of Saint Lawrence.[20] Captain Roderick Mackenzie and his force surprised and captured over 330 Acadians in late 1761, but that accomplished little to lessen Anglo-American anxieties over the holdouts.[21]

In the spring of 1762, French marines temporarily seized Saint John's, Newfoundland. Anglo-American paranoia of a resurgent Acadian-Indian-French force swept over the colony. Belcher panicked, called out the militia, and ordered it to muster at the forts to parry what he saw as the threat of a French invasion and an Acadian-Indian rebellion. Of course, neither the invasion nor the rebellion materialized; they were more figments of Belcher's imagination than potential realities. Nonetheless, the Planters from King's County protested when Belcher ordered their militia to Halifax and thereby left them at the mercy of what they believed was "a Considerable Body of Indians [that] were assembled together menacing the Inhabitants with Destruction."[22] Old patterns, especially the fear of the Acadian-Indian enemy, thus seem to have remained. Belcher conceded and allowed the militiamen to return to their homes. He also ordered 600 Acadian men—their wives and children remained under arrest in Halifax—deported to Massachusetts. The Bay Colony, which already had taken in 1,105 exiles (at a cost of nearly ten thousand pounds), did not allow the Acadians to land. Six weeks later the transports and refugees returned to Halifax.[23]

Massachusetts' refusal to accept the Acadians in late 1762 pointed to the need for a new Acadian policy. Then, in February 1763, France ceded all its claims to land in northeastern North America except for Miquelon and Saint-Pierre islands, two small outposts that French fishermen could use in the Gulf of Saint Lawrence.[24] With the ratification of the Treaty of Paris, the Anglo-American authorities in Nova Scotia could no longer legally treat the Acadians as rebels or enemies. Belcher and his replacement, Montague Wilmot, turned to the council for its recommendation on what to do with the Acadians. Their preference centered on finding a means within the law to compel the Acadians to leave.

In summer 1764, the British presented the Acadians with the same options that had been given to their grandfathers fifty years earlier: if the Acadians would take an unqualified oath of allegiance, they could settle in any of the king's colonies and thereby become British subjects. Any Acadian who did not want to take the oath was free to leave for France or any of France's colonial possessions except Miquelon or Saint-Pierre.[25] The oath of 1764 offered no provisions regarding property rights, neutrality, or freedom of religion. The Acadians were a conquered people and would have to acknowledge that or leave the colony.

Many Acadians chose exile over the oath. A group of five hundred Acadians who had been banished to Georgia and South Carolina sailed for Saint Domingue. The first group of around twenty Acadians who reached Louisiana (in February 1764) had been exiles in New York. Beausoleil Broussard's living relatives in the Maritimes left in 1765 and sailed first to Haiti and then to Louisiana. The Broussard party took up residence in the Attakapas District, where they focused on livestock ranching. Between 1766 and 1770, nearly four hundred Acadians followed suit and spread across Louisiana.[26] The landscape was certainly different from that of Nova Scotia and New Brunswick, but at least the Louisiana Acadians, eventually to become the Cajuns, were free of the British and Yankees.

Much like the first Anglo-Americans who arrived in Nova Scotia after the 1710 conquest, Wilmot and the Yankee settlers of the new Nova Scotia soon found that they too needed the Acadians. Nova Scotia again promised to bloom into a productive agricultural zone, but the Yankees needed to repair and make full use of the dykes, which few of them had the slightest idea how to work. Thus, because the Acadians possessed skills the Yankees lacked, Anglo-Americans tentatively welcomed some of them into the new Nova Scotia. Of course, the welcome the Yankees proffered was hardly a warm one. For the 1,700 Acadians who stayed behind, it must have been a bitter pill to swallow to work as laborers on the lands that once had been theirs.[27]

The sole remaining obstacle to British dominion in Nova Scotia was the Catholic Church. Priests still resided in Nova Scotia and New Brunswick, and Belcher and Wilmot understandably watched them closely. The governors employed both coercion and bribery to keep the priests under their control. Although in 1760 Father Jean Manach had brought many Indians to the peace table, in April 1761, as the British were in the midst of more treaty negotiations with the Indians, Belcher arrested him on charges that he had been "exciting the Indians and Acadians to rebellion."[28] Manach had made several statements that the administration, concerned as it was with the Acadian privateers at Restigouche, interpreted as incendiary. The British took Manach first to New York and then to Portsmouth, England, where he remained in prison until August 1761.[29]

Father Pierre Maillard navigated the waters of the new relationship with the British much better than his old understudy, Manach. Maillard brought his Indian flock to the peace table and in the autumn of 1760 accepted an annual salary of £150 from the British. Belcher perhaps knew of Machiavelli's dictum, "An enemy should be destroyed or bought—and never made a martyr." In return for his being bought, Maillard received permission to convert an old gun battery in Halifax into an oratory where he held regular masses. He certainly won the respect and friendship of the Anglo-Americans. When he died unexpectedly in 1762, the colony gave him a state funeral in which Belcher and members of the council served as pallbearers.[30]

Bribery thereafter proved the Anglo-Americans' preferred approach to dealing with the Catholic clergy. In 1768, Governor Michael Francklin gave a Father Baillie a gift of fifty pounds upon Baillie's arrival in the colony. Francklin also suggested that the Crown transfer Maillard's old pension to Baillie "as a means of inducing him to exert himself in the service of Government."[31] The Board of Trade concurred, and Baillie was soon in Francklin's pocket.[32] With the influence of France wiped from the table in Nova Scotia, the priests not unsurprisingly had become more amenable to abiding by the British understanding of Matthew 22:21. Like the Indians and Acadians, they posed little opposition to British rule in Nova Scotia.

By 1768, Anglo-Americans' dominion over Nova Scotia was total. No other colony in North America had as homogeneous an Anglo and pro-British population as Nova Scotia. American Indians were virtually nonexistent in Planter areas, Africans and African Americans had yet to show a significant presence in the colony, and a draconian conquest had thoroughly subjugated the Acadians. Indeed, where formerly they had been the masters of Acadia, Acadians had become little more than day laborers for Anglo-Americans. Yankees thoroughly dominated the colony's social, political, and economic fabric.

Yet the Yankees of Nova Scotia were different from those who stayed behind in New England. Whereas by the mid- to late 1760s, New England Yankees were growing increasingly factious and troublesome for the Crown, Nova Scotia Yankees rejoiced in being part of the British Empire. Part of that disconnect can be attributed to the differences in the respective colonies' government structures. The empire's administrators hoped to avoid the factiousness endemic to the New England colonies; they therefore centered decision making not at the town level (as in New England) but instead at the county level. Unlike the New England towns that met regularly to elect officials and debate the pressing issues of the day, Nova Scotia town meetings normally were only annual occurrences to set poor rates.[33]

Just as important as the mechanisms of government to the Nova Scotia Yankees were the costs involved in conquest; the Yankees appreciated their membership in the age's most powerful empire. When the War Office ordered the troops from Nova Scotia to quell the turmoil in Boston in 1768, the Yankees of Nova Scotia were alarmed. The settlers irrationally feared that with the regulars out of the colony, the Indians and Acadians would rise in arms and, with the assistance of the French forces on Miquelon and Saint Peters, retake the province. Governor William Campbell pleaded for the Crown to pay proper attention to his "infant struggling Province."[34]

Officials in London and imperial administrators in America found, however, that they faced more pressing issues than Nova Scotia. As a result, Nova Scotia entered a period of salutary neglect between 1768 and 1775. The empire could afford to adopt that policy, or lack of policy, only because its hold on Nova Scotia was so strong. Indeed, by 1768 Nova Scotia could rightfully stand as a model of how a prosperous, secure, and thoroughly loyal colony should look. Its experience with the fifty years' war, in which it had driven out or subjugated all non-Anglo elements, had given it an indelible pro-British character. Ironically, at the very moment that Nova Scotia stood on the verge of becoming fully integrated into the empire, of becoming the fourteenth colony,[35] the thirteen colonies that became the United States left Nova Scotia alone in carrying the mace of the British Empire in North America.

Abbreviations Used in Notes

A&NS	Aikens, *Acadia and Nova Scotia.* The documents in *A&NS* are reprints of the documents originally published in *Selections from the Public Documents of the Province of Nova Scotia* (Aikens, *NS Docs.*).
Bax. MSS	Baxter, *Collections of the Maine Historical Society.*
BT	Board of Trade (Council of Trade and Plantations).
CCA	Casgrain, *Collection de documents inédits sur le Canada et l'Amérique.*
CNF	Québec Province, *Collection des manuscrits contenants lettres, mémoires, et autres documents historiques relatifs à la Nouvelle-France recueilles aux archives de la province de Québec, ou copiés à l'étranger.* Note that the *CNF* is an abridgement of documents; as with the *CSP* noted below, certain points may be missing from the documents.
CO 217A	Great Britain, Public Record Office, Colonial Office Papers 217, Nova Scotia and Cape Breton, Original Correspondence, "Nova Scotia A," National Archives of Canada (NAC), Ottawa. CO 217A at the NAC differs from other copies of CO 217 from the British Public Record Office (PRO). CO 217A includes copies of documents from the British Museum, Lambeth Palace, and from earl of Dartmouth's personal collection. The NAC originally intended CO 217A as a composite set of documents for Nova Scotia but abandoned the idea after the PRO reorganization of 1908–10. For documents prior to 1801, CO 217A at the NAC contains some documents not included in CO 217 from the PRO.

CO 218	Great Britain, Public Record Office, Colonial Office Papers 218, Nova Scotia and Cape Breton, Entry Books, National Archives of Canada, Ottawa.
CO 220	Great Britain, Public Record Office, Colonial Office Papers 220, Nova Scotia and Cape Breton, Sessional Papers, National Archives of Canada, Ottawa.
CSP	Sainsbury, *Calendar of State Papers, Colonial Series, American and West Indies.* Volumes bear inclusive dates rather than numbers. The materials in *CSP* are guides and synopses of documents rather than complete copies of the documents themselves. As incomplete transcriptions of the original manuscripts, they may be missing some nuances, although the collections of eighteenth-century documents are much better than those for the seventeenth century and are more than adequate. My comparisons of the eighteenth-century documents I used as printed in the *CSP* showed them to be nearly identical with the manuscript versions. The printed copies, as opposed to the original manuscript, provide more easily accessible and widely available resources.
CWNA	*Colonial Wars of North America, 1512–1763: An Encyclopedia.* Note that encyclopedias such as *CWNA* and the *Dictionary of Canadian Biography* (*DCB*) generally are not included in bibliographies. I have followed that precedent.
DCB	*Dictionary of Canadian Biography.* The National Archives of Canada offers an on-line version of the *DCB* in English at http:///www.biographi.ca/EN. I have used the on-line version for all *DCB* citations; they therefore contain neither volume nor page numbers.
DRCEFNS	Board of Historical Publications, *Documents Relating to Currency, Exchange and Finance in Nova Scotia.*
DRCHNY	O'Callaghan and Fernow, *Documents Relative to the Colonial History of the State of New York.*
GB:FP	Wiener, *Great Britain: Foreign Policy and the Span of Empire, 1689–1971.*
MANA	Pargellis, *Military Affairs in North America.*
Northcliffe	Public Archives of Canada, *The Northcliffe Collection.*
NSAIV	Fergusson, *Nova Scotia Archives IV.*
NSARM MSS	Nova Scotia Papers, Nova Scotia Archives and Records Management. The Nova Scotia Archives and Records Management (NSARM) formerly was known as the Public Archives of Nova Scotia, or PANS.
NS Docs.	Aikens, *Selections from the Public Documents of the Province of Nova Scotia.*
PANS	Public Archives of Nova Scotia.
PDBP	Stock, *Proceedings and Debates of the British Parliaments Respecting North America.*

PRO	Public Record Office.
RCA, 1894	Brymner, *Report on Canadian Archives, 1894.*
RCCA, 1905	Gaudet, *Report Concerning Canadian Archives for the Year 1905.*
SLHQ	Société Littéraire et Historique de Québec.

Notes

PREFACE

1. The primary sources on Indian-Acadian *métissage* are sparse. Some historians, particularly Wicken (see "Encounters with Tall Sails," 236–39), question the degree to which métissage was widespread. Anglo-Americans, through the dark lenses through which they viewed the Acadian and Indian identity, undoubtedly saw many métis because of the Indian adaptation of Roman Catholicism and the French language.

2. Jacques-François de Monbeton de Brouillan au Ministre, June 1, 1703, *CNF,* 2:403–404. This governor Monbeton was the uncle of Joseph de Monbeton de Saint-Ovide de Brouillan, who was governor of Île Royale in the 1720s and 1730s.

3. For the difficulty involved in fixing the boundaries of Indian territories and hunting areas, see Thwaites, *Jesuit Relations,* 1:9.

4. The main Saint Lawrence Iroquois towns included Kahnawake, Kanasatake (with Algonquins and Nipissings), Akwesane, and Oswegatchie.

INTRODUCTION

1. The First British Empire spanned from 1689, when Britons witnessed a striking growth in Britain's worldwide interests, to 1815, when its "nineteenth-century hegemony outside Europe was clearly in place." Marshall, "Introduction," 2. American historians are tempted to suggest that the First Empire fell in 1783 with the loss of the colonies that became the United States in the

American War of Independence. However, Great Britain more than made up for its losses in North America with gains in India and Asia.

2. Scholars have engaged in a pointed debate over the different meanings of "frontier," "borderland," and "empire." Jeremy Adelman and Stephen Aron's forum essay "From Borderlands to Borders" offers a useful discussion to delineate the differences among those terms and places. They argue that borderlands more often saw accommodation between different ethnic groups. Frederick Jackson Turner's frontier thesis and its followers, they also argue, better took in the underlying "transformations" caused by the rise and fall of empires. Because this work focuses on the rise of the British Empire in Nova Scotia, I use "frontier" rather than "borderland." "Dominion," from Latin *dominium,* implies possession of a territory and the right to govern it. *Imperium,* from which "empire" derived, implies supreme power. "Suzerainty" did not enter the English lexicon until 1822 but is a useful term for understanding British aspirations in Nova Scotia in the eighteenth century; it suggests overlordship.

3. Some Canadians might question whether Acadia/Nova Scotia was a distant frontier in the eighteenth century. One reviewer of the manuscript version of this book suggested that the importance of the North Atlantic fishery and the "relative proximity of" Newfoundland and Nova Scotia to western Europe gave them an immediacy that was not necessarily shared by other frontiers. Nonetheless, the volume and value of British resources expended on Nova Scotia, as compared to the other colonies, suggests that Nova Scotia remained an imperial backwater until at least the mid-eighteenth century, if not until the era of the American War of Independence. Nova Scotia did not rank as high in importance by comparison to the empire's other colonies on mainland North America or in the Caribbean. It thus was a distant frontier in both the geographic and the metaphoric sense.

4. Marshall has shown that negotiation and the subsequent acquiescence of the peoples whom the British tried to rule stood as hallmarks of the eighteenth-century British Empire. In both North America and India, British rule depended on finding a modus vivendi with putatively conquered peoples. See Marshall, *Making and Unmaking of Empires.*

5. Hofstra wrote, "The frontier then was an imperial story" (" 'Extension of His Majesties Dominions,' " 1286, passim). Although Hofstra, as his title implies, focused on the Virginia backcountry, his work also has relevance to Nova Scotia's history. In the Virginia backcountry, settlers developed a society and culture that contrasted with that of the Tidewater region. A similar process occurred in Nova Scotia, especially after the American War of Independence; eighteenth-century Anglo-American settlers in postwar Nova Scotia created a unique society and culture of their own at odds with that of the other British mainland colonies. In both the Virginia backcountry and on the Nova Scotia frontier, imperial interests and settlers iteratively shaped the society and culture that developed.

6. For works that group the Caribbean with the mainland colonies, see O'Shaughnessy, *Empire Divided,* and Lenman, "Colonial Wars and Imperial Instability," 156. In Hinderaker and Mancall's excellent survey of the British backcountry, Nova Scotia receives only one paragraph; see Hinderaker and

Mancall, *At the Edge of Empire,* 113–14. Consider that in both the body of the essay and the extensive footnotes in Adelman and Aron's attempt to "disentangle frontiers from borderlands," there is no mention of Nova Scotia; see Adelman and Aron, "From Borderlands to Borders," 815, passim.

7. Haliburton, *History of Nova Scotia*; Murdoch, *History of Nova Scotia*; Allison, *History of Nova Scotia*; Calnek, *History of the County*; Eaton, *History of Kings County*; Herbin, *History of Grand Pré*; Brebner, *New England's Outpost*; Rawlyk, *Nova Scotia's Massachusetts*; Patterson's "In Search of" offers a useful review essay of New England–Nova Scotia relations; MacFarlane, "British Indian Policy."

8. For histories that have a strong nationalist flavor, see Arsenault, *History of the Acadians*; Paratte, *Acadians*; Reid, *Six Crucial Decades*; Faragher, *Great and Noble Scheme,* xix; Griffiths, *From Migrant to Acadian.* For two of Griffiths's earlier works, see *Acadians* and *Contexts of Acadian History.* On the Acadians, see Daigle, *Acadians of the Maritimes,* and Brasseaux, *Founding of New Acadia.* Consider, also, that among the six crucial decades in Nova Scotia's history since 1600, John Reid considers the 1750s, what he calls the "Decade of Expulsion," as worthy of attention. For the Acadians as warriors, see Sauvageau, *Acadie,* 147–70. For an example of an older work that excoriates the British for the deportation of the Acadians, see D'Arles, *La Déportation des Acadiens.*

9. Hutton, "Indian Affairs in Nova Scotia"; Upton, "Indian Affairs," "Indians and Islanders," and *Micmacs and Colonists.* Dickason describes her "Amerindians between French and English" as an expansion and reinterpretation of her "Louisbourg and the Indians" and "La 'Guerre navale.'" See also Wicken, "Encounters with Tall Sails."

10. Ghislain, *Les gardiens des portages,* 21. For the tendency to group the Maliseets and Mi'kmaq together, see Leavitt, *Maliseet and Micmac.*

11. Baker and Reid, "Amerindian Power."

12. Morrison, *Embattled Northeast*; McNeill, *Atlantic Empires*; Patterson, "Indian-White Relations in Nova Scotia," and "Colonial Wars and Aboriginal Peoples"; Robison, "Maritime Frontiers"; Plank, "Two Majors Cope," 21, and *Unsettled Conquest*; Reid, *"Conquest" of Acadia,* xi.

13. Note, for example, that "Nova Scotia" does not merit an entry of its own in *CWNA,* which has become the standard reference work for colonial American military history. For a naval history of Nova Scotia that focuses on the period after my narrative's end, see Gwyn, *Frigates and Foremasts.*

14. Shy, "American Colonies," 300–301.

15. The middle ground of Nova Scotia resembled the accommodation that defined, for a brief period, the *pays d'en haut* in White's *Middle Ground.*

16. I first introduced the conflict in Nova Scotia from 1748 to 1755 as Father Le Loutre's War in Grenier, *First Way of War,* chap. 2.

CHAPTER 1. THE FIRST DECADE OF BRITISH RULE, 1710–1722

1. Penhallow, *History of the Indian Wars,* 56. For the growing influence of New England on British imperial policies in the early eighteenth century, see Haffenden, *New England,* chap. 7. For the permanence of the idea of

Acadia as New Scotland, its place in imperial imperatives of early eighteenth-century Britain, and Scotland's role in the new (after 1707) British state, see Reid, "Conquest of 'Nova Scotia.'" Regarding the prosperity of Acadia, Naomi E. S. Griffiths writes that in 1688, two years before the Yankees occupied Port Royal, "Acadia was in the best condition it had ever been, boasting a growing population with an established subsistence economy, capable of some commercial enterprise, and a lucrative fur trade" (*From Migrant to Acadian,* 146).

2. Almost from the start of the European presence in Acadia, Englishmen had claimed all of Acadia. In 1621, James I of England granted Sir William Alexander proprietary rights to Acadia, which Alexander christened "New Scotland" ("Nova Scotia," or "Nouvelle-Écosse" in French). The Acadians had abandoned Port Royal and congregated on Cape Sable under the leadership of Charles de Saint Etienne de la Tour. The Treaty of Saint Germain-en-Laye returned Acadia to France.

3. For Phips's campaign against Quebec, see Revolutionary Government at New York to the Earl of Shrewsbury, June 23, 1690, *CSP, 1689–1692,* no. 955; Savage, *Expedition against Québec, 1690,* 256–59.

4. For New England's "mournful decade" during King William's War, see Mather, *Decennium Luctuosum.*

5. *CWNA,* s.v. "Port Royal, Acadia (Annapolis Royal, Nova Scotia)."

6. Fort Anne sits around nine miles upstream from the entrance of the Annapolis River (rivière Dauphin to the French) at the Bay of Fundy. The Fort Anne site has existed since 1629, when Scottish settlers constructed Charles Fort. The French built four successive forts on the same site. In 1702, the French began the fort that the English captured in 1710. It was an earthwork star-shaped Vauban fort with four bastions and a ravelin. See Dunn, "1711: Fort Anne/Annapolis Royal (NS)," in DePlanne and Vance, *Colonial Fortifications in North America.*

7. Geoffrey Plank provides perspective on the degree of Anglo-American interest in Nova Scotia: "Only a minority of New Englanders concerned themselves with the affairs of Acadia or Nova Scotia, and that minority grew smaller, proportionately, as the colonies expanded to the north and west"; Plank, "New England and the Conquest," 68.

8. The Western Design—the English attempt to take Hispaniola from the Spanish—stands as "the first deployment of the military resources of the British state in the interests of transoceanic, as opposed to Irish, colonization"; Canny, "Origins of Empire," 20.

9. Curtin's description of the four main forms of cultural encounter between European and non-Western societies is useful in this context. Curtin writes that there were trade diasporas of merchants scattered along trade routes; settlement empires in which natives were few and alien immigrants many ("the United States is the obvious type case," in his opinion); the plantation complex, in which Europeans first conquered, then replaced the vanishing peoples with non-European settlers; and, finally, outright military conquest and rule over an alien society (Curtin, *Rise and Fall,* 14–15).

10. For British success in, failures in, and attitudes toward Ireland, see Bartlett, " 'This Famous Island,' " 253–75.

11. For the state of the theory of empire circa 1710, see Greene, "Transatlantic Colonization," 267, 275.

12. Anderson and Cayton, *Dominion of War*, 42.

13. Samuel Vetch to Lord Dartmouth, June 14, 1711, *CSP, 1710–1711*, no. 879. For a more detailed narrative of the Anglo-American operations at Port Royal, see Reid, " 'Conquest' of Acadia: Narratives," 3–22.

14. Articles of Capitulation, October 2, 1710, *CSP, 1710–1711*, no. 412. Captain William Eyre of the British Army, during the Seven Years' War, described the protocol for determining the honors of war in the *siège en forme*: "The honours of War are colors flying, Drums a beating, with one or two Pieces of Cannon and Match lighted & so many Rounds, and Days provisions; and the whole to march thro the Breach; But this is never alow'd to any, but those who make an obstinate defence" (quoted in Steele, *Betrayals*, 64).

15. The entire text of the Treaty of Ryswick can be found in *GB:FP*, 15–18. Article VII returned within six months to both sides any territories the other side had captured during the war.

16. Articles of Capitulation, October 2, 1710, *CSP, 1710–1711*, no. 412. When William Phips captured Port Royal in 1690, he required all Acadian males to swear allegiance to King William and Queen Mary (Basque, "Family and Political Culture," 55). The oath read, "You and everyone of you do swear by the dreadful Name of the Ever Living God, that you will bear true Faith & Allegiance to Their most excellent Majesties William and Mary of England, Scotland, Ireland King and Queen: so help you God in our Lord Jesus Christ." Quoted in Griffiths, *From Migrant to Acadian*, 154.

17. For the dynamics of Jacobitism, see Szechi, *1715*.

18. Proclamation by General Nicholson, October 12, 1710, *CSP, 1710–1711*, no. 419.

19. Council of War at Annapolis Royal to Vaudreuil, October 11, 1710, ibid., no. 427i. For the story of Eunice Williams, see Demos, *Unredeemed Captive*, and Haefeli and Sweeney, *Captors and Captives*.

20. The best biography of Vetch is Waller, *Samuel Vetch*. Vetch continually sought out schemes and alliances that would increase his wealth and standing in both colonial and British society.

21. Vetch, Canada Survey'd, July 27, 1708, *CSP, 1708–1709*, no. 60.

22. Description of Fortifications, January 15, 1710/11, *CSP, 1710–1711*, no. 613i.

23. Vetch to [William Legge, 1st earl of] Dartmouth, June 14, 1711, ibid., no. 879. For the text of the oath, see Oath Taken by the French Inhabitants of Annapolis Royal, January 22, 1715, *CCA*, 1:110. McCusker and Menard (in *Economy of British America*, 112, table 5.3) estimate the Acadian population as approximately 3,400. Reid (in *"Conquest" of Acadia*, ix) lists it at 2,000. I have used the more recently published figures, which are more in line with Canada's historical census at www.statcan.ca/english/freepub/98-187-XIE/earlyeng.htm.

24. Vetch to Dartmouth, January 22, 1711, *CSP, 1710–1711*, no. 613.

25. Plank, "New England and the Conquest," 75.

26. Vetch to Dartmouth, January 22, 1711, *CSP, 1710–1711*, no. 613. For

complaints regarding French privateers, see Vetch to [Alured] Popple, June 15, 1711, ibid., no. 884.

27. Vetch to Dartmouth, June 14, 1711, ibid., no. 879.

28. Ibid.; *DCB,* s.v. "Durand, Justinien."

29. Vetch to Dartmouth, November 16, 1711, *CSP, 1711–1712,* no. 175.

30. Livingston quotation from *DCB,* s.v. "Livingston, John"; quotation from Vetch to Dartmouth, June 14, 1711, *CSP, 1710–1711,* no. 879.

31. Vetch to Dartmouth, June 18, 1711, *CSP, 1710–1711,* no. 887.

32. *DCB,* s.v. "Abbdie de Saint-Castin, Bernard-Anselme, d'."

33. Vetch to BT, November 26, 1711, *CSP, 1711–1712,* no. 192.

34. Ibid.

35. Vetch to Dartmouth, January 3, 1712, ibid., no. 253; Vetch to Dartmouth, February 9, 1712, ibid., no. 303.

36. In the eighteenth century, British infantry units were organized on the regiment system and, until the middle of the century, named after their commanders. British regiments in Europe generally were one-battalion units consisting of thirteen companies divided among one company of grenadiers and a dozen line companies, each ranging between forty and sixty officers and enlisted men. See Chandler, *Art of Warfare,* 96. In North America, most regiments did not have their full allotment of men or companies.

37. Dunn, "Mohawk Fort (NS)."

38. Vetch to Dartmouth, June 24, 1712, *CSP, 1711–1712,* no. 457.

39. Ibid.

40. Great Britain signed separate treaties with France and Spain. For the treaty with France, see *GB:FP,* 34–39; for the treaty with Spain, see ibid., 40–44.

41. For the importance of the treaties of Utrecht on the changing nature of Britain's economic and military policies vis-à-vis its empire, see Brewer, *Sinews of Power,* 172–73. See also Mancke, "Empire and State," 185, and "Negotiating and Empire," 235–65; and Mancke and Reid, "Elites, States," 25–47.

42. Black, *British Foreign Policy.*

43. Szechi, *1715,* 48.

44. For Acadia/Nova Scotia's particular place in the negotiations at Utrecht, see Reid, "Imperialism, Diplomacies," 101–23.

45. Balen, *Secret History,* 134.

46. Eccles, "Fur Trade and Imperialism"; Miquelon, *New France, 1701–1744.* For the ways in which Louis XIV's wars of *Glorie* affected French strategy in Europe, and thus North America, see Lynn, *Wars of Louis XIV,* chaps. 2–3.

47. Article XIV, Treaty of Utrecht, *GB:FP,* 39. For the trade relations between the Yankees and Acadians, see Daigle, "Nos amis les ennemis." For the differences within the Acadian community, see Basque, "Third Acadia." For the "zeal" quotation, see Memoir sur les habitants de l'Acadie, 1714, *CNF,* 3:9.

48. Letter of Queen Anne, June 23, 1713, *A&NS,* 15.

49. Griffiths, *From Migrant to Acadian,* 160, 201.

50. See Wood, *Creation of the American Republic.*

51. For the tortured history of the struggle for religious toleration in seventeenth- and eighteenth-century Britain, see two essays in Morgan, *Oxford History of Britain*: John Morrill, "The Stuarts (1603–1688)" and Paul Langford, "The Eighteenth Century (1688–1789)."

52. Griffiths, *Contexts of Acadian History,* 39.

53. XIV Article, Treaty of Utrecht, *GB:FP,* 39.

54. *DCB,* s.v. "Espiet de Pensens, Jacques d'."

55. Vetch to BT, November 24, 1714, *CSP, 1714–1715,* no. 94. Vetch reiterated his concerns several months later; see March 9, 1715, ibid., no. 263.

56. For Acadian migration to Île Royale following the conquest of 1710, see Pothier, "Acadian Emigration." For the construction of Louisbourg, see Moore, *Louisbourg Portraits,* 209–30.

57. Vetch to Dartmouth, May 22, 1713, *CSP, 1713–1714,* no. 347; Vetch's Order to Peter Mason, May 22, 1713, ibid., no. 347i.

58. Oath Taken by the French Inhabitants of Annapolis Royal, January 22, 1715, *CCA,* 1:110.

59. Caulfield to BT, January 3, 1715, *CSP, 1714–1715,* nos. 142–142x; Answer of the Inhabitants of Mines, January 3, 1715, and Réponse des Habitants de Beaubassin, March 28, 1715, *CCA,* 1:111–12.

60. Copy of H.M. Establishment of the Garrison and Four Companies at Annapolis Royal, July 30, 1712, *CSP, 1714–1715,* no. 409; John Mulcaster to [BT], May 13, 1715, ibid., no. 411; Foote, "American Independent Companies."

61. David Jefferies and Charles Shepreve, July 6, 1715, *CSP, 1714–1715,* no. 568i; Nicholson to Popple, August 13, 1715, ibid., no. 568.

62. Caulfield to BT, November 1, 1715, ibid., no. 658.

63. Anderson and Cayton, *Dominion of War,* 27.

64. Caulfield to BT, November 1, 1715, *CSP, 1714–1715,* nos. 658, 658i, and 658ii. For the impact of the North Atlantic fisheries on New England's economy, see Vickers, *Farmers and Fishermen.* Vickers (table 4, p. 154) estimates that Massachusetts fishermen took 120,000 quintals of fish in 1716 and 150,000 in 1719.

65. For the clearest elucidation of the garrison government thesis, see Webb, *Governors-General.*

66. Steele, "Anointed," 115.

67. Copy of the Declaration sent to the French Acadians for Signature, *A&NS,* 14.

68. Doucett to BT, November 6, 1717, *CSP, 1717–1718,* no. 185.

69. Ibid.

70. French Inhabitants of Minnes to Doucett, February 10, 1718, ibid., nos. 371i, 371ii, and 371iv.

71. Faragher, *Great and Noble Scheme,* 59; Griffiths, *From Migrant to Acadian,* 79–83; *DCB,* s.v. "Sedgwick, Robert."

72. Doucett to BT, November 6, 1717, *CSP, 1717–1718,* no. 185.

73. Ibid.

74. French Inhabitants to Doucett, n.d., ibid., no. 185ii.

75. Doucett to Vaudreuil, April 15, 1718, ibid., no. 565v; Doucett to

Saint-Ovide, May 15, 1718, ibid., 565iv. For the different methods employed in the cod fisheries (the "green fishery" and the "dry fishery"), see Vickers, *Farmers and Fishermen,* 87–88.

76. Doucett to Père Félix [Pain], March 29, 1717/18, *CSP, 1717–1718,* no. 565iii.

77. Voltaire, "Revocation of the Edict of Nantes," 1415.

78. Doucett to BT, November 6, 1717, *CSP, 1717–1718,* no. 185.

79. Griffiths, *From Migrant to Acadian,* 272, 273, 311–12, 331.

80. Doucett to BT, November 6, 1717, *CSP, 1717–1718,* no. 185.

81. Ibid.

82. Dickason, "Amerindians between French and English," 38.

83. Doucett to BT, February 10, 1718, *CSP, 1717–1718,* no. 371.

84. Ibid.

85. BT to George I, May 30, 1718, ibid., no. 550; Philipps's Memorial, February 21, 1718, ibid., no. 551.

86. BT to Secretary [of State for the Southern Department James] Craggs, April 30, 1719, *CSP, 1719–1720,* no. 172. The secretary of state for the Southern Department was responsible for the colonies, while the secretary of state for the Northern Department handled relations with northern Europe. In 1768, the British created the secretary of state for the American Department to handle the mainland North American colonies.

87. Philipps to BT, March 11, 1719, ibid., no. 102.

88. Doucett to Philipps, November 1, 1718, ibid., no. 129i(a).

89. Doucett to BT, November 15, 1718, ibid., no. 102i.

90. Doucett to Philipps, n.d., ibid., no. 129i(c).

91. The conflict that came to be known as the War of the Quadruple Alliance originated with Philip V of Spain's desire to reclaim the European territories that Spain had lost in the War of the Spanish Succession; Kamen, *Empire,* 453–55. Great Britain, France, and the Netherlands, in 1717, joined in the Triple Alliance to oppose the Spanish and maintain the balance of power established at Utrecht; see Article V of the Treaty of the Triple Alliance, *GB:FP,* 51. In August 1718, the Holy Roman Empire and Savoy joined the alliance, and the Netherlands withdrew, thus making the Quadruple Alliance. Spanish forces landed in Scotland and joined 1,000 Highlanders in the "Little Rising" of 1719, but a British army defeated them at Glenshiel. France, Great Britain, and Holland also formed the League of Hanover in 1725 to recommit themselves to opposing Spanish designs in Europe.

92. Vaudreuil to Louis Allain, September 22, 1718, *CSP, 1717–1718,* no. 789iii; Vaudreuil to Allain, September 22, 1718, ibid., no. 789iv.

93. Doucett to Philipps, December 13, 1718, ibid., no. 789.

94. Article XII, Treaty of Utrecht, *GB:FP,* 38.

95. Doucett to Philipps, November 1, 1718, *CSP, 1719–1720,* no. 129i(a).

96. For the background to the 1718 confrontation off Canso, see Robison, "Maritime Frontiers," chap. 1.

97. Memorandum by Capt. Southack, n.d., *CSP, 1719–1720,* no. 137v(d).

98. Memorandum, *Bax. MSS,* 9:429.

99. Maurepas quoted in *DCB,* "Monbeton de Brouillan, *dit* Saint-Ovide, Joseph de."

100. Deposition of Nathaniel Cunningham, October 27, 1718, *CSP, 1719–1720,* no. 213i(a).

101. Deposition of John Henshaw and Jonathan Rowse, October 30, 1718, ibid., no. 213i(c); Memorial of James Pitts, Oliver Noyes, John Marshall, Nath[anie]l Cunningham, and Benjamin Alford, June 9, 1718, ibid, no. 213v.

102. Instructions Left by Saint-Ovide to the French Fishermen at Canso, June 2, 1718, *CNF,* 3:27.

103. Smart to Secretary Burchett, October 22, 1718, *Bax. MSS,* 9:433. A brigantine is a two-masted, square-rigged craft that differs from a brig in not carrying a square mainsail. A sloop is a single-mast craft with a single head-sail jib.

104. Shute to Saint-Ovide, n.d., *CSP, 1719–1720,* no. 213iv; Shute's Instructions to Smart, n.d., ibid., no. 213vii; Southack's Journal, ibid., no. 137vi; Article XII, Treaty of Utrecht, *GB:FP,* 38; Shute to Saint-Ovide, August 24, 1718, *CNF,* 3:29.

105. Saint-Ovide to Shute, November 22, 1718, *CNF,* 3:34.

106. Nathaniel Shannon to George Vaun [Vaughan], October 22, 1718, *Bax. MSS* 9:432.

107. Vaughan to Craggs, November 29, 1718, *Bax. MSS,* 9:440–41.

108. Southack to Philipps, January 27, 1719, *CSP, 1719–1720,* no. 137i; Southack's Journal, ibid., no. 137vi; Resumé de la declaration du Sieur Domincé, Basque captain, December 28, 1718, *CNF,* 3:38.

109. Saint-Ovide to Philipps, July 23, 1718, *CSP 1719–1720,* 213viii.

110. Saint-Ovide to Shute, September 23, 23, 1718, *CNF,* 3:30.

111. Capt Aldrige to Philipps, December 24, 1718, *CSP, 1719–1720,* no. 129i(b).

112. BT quoted in *DCB,* s.v. "Smart, Thomas."

113. Louis XV à Saint-Ovide, July 2, 1720, *CNF,* 3:45.

114. Saint-Ovide to Philipps, June 8, 1720, *CSP 1720–1721,* no. 177i; "made light" quotation from Memorial of John Henshaw, William Taylor and Richard Pieke, n.d., ibid., no. 241i.

115. English Merchants and Residents at Port Canso to Saint-Ovide, ibid., no. 241ii.

116. CO 220B/1, 30, August 27, 1720.

117. Deposition of François Pitrelle, n.d., *CSP, 1720–1721,* no. 241v.

118. Philipps to BT, September 27, 1720, ibid., no. 241.

CHAPTER 2. THE MALISEET-MI'KMAW WAR, 1722–1726

1. Philipps to BT, January 3, 1720, *CSP, 1720–1721,* no. 504.

2. Ibid.

3. The term "small wars" derives from the French *petite guerre.* Traditionally, "guerrilla" (the Spanish diminutive translation of the French term) was used to describe small wars. But, as noted in the introduction and will be seen in more detail later, the adjective "guerrilla" implies a specific type of warfare, albeit one that is often found in the context of small wars.

4. BT to Lords Justices, June 19, 1719, *CSP, 1719–1720,* nos. 255, 255i, 255ii.

5. BT to Philipps, July 21, 1720, *CSP, 1720–1721,* no. 158.

6. Philipps to BT, August 6, 1720, ibid., no. 177.

7. Ibid.

8. Louis XV à Vaudreuil et [Michel] Bégon [de La Picardière], May 23, 1719, *CNF,* 3:40.

9. Morrison, *Embattled Northeast,* 166. The First Anglo-Abenaki War ran concurrently with King Philip's War (1675–1676) and the second with King William's War (1689–1697).

10. Rapport de Vaudreuil et Bégon, October 26, 1719, *CNF,* 3:41.

11. Morrison, *Embattled Northeast,* 159.

12. Memoire sur les limits de l'Acadie, October 29, 1720, *CNF,* 3:49.

13. Memoir du Roy aux Sieurs de Vaudreuil et Bégon, June 2, 1720, ibid., 3:44–45; *DCB,* s.v. "Rale, Sébastien." Technically, it would have been the favor of Philippe II, duc d'Orléans, the regent of France, because the regency officially did not end until 1723.

14. Memoire sur les limits de l'Acadie, October 29, 1720, *CNF,* 3:49.

15. CO 220B/1, 24, June 29, 1720.

16. Indians to Philipps, October 2, 1720, *CNF,* 3:46–47.

17. Vaudreuil et Bégon au ministre, October 26, 1720, ibid., 3:48–49; Louis XV à Vaudreuil et Bégon, June 8, 1721, ibid., 3:54.

18. Shute to Vaudreuil, September 22, 1721, ibid., 3:56.

19. Philipps to BT, August 16, 1721, *CSP, 1720–1721,* no. 614.

20. Massachusetts, *Laws and Orders,* July 1720, 14.

21. Ibid., August 1721, 112; July 1720, 14; November 1721, 126; May 1722, 204; and August 1722, 258.

22. Vaudreuil and Bégon to the Council of Marine, October 17, 1722, *DRCHNY,* 9:910.

23. Quoted in *CWNA,* s.v. "Dummer's War." Emphasis in original.

24. Philipps to BT, September 19, 1722, *RCA, 1894,* 53.

25. Doucett to BT, June 29, 1722, *CSP, 1722–1723,* no. 205.

26. Journal of Hibbert Newton, June 16, 1722, ibid., no. 205i; Doucett to BT, June 29, 1722, ibid., no. 205; Deposition of George Lynham, June 27, 1722, ibid., no. 205iii; Deposition of Joseph Bissell, June 24, 1722, ibid., no. 205iv; Winniett to Doucett, July 1, 1722, ibid., no. 209i. For the Maliseets' attack on Fort Saint George, see John Penhallow to Shute, July 4, 1722, *Bax. MSS,* 10:150–51.

27. Doucett to BT, June 29, 1722, *CSP, 1722–1723,* no. 205.

28. Ibid.

29. Doucett to BT, June 29, 1722, ibid., no. 209.

30. Ibid.

31. Gaulin to Doucett, March 13, 1722, ibid., no. 209iii.

32. Doucett to Gaulin, March 14, 1722, ibid., no. 209v.

33. Winniett to Doucett, July 1, 1722, ibid., no. 209i.

34. Gaulin to Doucett, September 7, 1722, ibid., no. 209ii.

35. John Wheelwright to Shute, July 6, 1722, *Bax. MSS,* 10:151–52.

36. Journal of the House of Representatives, July 8, 1722, ibid., 10:152–53. For the rangers on the Maine frontier, see Grenier, *First Way of War,* 47–52.

37. Westbrook to Shute, September 23, 1722, *Bax. MSS,* 10:153–55.

38. Penhallow, *History of the Indian Wars,* 92–93.

39. Ibid., 94.

40. BT to Lord Carteret, September 26, 1722, *CSP, 1722–1723,* no. 301.

41. Ibid.

42. Harmon to Dummer, February 25, 1722/23, *Bax. MSS,* 9:469–70.

43. John Penhallow to Dummer, February 28, 1722/23, ibid., 9:472–73; Westbrook to Dummer, February 27, 1722/23, ibid., 9:471; *DCB,* s.v. "Lauverjat, Étienne."

44. Robison, "Maritime Frontiers," 79.

45. Philipps to Lord Carteret, February 1724, *CSP, 1724–1725,* no. 69; Doucett to Mascarene, April 18, 1723, *RCA, 1894,* 54; Doucett to Mascarene, October 25, 1723, ibid., 55; Report on Ordinance, October 31, 1723, ibid.

46. Scheme for a Settlement, [August 20, 1723], *CSP, 1722–1723,* no. 686.

47. Philipps to Lord Carteret, February 1724, *CSP, 1724–1725,* no. 69.

48. Gwyn, *Frigates and Foremasts,* 8.

49. BT to Treasury, September 3, 1724, *RCA, 1894,* 56.

50. Philipps to BT, March 12, 1724, *CSP, 1724–1725,* no. 86.

51. Griffiths, *From Migrant to Acadian,* 299.

52. Rapport de M. Bégon au ministre, July 4, 1724, *CNF,* 3:104; Grenier, *First Way of War,* 78–80; *DCB,* s.v. "Mog."

53. Vaudreuil au ministre, October 25, 1724, *CNF,* 3:110.

54. Grenier, *First Way of War,* 81–84.

55. Vaudreuil au ministre, November 18, 1723 [*sic,* 1724], *CNF,* 3:111–12.

56. Ibid., 3:112.

57. Armstrong to BT, September 5, 1725, *CSP, 1724–1725,* no. 718; *DCB,* s.v. "Petitpas, Claude."

58. Armstrong to Saint-Ovide, August 12, 1725, *CSP, 1724–1725,* no. 718iv.

59. Articles to Be Demanded of the Indians, November 3, 1724, ibid., no. 718vii; Instructions, August 12, 1725, ibid., no. 718v.

60. Proceedings of Newton and Bradstreet, ibid., no. 718viii.

61. Ibid.

62. Bégon au ministre, April 21, 1725, *CNF,* 3:117; Morrison, *Embattled Northeast,* 185; [Charles Le Moyne de Longueuil, Baron de] Longeueil et Bégon au ministre, October 31, 1725, *CNF,* 3:125; Note de ministre sur les despeches de l'année dernierre, May 2, 1726, ibid., 3:127; Louis XV à [Charles de] Beauharnois [de la Boische] et [Claude-Thomas] Dupuy, May 14, 1726, ibid., 3:128.

63. Instructions, August 31, 1725, *CSP, 1724–1725,* no. 718vi.

64. Robison, "Maritime Frontiers," 80.

65. The provisions of the Treaty of 1725 can be found in Daugherty, *Maritime Indian Treaties.*

66. For his personal relations with the Indians, see Gyles, *Ordeal of John Gyles.*

67. *DCB,* s.v. "Gray Lock"; ibid., s.v. "Wenemouet"; ibid., s.v. "Sauguaaram"; Abstract of Despatches, March 16, 1728, *DRCHNY,* 9:990–94.

68. Armstrong to BT, July 27, 1726, *CSP, 1726–1727,* no. 323.

69. www.canadiana.org/ECO/PageView/91943/0231.

70. Dickason, "Amerindians between French and English," 33.

71. Daugherty, *Maritime Indian Treaties,* 75–78.

72. Doucett to BT, August 16, 1726, *CSP, 1726–1727,* no. 268.

73. Instrument signed by Doucett, June 4, 1726, ibid., no. 268ii.

74. Wicken, "Mi'kmaq Decisions," 95.

75. For the Indian perspective on the sovereignty question, see Dickason, "Amerindians between French and English," 35. For the "have patterns" quotation, see Countryman, "Indians, the Colonial Order," 354. Countryman writes about a later period in the history of the empire, but his observations on Indians' place in Revolutionary War–era society also apply to the Mi'kmaw-Maliseet experience in the half century following Mascarene's Treaty.

CHAPTER 3. ANGLO-AMERICANS AND ACADIANS IN NOVA SCOTIA, 1720–1744

1. Griffiths, "Golden Age," 21–34.

2. Copy of the Declaration Sent to the French Acadians, 1717, *A&NS,* 14; Copy of the Answer of the Above Declaration, 1717, ibid., 15–16.

3. Inhabitants of Acadia to Saint-Ovide, May 6, 1720, ibid., 25–26.

4. Philipps to BT, May 26, 1720, ibid., 31.

5. Philipps received permission to grant the Acadians up to 24 deputies—Annapolis Royal would get 6, Cobequid 4, Minas 12, and Beaubassin 2; Daigle, *Acadians of the Maritimes,* 36.

6. Inhabitants of Minas to Philipps, May 1720, *A&NS,* 29; CO 220, April 29, 1720, 1:11; ibid., April 30, 1720, 1:15; ibid., May 4, 1720, 1:17.

7. Philipps to BT, May 26, 1720, *RCA, 1894,* 40.

8. Basque, "Third Acadia," 156. Members of the Robichaud clan often served as Acadian deputies; ibid., 175.

9. For the La Tour family's significant role in the founding of Acadia, see MacDonald, *Fortune and La Tour,* chap. 2.

10. Godfrey, *Pursuit of Profit,* 1–9.

11. Philipps to BT, May 26, 1720, *RCA, 1894,* 40.

12. Ibid.

13. Council Minutes, September 25, 1726, *A&NS,* 66.

14. Ibid., 67.

15. Ibid.

16. Armstrong to Deputies of Minas &c, June 1, 1727, ibid., 73.

17. Armstrong to Newcastle, April 30, 1727, *CSP, 1726–1727,* no. 528.

18. Order by Armstrong, July 29, 1727, ibid., no. 789iii.

19. Council Minutes, July 25, 1727, *A&NS,* 75.

20. Armstrong to Dartmouth, November 17, 1727, ibid., 79.

21. Matt. 22:21.

22. Armstrong to Dartmouth, November 17, 1727, *A&NS,* 80. The oath, in the original French, was "Je promets & jure sincèrement que je serai fidèle & obéirai véritablement à sa Majesté Le Roy George Second."

23. Armstrong to Dartmouth, November 17, 1727, ibid., 80.

24. Ibid.
25. Ibid.
26. *DCB,* s.v. "Bourg, Alexandre."
27. Various correspondence, autumn 1727, *CSP, 1726–1727,* nos. 789vi–viiii.
28. Ensign Wroth's Articles, May 10, 1728, *CSP, 1730,* no. 3iii.
29. Armstrong to BT, June 23, 1729, *A&NS,* 82.
30. *DCB,* s.v. "Breslay, René-Charles, de."
31. Address of the French Inhabitants, *CSP, 1730,* no. 3ii.
32. Philipps to BT, August 3, 1734, *A&NS,* 102.
33. Certificat donné au R. P. De Breslay, 1730, *CNF,* 3:150.
34. *DCB,* s.v. "Philipps, Richard."
35. Philipps to Newcastle, January 3, 1729 (o.s), *A&NS,* 83.
36. Oath of Allegiance, n.d., *CSP, 1730,* no. 3i.
37. Philipps to BT, September 2, 1730, ibid., no. 411.
38. Ibid.
39. The Minas oath: "Nous serons entièrement fidèles et nous soumettrons véritablement à sa Majesté George le second *etc.,* que nous reconnoissons pour le souverain seigneur de la Nouvelle Ecosse et l'Accadie." Oath of Allegiance to King George, *CSP, 1730,* no. 411iii; *DCB,* s.v. "La Goudalie."
40. Philipps to Newcastle, September 2, 1730, *A&NS,* 86.
41. Philips to BT, January 3, 1730, *CSP, 1730,* no. 3.
42. Popple to Philipps, May 20, 1730, ibid., no. 248. Popple wrote to Philipps in response to the latter's report of January 1730, which the Board of Trade did not receive until April 25 and did not read until May 11; see Philipps to BT, January 3, 1730, ibid., no. 3. By May, Philipps already had traveled to Minas and Chignecto to extract the oath from the Acadians there. We do not know the exact date Philipps received Popple's letter. Philipps's response was not received in London until February 23, 1731. It was read the same day.
43. Philipps to BT, November 26, 1730, *CSP, 1730,* no. 562.
44. See Philipps to BT, August 3, 1734, *A&NS,* 102.
45. Address of the French Inhabitants, *CSP, 1730,* no. 3ii.
46. Armstrong to Deputies, August 30, 1731, *A&NS,* 88.
47. Armstrong to Deputies, August 30, 1731, ibid., 89.
48. Council Minutes, July 25, 1732, ibid., 98.
49. Armstrong to Newcastle, November 15, 1732, ibid., 101.
50. *DCB,* s.v. "La Goudalie."
51. Armstrong to Godalie [La Goudalie], April 20, 1732, *A&NS,* 95.
52. *DCB,* s.v. "Breslay, René-Charles de."
53. Armstrong to Saint-Ovide, June 17, 1732, *A&NS,* 96.
54. Armstrong to Bishop of Québec, November 21, 1732, ibid., 99.
55. Council Minutes, May 18, 1736, ibid., 103.
56. *NSAIV,* October 25, 1736, 9.
57. *DCB,* s.v. "Chauvreulx, Claude-Jean-Baptiste."
58. *NSAIV,* April 20, 1737, 11–12.
59. Ibid., March 22, 1739/40, 25.
60. For a biography of Mascarene, see Moody, " 'Just and Disinterested Man.' "

61. Mascarene quoted in Griffiths, *From Migrant to Acadian,* 334.

62. Mascarene to Secretary of State, November 15, 1740, *A&NS,* 108–109.

63. Griffiths, *Contexts of Acadian History,* 46, 60.

64. Mascarene to Secretary of State, November 15, 1740, *A&NS,* 108–109.

65. *NSAIV,* July 31, August 2, August 4, and August 7, 1740, 29–32.

66. Ibid., April 23, 1740, 27.

67. Mascarene to Desenclaves, June 29, 1741, *A&NS,* 111.

68. *NSAIV,* July 1, 1740, 29.

69. Mascarene to Desenclaves, September 5, 1741, *A&NS,* 113.

70. For British grievances against the Spanish, see Speech of Sir John Bernard in the House of Commons, March 3, 1738, *GB:FP,* 70–72; see also *NSAIV,* May 12, 1740, 28.

71. *NSAIV,* September 18, 1740, 32.

72. Ibid., April 11, November 19, and November 21, 1741, 35–36.

73. *DCB,* s.v. "La Goudalie."

74. *NSAIV,* November 30, 1742, 39.

75. Ibid., April 9, 1742, 37–38.

76. Ibid., April 29, 1742, 39.

77. Anon., "Account of Nova Scotia," 106.

CHAPTER 4. KING GEORGE'S WAR, 1744–1748

1. Ordonnance du Roi portant déclaration de guerre contre le Roi d'Angleterre, March 15, 1744, *CNF,* 3:196.

2. For central European aspects, see Browning, *War of the Austrian Succession.* Historians of early America have embraced a synthesis that explains the interplay between the British wars for trade and empire with those for maintaining the balance of power in Europe; see, for example, Gould, *Persistence of Empire,* 2–3. "Shifting complex" quotation from Leach, *Arms for Empire,* 206.

3. William Shirley to Newcastle, May 22, 1746, NSARM MSS, vol. 13, no. 22. In 1746, the British bomb ketch *Comet* captured the privateer with four soldiers on it. Mascarene sat as the senior judge on the court-martial that sentenced them to death, but he recommended pardons for some of the soldiers. He recommended that at least one of the offenders be executed, as "traitorous" behavior "may otherwise grow too fast in these remote Parts of his Dominions if the least Notion should prevail among the Soldiers that they can't be punished for it here."

4. *DCB,* s.v. "Heron, Patrick"; Capitulation le Canso, May 24, 1744, *CNF,* 3:201.

5. Mascarene to Shirley, December 1744, *A&NS,* 141.

6. Shirley to General Court of Massachusetts, May 31, 1744, in Shirley, *Correspondence,* 1:122; Mascarene to Shirley, July 7, 1744, *RCA, 1894,* 101.

7. Historians recently have questioned whether Le Loutre or Father Pierre Maillard was at the head of the Mi'kmaq in the summer of 1744. Faragher credits Maillard, contending that Le Loutre, in his autobiography,

claimed 1745 as the year he first began his military activities. That autobiography, however, was published in 1933 by John Clarence Webster and unfortunately has several inconsistencies in it. Perhaps that is why Faragher calls Le Loutre "Louis-Joseph Le Loutre," when in fact his name was Jean-Louis Le Loutre; see Faragher, *Great and Noble Scheme,* 514n16. We can explain Le Loutre's reluctance to be too closely associated with the 1744 operation due to its failure. Moreover, contemporaries were convinced that Father Le Loutre was the one who led the Mi'kmaq. In the autumn of 1743, Le Loutre had threatened Mascarene that the Indians were ready to raise the hatchet against the English. Edward Cornwallis observed in 1749 that "De Loutre [*sic,* Le Loutre], the same that led them before Annapolis Royal, has once more persuaded them [Mi'kmaq] to begin hostilities"; Cornwallis to BT, October 17, 1749, NSARM MSS, vol. 40, no. 9. Finn, in "Jean-Louis Le Loutre," takes a less critical view of Le Loutre than the one I hold. It remains my opinion that Father Le Loutre was an extremist, who at the most basic level asked others to kill and terrorize in his name.

8. Le Loutre to Séminaire des Missions Étrangers, October 1, 1738, and Le Loutre to Séminaire des Missions Étrangers, October 3, 1740, *CCA,* 1:19, 25.

9. Mascarene to BT, September 20, 1744, *NS Docs.,* 131.

10. Mascarene to Shirley, December 1744, *A&NS,* 141.

11. Ibid.

12. Ibid., 140–42.

13. Pothier, *Course à L'Accadie,* 38.

14. Ibid., 36.

15. Eccles, "Social, Economic, and Political Significance," 1.

16. Competency was not financial self-sufficiency but financial and familial independence; see Vickers, "Competency and Competition."

17. Orders, August 27, 1744, *A&NS,* 134.

18. *DCB,* s.v. "Leblanc, 'Le Maigre,' Joseph." In the 1980s, a band of Acadian folk musicians took the name Beausoleil to honor the memory of Joseph Broussard.

19. *NSAIV,* May 5, 1744, 46.

20. Mascarene to Shirley, December 1744, *A&NS,* 142.

21. Ibid., 143.

22. Ibid.

23. Ibid.

24. Ibid., 144.

25. Ibid.

26. Ibid., 145.

27. Two French ships sailed into the river in November but left after three days spent gathering wood and watching the British from afar. The Acadians told Mascarene that those ships carried three mortars. Yet mortars alone did not offer enough firepower to take Fort Anne, because they could not breach the walls of the fort.

28. Mascarene to BT, September 20, 1744, *A&NS,* 131.

29. Mascarene to ?, December 1744, ibid., 149.

30. Ibid., 147.

31. Mascarene to Shirley, December 1744, ibid., 146.

32. Ibid.

33. Mascarene to ?, December 1744, ibid., 147.

34. Minas Deputies to de Gannes, October 10, 1744, ibid., 135.

35. Mascarene to ?, December 1744, ibid., 148–49.

36. *NSAIV,* December 11, 1744, 52.

37. Mascarene to Minas Deputies, October 13, 1744, *A&NS,* 137.

38. Ibid.

39. Ibid., 138.

40. *NSAIV,* January 21 and 23, 1744/45, 56–57.

41. Shirley to duke of Newcastle, May 22, 1746, NSARM MSS, vol. 13, no. 22.

42. Mascarene to Minas Deputies, October 13, 1744, *A&NS,* 137.

43. Mascarene to Chignecto Deputies, October 26, 1744, ibid., 138.

44. Mascarene to Chignecto Deputies, November 16, 1744, ibid., 139.

45. Faragher (*Great and Noble Scheme,* 219) writes that Gorham hailed from Maine, but he was from Massachusetts.

46. *NSAIV,* April 1, 1738, 18. Le Mercier first asked for proprietorship on Cape Sable in 1729. Governor Philipps, always in search of settlers for Nova Scotia, recommended that Le Mercier receive 5,000 acres, but nothing came of that. Le Mercier and Gorham's petition nine years later included a statement that they would pay a penny for each acre; Sable Island Papers, MHS.

47. Copy of Minutes of Council, December 6, 1744, NSARM MSS, vol. 11, no. 16.

48. Ibid.

49. *NSAIV,* January 4, 1744/45, 55.

50. Ibid.

51. Ibid., December 21, 1744, 53–54.

52. Grenier, *First Way of War,* 72.

53. [Charles de Beauharnois de La Boische, marquis de] Beauharnois to [Minister of the Marine] Count de Maurepas, June 18, 1745, *DRCHNY,* 10:1.

54. Gorham, "Col. John Gorham's 'Wast Book,'" 198.

55. Extrait en forme de journal de ce qui s'est passé d'interssant dans la nouvelle-France les années 1745, 1746, 1747, 1748, *CNF,* 3:217–18.

56. *NSAIV,* May 25, 1745, 71.

57. Beauharnois to Maurepas, September 12, 1745, *DRCHNY,* 10:4.

58. *NSAIV,* June 19, June 27, and August 7, 1745, 73–75.

59. Linda Colley, in *Britons,* shows convincingly that as the eighteenth century progressed, Britons defined themselves as the antithesis of the "unfree" Catholic French.

60. Beauharnois to Maurepas, September 12, 1745, *DRCHNY,* 10:4.

61. Warren to Duchambon, June 19, 1745, *CNF,* 3:209.

62. Balcom, "Mi'kmaq."

63. *NSAIV,* August 24, 1745, 77.

64. Abstract of Despatches Received from Canada, *DRCHNY,* 10:77.

65. Robert Sanders to William Johnson, November 28, 1745, in Johnson, *Papers,* 1:43; Abstract of Despatches Received from Canada, *DRCHNY,* 10:76; Military and Other Operations in Canada during the Years 1745–1746, *DRCHNY,* 10:38.

66. Steele, *Warpaths,* 172.

67. Warren and Pepperrell to Newcastle, January 18, 1746, *RCA, 1894,* 110; Gorham, "Col. John Gorham's 'Wast Book,'" 198.

68. Extrait en forme . . . , 1746, *CNF,* 3:272–74.

69. Extrait en forme . . . , 1746, ibid., 3:276–79.

70. The Anglo-American plan fell apart when Lieutenant General James St. Clair's British regulars—troops that Whitehall had promised to support the invasion up the St. Lawrence—never arrived at Louisbourg. See John Rutherford to William Johnson, June 12, 1746, in Johnson, *Papers,* 1:52. Without the support of the eastern thrust, Shirley called off the campaign. Still, he presented Parliament a bill for over £220,000 for what was little more than an American campout in New York; PDBP, March 12, 1749/50, 415–18; Extrait en forme . . . , 1746, *CNF,* 3:298–99.

71. *NSAIV,* November 8, 1745, 84.

72. Ibid., September 22, 1746, 88; *Gentleman's Magazine,* 1746, 685.

73. *Gentleman's Magazine,* 1746, 577–78; *DCB,* s.v. "La Rochefoucauld de Roye, Jean-Baptiste-Louis-Frédéric de, marquis de Roucy, duc D'Anvillve"; ibid., s.v. "Taffanel de La Jonquière, Jacques-Pierre de, marquis de La Jonquière"; ibid., s.v. "Barrin de La Galissonière, Roland-Michel, marquis de La Galissonière." Pritchard's *Anatomy of a Naval Disaster* is the best study of the 1746 expedition.

74. Mascarene to Newcastle, December 9, 1745, *RCA, 1894,* 109.

75. Shirley to Newcastle, May 22, 1746, NSARM MSS, vol. 13, no. 22.

76. William Bollan to Newcastle, August 17, 1747, *Bax. MSS,* 11:387–88.

77. Shirley to Newcastle, August 15, 1746, in Shirley, *Correspondence,* 1:336; Gorham to Shirley, November 15, 1746, NSARM MSS, vol. 13, no. 34.

78. *NSAIV,* November 8, 1745, 84.

79. Gorham to Shirley, October 4, 1746, Gorham Papers.

80. *NSAIV,* September 29, 1746, 90–91.

81. Gorham to Shirley, October 4, 1746, Gorham Papers.

82. *NSAIV,* October 27, 1746, 92.

83. Ibid., November 14, 1746, 94.

84. Ibid., October 31, 1746, 92.

85. Ibid., November 14, 1746, 94.

86. Ibid., December 29, 1746, and January 15, 1746/47, 97–98.

87. Griffiths, in *From Migrant to Acadian,* 363, confuses Joseph Coulon de Villiers de Jumonville with his older brother by ten years, Nicholas-Antoine Coulon de Villiers. Nicholas-Antoine commanded the French and Indian forces at the Battle of Grand Pré; she mistakenly writes that it was Joseph. The younger Coulon, Joseph, was killed by, in the words of Horace Walpole, "a volley fired by a young Virginian in the backwoods of America [that] set the world on fire." Of course, that young Virginian was George Washington, and the fire was the Seven Years' War; *DCB,* s.v. "Coulon de Villiers, Nicolas-Antoine" and "Coulon de Villiers de Jumonville, Joseph."

88. Journal of Occurrences in Canada, 1746, 1747, *DRCHNY,* 10:92; Capitulation of the Garrison at Grand Pré, Nova Scotia, ibid., 10:78. For French and Anglo-American reports of the battle, see Trask, "Battle of Minas"; Parkman Papers, New France I: Acadia 1713–1767. Daniel-Hyacinthe-Marie

Liénard de Beaujeu's Journal de la campagne du détachement de Canada à l'Acadie aux Mines, in which he discussed the march to Grand Pré and the battle, is printed in full in *CCA,* 2:16–75. Beaujeu died a hero's death for the French in the opening moments at the battle of the Monongahela in 1755.

89. Mascarene to the Commander and All the Other Officers of the Part Returning from Minas, February 7, 1746, NSARM MSS, vol. 13, no. 38.

90. Bates, "John Gorham," 42; Gorham to ?, March 1746/47, Gorham Papers.

91. Shirley to Newcastle, February 27, 1747, quoted in Bates, "John Gorham," 42.

92. Bedford to Newcastle, September 11, 1747, *Bax. MSS,* 11:389.

93. Bates, "John Gorham," 44; Gorham, "Col. John Gorham's 'Wast Book,'" 198.

94. Extrait en forme . . . , 1747, *CNF,* 3:331–56.

95. Word of the peace would have reached Annapolis Royal relatively quickly. Following Queen Anne's War, Great Britain had created a regular packet service that carried mail and government communications between Great Britain and the North American colonies.

96. Mascarene to Bedford, September 8, 1748, *NS Docs.,* 164; Gorham to Capt Bourn, December 13, 1748, Gorham Papers.

CHAPTER 5. FATHER LE LOUTRE'S WAR, 1749–1755

1. Article IX, Treaty of Aix-la-Chapelle, *GB:FP,* 93.

2. Half a century ago, Guy Frégault argued essentially my same point. He wrote, "La nouvelle écosse est en guerre et elle s'engage dans un movement de colonisation intensive. Le dispersion des Acadiens constitute un episode de cette guerre et le ce mouvement"; Frégualt, *La Guerre de la Conquête,* 272. See also Frégualt, "L'Empire britannique."

3. Ordannance du Roy concernant la suspension d'armes par mer, May 26, 1748, *CNF,* 3:420.

4. Pitt to Henry Pelham, August 17, 1746, www.longford.nottingham.ac.uk.

5. Mascarene to Acadian Deputies, August 30, 1748, *A&NS,* 162.

6. La Galissonière to Mascarene, January 15, 1749, ibid., 362–64; Mascarene to La Galissonière, April 25, 1749, ibid., 365–67; Shirley to La Galissonière, May 9, 1749, in Shirley, *Correspondence,* 1:481; Shirley to La Galissonière, May 9, 1749, *Bax. MSS,* 11:465; Mascarene to Bedford, September 8, 1748, *NS Docs.,* 164.

7. Gilles Hocquart estimated in 1737 that there were 500 men of fighting age within the three major Mi'kmaw villages in the Miramischi and Ristigouche River valleys and on Chignecto. For Hocquart's estimation, see SLHQ, *Publies,* 10. By contrast, 1,000 are listed in Description de l'Acadie avec le nom des paraisses et le nombre des habitants, 1748, Parkman Papers, New France I: Acadia 1713–1767.

8. Vaughan, "Essay," *Gentleman's Magazine,* 1748, 29–30.

9. Gwyn, *Frigates and Foremasts,* 29.

10. Burke quoted in Salusbury, *Expeditions of Honor,* 15.
11. *Gentleman's Magazine,* 1749, 112–13.
12. For the "pleasant passage" quotation, see ibid., 571. See also ibid., 138–76, 235, 408; July 29, 1749, *CNF,* 3:437.
13. Edwards, "Militia of Nova Scotia," 65. By 1749, the British army had begun to refer to regiments by their numerical designator, although the practice of also listing them by their commander's name continued.
14. Prise de possession de Louisbourg par les Françoise, 1749, *CNF,* 3:430.
15. [John, 8th earl and 4th duke of] Bedford to [William Augustus, Duke of] Cumberland, October 11, 1748, *MANA,* 6–7.
16. Akins, "First Council," 17–30; *DCB,* s.v. "Salusbury, John."
17. Declaration, July 14, 1749, *A&NS,* 165.
18. Copy of Oath, July 14, 1749, ibid., 167.
19. Council Minutes, July 31, 1749, ibid., 169.
20. Council Minutes, August 1, 1749, ibid., 170.
21. Council Minutes, September 6, 1749, ibid., 172.
22. Ibid.
23. *DCB,* s.v. "Rous, John."
24. Shirley to La Galisonnière, May 9, 1749, *CNF,* 3:423; Rous to [Charles des Champs de] Boishébert, July 3, 1749, *CNF,* 3:428; Boishébert to Cornwallis, August 12, 1749, ibid., 3:450.
25. Campbell, *Road to Canada,* 26.
26. Salusbury, *Expeditions of Honor,* August 13, 1749, 59.
27. Ibid., August 18, 1749, 60.
28. Le Loutre au ministre, July 29, 1749, *RCCA, 1905,* appx. N, 283.
29. Le Loutre to ?, October 4, 1749, *CNF,* 457; Boishébert, *Memorial,* 13.
30. *DCB,* s.v. "Le Loutre, Jean Louis."
31. A Short Account of What Passed at Cape Breton from the Beginning of the Last War until the Taking of Louisbourg by the English in 1758, *CNF,* 3:466.
32. William Tutty to SPG, September 29, 1749, in Anon., "Letters," 97.
33. Bumsted, *Peoples of Canada,* 128.
34. July 29, 1749, *CNF,* 3:438; October 4, 1749, ibid., 3:460.
35. Salusbury, *Expeditions of Honor,* September 18, 1749, 65.
36. Ibid., August 23, 1749, 61.
37. The "Declaration de Guerre des Micmacs aux Anglois, 1749," as it was titled in *CCA,* 1:17–19, was not listed as such in the orginal; the title was added later by a compiler.
38. *DCB,* s.v. "Maillard, Pierre."
39. Cornwallis to Robert Napier [aide to the commander-in-chief, the duke of Cumberland], December 6, 1749, *MANA,* 8–9.
40. Mascarene had retired to Boston with the brevet rank of colonel; *DCB,* s.v. "Mascarene, Paul."
41. Cornwallis to BT, October 17, 1749, NSARM MSS, vol. 40, no. 9.
42. Piers, "Old Peninsular Blockhouses," 99.
43. *DRCEFNS,* 281.
44. Salusbury, *Expeditions of Honor,* September 30, 1749, 67.

45. Cornwallis to BT, October 17, 1749, NSARM MSS, vol. 40, no. 9.

46. *Gentleman's Magazine,* 1749, 574; Cornwallis to BT, October 17, 1749, NSARM MSS, vol. 40, no. 9.

47. Tutty to SPG, September 29, 1749, in Anon., "Letters," 101.

48. Salusbury, *Expeditions of Honor,* October 2, 1749, 68.

49. Ibid., October 22, 1749, 70.

50. Eaton, *Lt.-Col. Otho Hamilton,* 15; Salusbury, *Expeditions of Honor,* December 10, 1749, 74. For "strange that a party" quotation, see Cornwallis to BT, December 10, 1749, NSARM MSS, vol. 40, no. 15.

51. Cornwallis to BT, December 10, 1749, NSARM MSS, vol. 40, no. 15.

52. Cornwallis to BT, March 19, 1749/50, NSARM MSS, vol. 35, no. 11.

53. Salusbury, *Expeditions of Honor,* December 10, 21, and 25, 74–75.

54. Cornwallis to BT, March 19, 1749/50, NSARM MSS, vol. 35, no. 11.

55. Salusbury, *Expeditions of Honor,* January 6, 1750, 76.

56. Cornwallis to BT, March 19, 1749/50, NSARM MSS, vol. 35, no. 11.

57. Cornwallis to Cobb, January 13, 1749/50, in Webster, *Thomas Pichon,* 178–79.

58. Salusbury, *Expeditions of Honor,* February 9, 1750, 78.

59. Cornwallis to BT, March 19, 1749/50, NSARM MSS, vol. 35, no. 11.

60. Cornwallis to duke of Bedford, March 24, 1749/50, NSARM MSS, vol. 40, no. 21.

61. Ibid.; Salusbury, *Expeditions of Honor,* March 28, 1750, 80.

62. Cornwallis to duke of Bedford, March 24, 1749/50, NSARM MSS, vol. 40, no. 21.

63. Cornwallis to BT, March 19, 1749/50, NSARM MSS, vol. 35, no. 11.

64. Salusbury, *Expeditions of Honor,* April 9, 1750, 83.

65. Ibid., April 30, 1750, 86.

66. *DCB,* s.v. "Rous, John."

67. www.immigrantships.net/1700/merryjacks17490600.html; Anon., "Readers' Questions," 45.

68. Salusbury, *Expeditions of Honor,* April 19, 1750, 88; La Corne à [Charles] Des Herbiers [de La Ralière], 1750, *CNF,* 3:499.

69. Salusbury, *Expeditions of Honor,* April 22, 1750, 90.

70. Ibid., 91.

71. Ibid., May 13, 1750, 96.

72. *DCB,* s.v. "Lawrence, Charles."

73. Cornwallis to Bedford, August 19, 1750, *RCA, 1894,* 165.

74. For the questions over who murdered Edward How, see Plank, "Two Majors Cope," 21; *DCB,* s.v. "Bâtard, Étienne."

75. *Boston Weekly News Letter,* October 4, 1750; emphasis in original. Although Massachusetts currency was hopelessly inflated against sterling in 1750, £500 of Massachusetts currency for scalping an Indian was impressive, particularly when compared to the daily wage of 17.5 pence sterling that an unskilled farm laborer would earn for his labors; see Main, "Gender, Work, and Wages," 48.

76. Journal de ce qui s'est passé à Chinectou et autre parties des frontières de l'Acadie depuis le 15 septembre 1750 jusqu'au 28 juillet 1751, *RCCA, 1905,* appx. N, 325; M. Prevost au ministre, October 15, 1750, *CNF,* 3:497.

77. Cornwallis to duke of Bedford, June 24, 1751, NSARM MSS, vol. 40, no. 32.

78. For Mi'kmaq hunting practices, see Clark, *Acadia,* 59–63.

79. La Corne à Des Herbiers, 1750, *CNF,* 3:501. Le Loutre estimated that there were 1,114; see [Charles Le Moyne de Longueuil, Baron] de Lonqueuil au ministre, April 26, 1752, *CNF,* 3:508–509.

80. Halifax to BT, November 8, 1750, *DRCEFNS,* 320.

81. In February, based on a report from Cobb, the British learned that the Anglo-American garrison at Fort Lawrence was in good health but many of the Acadians across the river were ill and all were running low on provisions; Salusbury, *Expeditions of Honor,* 104.

82. Wilson, *Genuine Narrativet,* 15; Salusbury, *Expeditions of Honor,* May 13, 1751, 106, 109, 111; Tutty to SPG, July 5, 1751, in Anon., "Letters," 122; "Ransom," *DRCEFNS,* 346.

83. Salusbury, *Expeditions of Honor,* May 29, 1751, 112.

84. Milner, "Records of Chignecto," 12; Cornwallis to Bedford, June 24, 1751, NSARM MSS, vol. 40, no. 32.

85. PDBP, February 27, 1750/51, 451–52; Ibid., March 7, 1749/50, 410–11.

86. Cornwallis to BT, November 18, 1751, NSARM MSS, vol. 35, no. 63; Cornwallis to BT, October 17, 1749, NSARM MSS, vol. 40, no. 9.

87. Gorham to Erasmus James Philipps, January 17, 1746/47, Gorham Papers. Gorham's heirs petitioned the treasury as late as 1759 for the money they thought they were due; see Memorial, March 21, 1759, *RCA, 1894,* 220.

88. Mascarene to Lutterell, August 24, 1751, *CNF,* 3:504.

89. Hopson to Monckton, August 17, 1752, in PAC, *Northcliffe,* 7.

90. Salusbury, *Expeditions,* October 24, 1752, 128. For the text of the 1752 treaty, see Davis, *Peoples of the Maritimes,* 67–69.

91. *DCB,* s.v. "Cope, Jean-Baptiste."

92. William Cotterell to Monckton, April 8, 1753, in PAC, *Northcliffe,* 11.

93. Griffiths, *From Migrant to Acadian,* 411.

94. Ibid., 412.

95. Ibid., 413.

96. Salusbury, *Expeditions of Honor,* October 24, 1752, 128.

97. Desbrisay, *History,* 16.

98. June 5, June 8, and June 9, 1753, Lawrence, "Journal and Letters," 1–6.

99. Lawrence to Monckton, December 18, 1753, in PAC, *Northcliffe,* 19.

100. MacDonald, "Memoir Lieut.-Governor Michael Francklin." Francklin spent three months as a captive. He used his captivity to improve his Mi'kmawi'simk.

101. "Acquisition and Trade of Halifax in 1755," from *Gentleman's Magazine,* 1755, in *DRCEFNS,* 453; emphasis in original.

102. Ibid.

103. Duquesne to Le Loutre, *NS Docs.,* 239–40.

104. Duquesne au ministre, October 10, 1754, *CNF,* 3:516–17.

105. For the British report of the negotiations, see Commissioners for Adjusting the Boundaries of Acadia, or Nova Scotia, *The Memorials of the English and French Commissioners Concerning the Limits of Nova Scotia or Acadia, &c.*

106. Le Loutre to Lawrence, August 26, 1754, Parkman Papers, New France I: Acadia 1713–1767.

107. Lawrence to Hussey, 1754, *NS Docs.*, 237.

108. *DCB*, s.v. "Le Loutre, Jean-Louis"; Pichon to George Scott, September 17, October 14, and November 2, 1754, in Webster, *Thomas Pichon*, 39, 44, 53.

109. Shirley to Thomas Robinson, May 23, 1754, *NS Docs.*, 382.

110. Lawrence to Halifax, August 23, 1754, *MANA*, 27–29.

111. Lawrence to Shirley, November 5, 1754, *NS Docs.*, 376–77; Loudon Papers, 477.

112. I have based my narrative of the Fort Beauséjour operations on Winslow, "Siege of Beauséjour," 113–246, and Thomas, *Journals of Beauséjour*, 46–49.

113. Griffiths observes, "By the middle of the twentieth century, more than two hundred articles, books, and pamphlets had been published on the subject and since then a great many more have seen the light of day"; Griffiths, *From Migrant to Acadian*, 431.

114. Plank, *Unsettled Conquest*, 149. Compared to the vast populations of Indians who lost their homes all along the Eastern Seaboard and the Trans-appalachian West, 6,500 is a relatively small number. Exact figures for the number of Acadians deported in 1755 and the years following are elusive. I have used Brasseaux's data from *"Scattered to the Wind,"* 8.

115. For Griffiths's even-handed estimate of Charles Lawrence's culpability, see *From Migrant to Acadian*, 419–30. Compare that with Faragher's unflattering description of Lawrence in *Great and Noble Scheme*, 280–81 and 294.

116. Some historians and Acadian nationalists have gone as far as to describe the Acadian proscription as akin to the Holocaust. A more apt comparison, however, resides in the Ottoman removal of the Armenians in 1915. The Young Turks, the coterie of military leaders who ruled the Ottoman Empire after the Revolution of 1908, espoused a nationalistic ideology that sought to cleanse Turkey of non-Turkish peoples and conquer a new Pan-Turanian empire. Their aim was not necessarily the elimination of the Armenian population but its removal. In a similar vein, the Acadian proscription focused on removal rather than extermination. Of course, in many cases, in both the Acadian and the Armenian experience, removal became inseparable from death.

117. Gorham to Mascarene, 1749, Gorham Papers.

118. Winslow to Lawrence, August 30, 1755, *RCCA, 1905*, appx. B, 17.

119. Winslow to Monckton, September 19, 1755, in PAC, *Northcliffe*, 53.

120. Knowles quoted in Arsenault, *History of the Acadians*, 106.

121. August 12, 1755, Thomas, "Thomas's Diary," 130. This John Thomas was a surgeon's mate in Winslow's battalion. The other John Thomas became a regimental commander later in the war. John Thomas the surgeon's mate died of smallpox while serving with the American army outside Quebec city in 1776.

122. Opinion of Chief Justice Belcher, July 28, 1755, *RCA, 1894*, 206.

123. Phips to Monckton, August 20, 1755, *DRCEFNS*, 52.

124. Griffiths, *From Migrant to Acadian,* 414–15.

125. Morris's Remarks Concerning the Removal of the French Inhabitants, Summer 1755, *CCA,* 1:130–37; *DCB,* s.v. "Morris, Charles."

CHAPTER 6. THE GUERRILLA WAR, 1755–1760

1. www.dtic.mil/doctrine/jel/doddict. The standard on guerrilla warfare remains Aspery's *War in the Shadows.* Ellis (in *Short History of Guerrilla Warfare,* 204–205) writes that fighting between the Austrian *Grenz* (border troops) and the French army in Bohemia during the War of the Austrian Succession (1744–48), along with the American campaign against the British in South Carolina in 1780–81 during the American War of Independence, are the "notable guerrilla wars" of the eighteenth century.

2. Leading thinkers and practitioners of counterinsurgency included the Frenchman Roger Trinquier, Sir Robert Thompson of Great Britain, and John Paul Vann of the United States.

3. The precept that guerrillas must depend on conventional forces for final victory manifested during the Second Indochina War in the 1968 Tet, 1972 Eastertide, and 1975 offensives by the North Vietnamese Army and Viet Cong.

4. John Rous to Monckton, June 25, 1755, *DRCEFNS,* 33.

5. July 1, 1755, Thomas, "Thomas's Diary," 127; Webster, *Abbé Le Loutre,* 49.

6. July 30, 1755, Willard, "Journal," 30–31; July 25, 1755, Thomas, "Thomas's Diary," 129.

7. Orders to Monckton, August 13, 1755, Parkman Papers, PRO 1755, 1756.

8. August 28, 1755, Thomas, "Thomas's Diary," 131.

9. Webster, *Boishébert,* 9.

10. September 1, 1755, "Thomas's Diary," 131; Jedediah Preble to John Winslow, September 5, 1755, in Winslow, "Journal"; Boishébert, *Memorial,* 18; Webster, *Boishébert,* 9.

11. Winslow to Halifax, June 27, 1755, in Winslow, "Siege of Beauséjour," 179. "It is unlikely" quotation from Anderson, *People's Army,* 144.

12. Murray to Winslow, September 8, 1755, in Winslow, "Journal," 108.

13. Webster, *Boishébert,* 10.

14. For example, on March 10, 1755, New Hampshire's governor ordered Robert Rogers to desist from recruiting rangers because of the necessity of raising troops for the provincial regiments; Winslow, "Journal," 119.

15. Anderson, *Crucible of War,* 88.

16. List of Men from Boston in Provincial Service, MHS Miscellaneous MSS.

17. October 23, 1755, Thomas, "Thomas's Diary," 134.

18. October 30, 1755, ibid., 135.

19. Light infantry companies, units of men trained as skirmishers and scouts who often conducted petite guerre, came into vogue in the European armies in the middle of the eighteenth century; see Grenier, *First Way of War,* chap 3.

20. November 13–17, 1755, Thomas, "Thomas's Diary," 136.

21. House of Representatives Proclamation, October 31, 1755, *NS Docs.*, 420.

22. Shirley to Fox, June 14, 1756, Parkman Papers, PRO 1755, 1756.

23. As late as 1760, Colonel John Thomas of the Massachusetts provincials had to devote nearly 25 percent of his regiment to garrison duty at Lunenburg; Orderly Book of John Thomas's Regiment of Massachusetts Provincials, Misc. MSS, MHS.

24. *DCB*, s.v. "Scott, George."

25. Boishébert, *Memorial*, 18.

26. The letter in *CNF*, 4:27, Montcalm au ministre, June 12, 1756, lists 1,000 refugees, while SLHQ, *Publies*, 82, lists 3,500. The smaller number seems more likely.

27. Montcalm au ministre, November 1, 1756, *CNF*, 4:81. Montcalm was technically subordinate to Governor-General Vaudreuil but responsible for army discipline, administration, and field operations.

28. *Boston Gazette*, March 15, 1756.

29. L'abbé Le Guerne à M. Prevost, March 10, 1756, Parkman Papers, New France I: Acadia 1713–1767; Lettre de Monsieur Cognard sur les affaires de Canada, n.d., *CNF*, 4:34; Clark, *Acadia*, 63.

30. Webster, *Boishébert*, 11.

31. L'abbé Le Guerne à M. Prevost, March 10, 1756, Parkman Papers, New France I: Acadia 1713–1767.

32. Speakman first served as a provincial in John Winslow's battalion. He later became a company commander in Rogers's rangers.

33. Shirley to [Major General James] Abercromby, June 27, 1756, Parkman Papers, PRO 1755, 1756.

34. L'abbé Le Guerne à M. Prevost, March 10, 1756, Parkman Papers, New France I: Acadia 1713–1767; Calnek, *History of the County*, 141; August 30, 1757, Knox, *Historical Journal*, 1:62–63; Boishébert, *Memorial*, 19.

35. Desbrisay, *History*, 30–31.

36. *DCB*, s.v. "Deschamps de Boishébert et de Raffetot, Charles."

37. Anderson, *Crucible of War*, 179–80.

38. Marble, *Surgeons, Smallpox*, 55.

39. Vice Admiral Francis Holburne to [Robert D'Arcy, 4th earl of] Holdernesse, August 4, and July 1, 1757, *MANA*, 388–89.

40. Loudoun to Cumberland, August 6, 1757, *MANA*, 393.

41. "Nothing seemingly prevented" quotation from Anderson, *Crucible of War*, 200.

42. Marble, *Surgeons, Smallpox*, 56.

43. Most of the companies of Rogers's rangers had accompanied Loudoun to Halifax. Loudoun used them primarily as foragers and as military police to apprehend deserters; Rogers, *Journals*, 39–40.

44. Witherspoon, "Journal," 31; July 29, 1757, and August 6, 1757, in Knox, *Historical Journal*, 1:39, 43.

45. Boishébert, *Memorial*, 20.

46. September 6–10, Knox, *Historical Journal*, 1:66–67.

47. December 12, 1758, ibid., 1:287.
48. September 8, 1757, ibid., 1:71.
49. September 21–22, 1757, ibid., 1:73–74.
50. October 10, 1757, ibid., 1:79.
51. October 13, 1757, ibid., 1:85; Webster, *Boishébert,* 12; October 23 and 28, 1757, Knox, *Historical Journal,* 1:100, 102.
52. October 28–November 13, 1757, ibid., 1:102–107.
53. December 6, 1757, ibid., 1:116–27; Letter of occurrences, ibid., 1:199–203.
54. January 17 and February 1, 1758, ibid., 1:133–34. Emphasis in original.
55. March 20, 1758, ibid., 1:143.
56. October 17, 1757, ibid., 1:65.
57. March 20 and April 1, 1758, ibid., 1:143, 145–48.
58. SLHQ, *Publies,* 98; Monckton to ?, March 22, 1758, Parkman Papers, PRO 1756–1758.
59. April 7, 1758, Knox, *Historical Journal,* 1:155–56.
60. May 12, 1758, ibid., 1:170.
61. Ibid.
62. Anderson, *Crucible of War,* 227.
63. March 30, 1738, Knox, *Historical Journal,* 1:145.
64. April 29, 1758, ibid., 1:162.
65. May 12, 1758, ibid., 1:174.
66. Monckton to Samuel Waldo, July 23, 1758, PAC, *Northcliffe,* 60.
67. *DCB,* s.v. "Deschamps de Boishébert et de Raffetot, Charles."
68. July 15, 1758, Amherst, *Journal,* 67.
69. Maillard quoted in Webster, *Boishébert,* 15.
70. June 9 and July 20, 1758, Witherspoon, "Journal," 33–34.
71. *DCB,* s.v. "Maillard, Pierre."
72. Piers, "Old Peninsular Blockhouses," 115.
73. Monckton to Boscawan, July 21, 1758, *DRCEFNS,* 55.
74. *DCB,* s.v. "Graham, Huge"; Milner, "Records of Chignecto," 32. For "one of the most" quotation, see Brown, "Papers Relating," 141.
75. Monckton to James Abercrombie, October 15, 1758, PAC, *Northcliffe,* 63.
76. September 23 and 28, 1758, Knox, *Historical Journal,* 1:263, 268; Lawrence to James Wolfe, June 30, 1759, PAC, *Northcliffe,* 56; Monckton to Abercromby, November 12, 1758, PAC, *Northcliffe,* 65; October 27, 1758, Knox, *Historical Journal,* 1:271.
77. Amherst to Monckton, August 27, 1758, PAC, *Northcliffe,* 62; Return of Forces under the Command of Monckton at River St. John, September 24, 1758, ibid., 62.
78. Monckton to Abercrombie, November 12, 1758, Report of the Proceedings of the Troops on the Expedition up St. John River in the Bay of Fundy under the Command of Col. Monckton, ibid., 102–107.
79. Monckton to Abercrombie, November 12, 1758, ibid., 64.
80. May 9 and 11, 1759, "Journal of the Voyage of His Excell'y Thos. Pownall, Esq, Capn General and Governor in Chief and Over His Majesty's

Province of the Massachusetts Bay, to Penobscot, and of His Proceedings in Establishing Possession of His Majesty's Right There in Behalf of Said Province," Pownall Papers, MHS.

81. Report of the Tour to Petitcoudiak River, November 19, 1758, PAC, *Northcliffe,* 99. For Monckton to Abercrombie letter, see ibid., 101.

82. Monckton to Pownall, November 20, 1758, ibid., 67.

83. September 23, 1758, Knox, *Historical Journal,* 1:263; Boishébert, *Memorial,* 22; *DCB,* s.v. "Rollo, Andrew." www.regiments.org, which provides quick access to the histories of the various regiments of the British army, contains no information on the operations of the regiments on the Gaspé Peninsula in late summer 1758. Understandably, most regular military units do not receive battle streamers for burning fields and houses.

84. Amherst to Monckton, December 25, 1758, PAC, *Northcliffe,* 113.

85. Amherst to Monckton, November 9, 1758, ibid.

86. January 20 and 21, 1759, Knox, *Historical Journal,* 1:289, 290.

87. Accounts of Events along St. John River, April 5, 1759, ibid., 1:296–97.

88. Wolfe to Amherst, June 19, 1759, Parkman Papers, PRO 1759, 1760.

89. General Wolfe's Scheme for Improving the Colony, PAC, *Northcliffe,* 110.

90. Wolfe to Monckton, August 6, 1759, ibid., 59.

91. Elisha Jackson Journal and Account Book, Misc. MSS, MHS; Orderly Book of Joseph Frye's Regiment, Misc. MSS, MHS; May 5, 1759, Knox, *Historical Journal,* 1:306.

92. Orderly Book of Jotham Gay's Company, Misc. MSS, MHS; Orderly Book of John Thomas's Regiment, Misc. MSS, MHS.

93. Boishébert, *Memorial,* 22.

94. Orderly Book of Joseph Frye's Regiment, Misc. MSS, MHS; Orderly Book of Jotham Gay's Company, Misc. MSS, MHS.

95. ? to John Thomas, September 7, 1759, Thomas Papers, MHS; Elisha Jackson Journal and Account Book, Misc. MSS, MHS.

96. *DCB,* s.v. "Manach, Jean."

97. Orderly Book of Joseph Frye's Regiment, Misc. MSS, MHS.

98. Frye to the Governor of Nova Scotia, March 7, 1760, MHS *Collections,* 1st ser., 10 (1809): 115.

99. For the Providentialism—"the belief that God guides all events, intervening in the natural world and in human life to make his will manifest to men"—of the Yankee provincials during the Seven Years' War, see Anderson, *People's Army,* 196, chap. 7.

100. Parkman Papers, PRO 1759, 1760.

101. Frye quoted in Steele, *Betrayals,* 134.

EPILOGUE: NOVA SCOTIA, 1760–1768

1. Traditionally, historians have seen the Anglo-American victory in Nova Scotia as decisive. An alternative to that argument can be found in Reid's "*Pax Britannica* or *Pax Indigena*?" Reid believes that the Indians stood as a potent force in Nova Scotia until they were overwhelmed by the Loyalist influx following the American War of Independence. I remain convinced that

it was a near-complete Anglo-American victory and that Anglo-Americans indeed had quashed Indian resistance.

2. Patterson suggests that it was land hunger that compelled the Yankees to emigrate to Nova Scotia; Patterson, "In Search of," 140.

3. Lawrence, "Proclamation."

4. The Planter era has come under great scrutiny by scholars, led by Margaret Conrad, since the late 1980s. Generally, Canadians see the Planter communities as successes; see Conrad, *They Planted Well, Making Adjustments,* and *Intimate Relations*; and Conrad and Moody, *Planter Links.* Jaffee, in his *People of the Wachusett,* examines Nova Scotia only superficially but nonetheless argues that the Planter communities were unsuccessful in replicating New England life in the Maritimes. Reid's "*Pax Britannica* or *Pax Indigena*?" is the first work to examine the interactions of the Planters and the Indians.

5. Anon., "General Return," 65; Fergusson, "Early Liverpool," 4; Alexander Grant to Ezra Stiles, May 1760, MHS *Collections,* 1st ser., 10 (1809): 79.

6. Fergusson, "Boundaries of Nova Scotia."

7. Elisha Jackson Journal and Account Book, 1759–1774, Misc. MSS, MHS; *DCB,* s.v. "Danks, Benoni"; Anon., "General Return," 65–70; *DCB,* s.v. "Glasier, Beamsley Perkins"; Glazier to John Fenton, March 1, 1765, St. John River Society Papers, MHS.

8. All the population figures for the Planter era are estimates. See Reid, "*Pax Britannica* or *Pax Indigena*?" 678, for Julian Gwyn's term "econocide"; Anon., "Estimate of the Inhabitants," 81–82. The 1755 population figure of 18,000 is Gwyn's, cited in Reid, "*Pax Britannica* or *Pax Indigena*?" 687. See also Marble, *Surgeons, Smallpox,* 261; Anon., "General Return," 59.

9. www.statcan.ca/english/freepub/98-187-XIE/acadians.htm#part2.

10. www.rism.org/isg/dlp/bc/background/1760.htm.

11. www.rism.org/isg/dlp/bc/background/1762.htm.

12. Upton, "Indians and Islanders," 23–24.

13. www.rism.org/isg/dlp/bc/background/1763.htm.

14. Charles Morris and Henry Newton to [Joshua] Mauger, August 5, 1763, *RCA, 1894,* 244. By 1763, Mauger had become Nova Scotia's agent to Parliament. He used his position to win large land grants in New Brunswick. Settlers named Maugerville in his honor; *DCB,* s.v. "Mauger, Joshua."

15. Piers, "Old Peninsular Blockhouses," 116; *DCB,* s.v. "Gorham, Joseph."

16. Anon., "Estimate of the Inhabitants," 82.

17. Anon., "General Return," 45, 56–57.

18. Bromley, "Address Delivered," 4.

19. For the Acadians who remained in Nova Scotia, see Brasseaux, "*Scattered to the Wind,*" 28–34.

20. Anderson, *Crucible of War,* 395; Belcher to BT, April 14, 1761, *RCA, 1894,* 226.

21. Belcher to [Algernon Seymor, earl of] Egermont, January 9, 1761, *RCA, 1894,* 229.

22. Quoted in Reid, "*Pax Britannica* or *Pax Indigena*?" 683.

23. Belcher to BT, July 2 and July 9, 1762, *RCA, 1894,* 233; Belcher to Egermont, October 20, 1762, ibid., 236; Lowe, "Massachusetts and the Acadians," 221.

24. Article VI, Treaty of Paris, *GB:FP,* 119.

25. BT to the King, June 19, 1764, *RCA, 1894,* 255; Order in Council, July 11, 1764, ibid., 256.

26. Brasseaux, *"Scattered to the Wind,"* 61–69, and *Founding of New Acadia.*

27. www.statcan.ca/english/freepub/98-187-XIE/acadians.htm#part1.

28. Belcher to BT, April 9, 1761, *RCA, 1894,* 226.

29. *DCB,* s.v. "Manach, Jean."

30. Ibid., s.v. "Maillard, Pierre."

31. Francklin to Hillsborough, July 20, 1768, *RCA, 1894,* 288.

32. Hillsborough to Campbell, October 12, 1768, ibid., 291.

33. For the growing tension between Yankees and the imperial officials in late-1760s Massachusetts, see Nicholson, *"Infamous Govener."* For the different post-1760 experiences with the empire between New England and Nova Scotia, see Mancke, *Fault Lines of Empire.*

34. Campbell to [William Wildman Shute, 2nd viscount] Barrington, September 22, 1768, *RCA, 1894,* 290.

35. Through 1776, Quebec, another candidate to become the fourteenth colony, remained a thoroughly "French" province. French-Canadians, the majority in Quebec, "continued to live under the power of a nation [Great Britain] whose religion, customs, language, and laws were very different from their own"; see Calloway, *Scratch of a Pen,* 122.

Bibliography

MANUSCRIPT COLLECTIONS

Gorham, John. Papers. William L. Clements Library, Ann Arbor, Michigan.

Great Britain, Public Record Office. Colonial Office Papers 217, Nova Scotia and Cape Breton, Original Correspondence. National Archives of Canada, Ottawa.

——. Colonial Office Papers 218, Nova Scotia and Cape Breton, Entry Books. National Archives of Canada, Ottawa.

——. Colonial Office Papers 220, Nova Scotia and Cape Breton, Sessional Papers. National Archives of Canada, Ottawa.

Loudoun, 4th earl of [John Campbell]. Papers. Henry E. Huntington Library, San Marino, California.

Miscellaneous Manuscripts. Massachusetts Historical Society, Boston.

Nova Scotia Papers. Nova Scotia Archives and Records Management, Halifax.

Parkman, Francis. Papers. Massachusetts Historical Society, Boston.

Pownall, Thomas. Papers. Massachusetts Historical Society, Boston.

Sable Island Papers. Massachusetts Historical Society, Boston.

St. John River Society. Papers. Massachusetts Historical Society, Boston.

Thomas, John. Papers. Massachusetts Historical Society, Boston.

PUBLISHED PRIMARY SOURCES

Aikens, Thomas B., ed. *Acadia and Nova Scotia: Documents Relating to the Acadian French and the First British Colonization of the Province, 1714–1758.* 1869. Reprint, Cottonport, La.: Polyanthos, 1972.

——. *Selections from the Public Documents of the Province of Nova Scotia.* Halifax: Charles Annand, 1869.

Amherst, Jeffery. *The Journal of Jeffery Amherst: Recording the Military Career of General Amherst in America from 1758 to 1763.* Ed. John C. Webster. Toronto: Ryerson Press, 1931.

Anon. "An Account of Nova Scotia in 1743." [Nova Scotia Historical Society] *Collections* 1 (1878).

——. "An Estimate of the Inhabitants of Nova Scotia, A.D. 1764." [Massachusetts Historical Society] *Collections,* 1st ser., 10 (1810).

——. "General Return of the Several Townships in the Province of Nova Scotia on the First Day of January, 1767, A." [Nova Scotia Historical Society] *Collections* 8 (1889–91).

——. "Letters and Other Papers Relating to the Early History of the Church of England in Nova Scotia." [Nova Scotia Historical Society] *Collections* 8 (1889–91).

Baxter, James Phinney, ed. *Documentary History of the State of Maine, Vols. 9–12, Containing the Baxter Manuscripts.* Collections of the Maine Historical Society, Second Series. Portland, Me.: LeFavor-Tower Company, 1907–1908.

Board of Historical Publications, comp. *Documents Relating to Currency, Exchange and Finance in Nova Scotia, with Prefatory Documents, 1675–1758.* Ottawa: J. O. Patenaude, 1933.

Boishébert, Charles des Champs de. *Memorial on Behalf of the Sieur de Boishébert, Captain, Chevalier de Saint-Louis, Former Commandant in Acadia.* Trans. Louise Manny and ed. John Clarence Webster. Historic Studies no. 4 of the New Brunswick Museum. Sackville: Tribune Press for the New Brunswick Museum, 1942.

Bromley, Walter. "An Address Delivered at the Free-Mason's Hall, Halifax, August 3, 1813, on the Deplorable State of the Indians." Halifax: Anthony Holland, 1813.

Brymner, Douglas, ed. *Report on Canadian Archives, 1894: Calendar of Papers Relating to Nova Scotia.* Ottawa: S. E. Dawson for the Public Archives of Canada, 1895.

Casgrain, Abbé Henri-Raymond, ed. *Collection de documents inédits sur le Canada et l'Amérique: Documents inédits publiés par le Canada Français.* 3 vols. Quebec: L.-J. Demurs and Frère, 1888–90.

Commissioners for Adjusting the Boundaries of Acadia, or Nova Scotia. *The Memorials of the English and French Commissioners Concerning the Limits of Nova Scotia or Acadia, &c.* London: n.p., 1755.

Fergusson, Charles Bruce, ed. *Nova Scotia Archives IV: Minutes of His Majesty's Council at Annapolis Royal, 1736–1749.* Halifax: Public Archives of Nova Scotia, 1967.

Frye, Joseph. "Letter to the Governor of Nova Scotia, March 7, 1760." [Massachusetts Historical Society] *Collections,* 1st ser., 10 (1809).

Gorham, John. "Col. John Gorham's 'Wast Book' and the Gorham Family." *New York Genealogical and Biographical Record* 28 (1897).

Grant, Alexander. "Letter to Ezra Stiles, May 1760." [Massachusetts Historical Society] *Collections,* 1st ser., 10 (1810).

Gyles, John. *The Ordeal of John Gyles: Being an Account of his Odd Adventures, Strange Deliverances &c. as a Slave of the Maliseets.* Ed. Stuart Trueman. Toronto: McClelland and Stewart, 1966.

Johnson, William. *The Papers of Sir William Johnson.* Ed. James Sullivan et al. 14 vols. Albany: University of the State of New York, 1921–65.

Knox, John. *An Historical Journal of the Campaigns in North America, for the Years 1757, 1758, 1759, and 1760.* Ed. Arthur G. Doughty. 3 vols. 1769. Reprinted as Publications of the Champlain Society nos. 8, 9, 10. Toronto, 1914.

Lawrence, Charles. "Journal and Letters of Colonel Charles Lawrence." *Bulletin of the Public Archives of Nova Scotia* 10 (1953).

——. "A Proclamation on Settling Vacated Lands." January 11, 1759, no. 41070. *Early American Imprints, Series 1, Evans (1639–1800).* Worcester, Mass.: American Antiquarian Society, 2002.

Massachusetts. *Laws and Orders of Massachusetts Bay Colony.* 736 microfiches. Buffalo: W. S. Hein, 1987.

O'Callaghan, E. B., and Berthold Fernow, eds. *Documents Relative to the Colonial History of the State of New York.* 15 vols. Albany, N.Y.: Weed, Parsons and Company, 1853–87.

Pargellis, Stanley, ed. *Military Affairs in North America, 1748–1765: Selected Documents from the Cumberland Papers in Windsor Castle.* New York: D. Appleton-Century, 1936.

Pothier, Bernard, ed. *Course à L'Accadie: Journal de campagne de François De Pont Duvivier en 1744.* Moncton, N.B.: Éditions d'Acadie, 1982.

Preble, Jedediah. "Letter to John Winslow, September 5, 1755." *New England Historical and Genealogical Register* 22 (1868).

Public Archives of Canada, comp. *The Northcliffe Collection: Presented to the Government of Canada by Sir Leicester Harmsworth, as a Memorial to His Brother the Right Honourable Alfred Williams Harmsworth, viscount of Northcliffe.* Ottawa: F. A. Acland, 1926.

Québec Province, ed. *Collection des manuscrits contenants lettres, mémoires, et autres documents historiques relatifs à la Nouvelle-France recueilles aux archives de la province de Québec, ou copiés à l'étranger.* 4 vols. Quebec: A. Côté, 1883–85.

Rogers, Robert. *Journals of Major Robert Rogers.* 1765. Reprint, New York: Corinth Books, 1961.

Sainsbury, W. Noel, et al., eds. *Calendar of State Papers, Colonial Series, American and West Indies.* 44 vols. to date. London: Longman Green, Longman and Roberts, 1860–.

Salusbury, John. *Expeditions of Honor: The Journal of John Salusbury in Halifax, Nova Scotia, 1749–1753.* Ed. Ronald Rompkey. Newark: University of Delaware Press, 1982.

Savage, Thomas. *Expedition against Québec, 1690.* 1691. Reprint, [Massachusetts Historical Society] *Collections,* 2d ser., 3. (1845).

Shirley, William. *The Correspondence of William Shirley.* Ed. Charles Henry Lincoln. 2 vols. New York: Macmillan, 1912.

Société Littéraire et Historique de Québec. *Publies de la Société Littéraire et Historique de Québec.* Quebec: T. Cary et Cie., 1838, and William Cowan et Fils, 1840.

Stock, Leo Francis, ed. *Proceedings and Debates of the British Parliaments Respecting North America,* vol. 5, *1739–1754.* Washington, D.C.: Carnegie Institution, 1941.

Thomas, John. *The Journals of Beauséjour: Diary of John Thomas, Journal of Louis Courville.* Ed. John C. Webster. Halifax: Public Archives of Nova Scotia, 1937.

Thomas, John. "Thomas's Diary of the Expedition of 1755 against the Acadians." [Nova Scotia Historical Society] *Collections* 1 (1878).

Thwaites, Reuben Gold, ed. *The Jesuit Relations and Allied Documents: Travels and Explorations of the Jesuit Missionaries in New France, 1610–1791.* 73 vols. Cleveland: Burrows Bros., 1896–1901.

Vaughan, William. "Essay on the Importance of Nova Scotia." *Gentleman's Magazine* (1748).

Webster, John C., ed. *The Career of the Abbé Le Loutre in Nova Scotia: With a Translation of His Autobiography.* Shediac, N.B.: privately printed, 1933.

Wiener, Joel H., ed. *Great Britain: Foreign Policy and the Span of Empire, 1689–1971, A Documentary History,* vol. 1. New York: Chelsea House, 1972.

Willard, Abijah. "Journal of Abijah Willard, 1755." John C. Webster's private reprinting of the *Collections of the New Brunswick Historical Society* 13, 1930.

Wilson, John. *A Genuine Narrative of the Transactions in Nova Scotia since the Settlement, June 1749 till August the 5th 1751.* London: A. Henderson, 1751.

Winslow, John. "Journal of Colonel John Winslow." [Nova Scotia Historical Society] *Collections* 3 (1882–83).

——. "Journal of Colonel John Winslow of the Provincial Troops, While Engaged in the Siege of Beauséjour." [Nova Scotia Historical Society] *Collections* 4 (1884).

Witherspoon, John. "Journal of John Witherspoon." [Nova Scotia Historical Society] *Collections* 2 (1879–80).

SECONDARY SOURCES

Adelman, Jeremy, and Stephen Aron. "From Borderlands to Borders: Empires, Nation-States, and the Peoples in between in North American History." *American Historical Review* 104 (1999): 814–41.

Akins, Thomas B. "The First Council." [Nova Scotia Historical Society] *Collections* 2 (1881).

Allison, David. *History of Nova Scotia.* Halifax: Bowen, 1916.

Anderson, Fred. *Crucible of War: The Seven Years' War and the Fate of Empire in British North America, 1754–1766.* New York: Alfred A. Knopf, 2000.

——. *A People's Army: Massachusetts Soldiers and Society in the Seven Years' War.* Chapel Hill: University of North Carolina Press for the Institute of Early American History and Culture, 1984.

——, and Andrew Cayton. *The Dominion of War: Empire and Liberty in North America, 1500–2000.* New York: Viking, 2005.

Anon. "Readers' Questions." *Journal of the Society of Army Historical Research* 32 (1954): 45.

Arsenault, Bona. *History of the Acadians.* Ottawa: Leméac, 1978.

Aspery, Robert. *War in the Shadows: The Guerrilla in History.* 2nd ed. New York: William Morrow, 1994.

Baker, Emerson W., and John G. Reid. "Amerindian Power in the Early Modern Northeast: A Reappraisal." *William and Mary Quarterly* 61 (2004): 77–106.

Balcom, B. A. (Sandy). "The Mi'kmaq and the First Siege of Louisbourg, 1745." Paper presented at the 2003 Spring Heritage Conference, Amherst, N.S.

Balen, Malcolm. *The Secret History of the South Sea Bubble: The World's First Great Financial Scandal.* London: Fourth Estate, 2004.

Bartlett, Thomas. "'This Famous Island Set in a Virginian Sea.'" In Louis, *Oxford History of the British Empire,* vol. 2.

Basque, Maurice. "Family and Political Culture in Pre-conquest Acadia." In Reid, *"Conquest" of Acadia.*

——. "The Third Acadia: Political Adaptation and Societal Change." In Reid, *"Conquest" of Acadia.*

Bates, John. "John Gorham, 1709–1751: An Outline of His Activities in Nova Scotia, 1744–1751." [Nova Scotia Historical Society] *Collections* 30 (1954).

Black, Jeremy. *British Foreign Policy in the Age of Walpole.* Edinburgh: John Doland, 1985.

Brasseaux, Carl A. *The Founding of New Acadia: The Beginnings of Acadian Life in Louisiana, 1765–1803.* Baton Rouge: Louisiana State University Press, 1987.

——. *"Scattered to the Wind": Dispersal and Wanderings of the Acadians, 1755–1809.* Lafayette: Center for Louisiana Studies, 1991.

Brebner, John B. *New England's Outpost: Acadia before the Conquest of Canada.* New York: Columbia University Press, 1927.

Brewer, John. *The Sinews of Power: War, Money and the English State, 1688–1783.* Cambridge, Mass.: Harvard University Press, 1988.

Brown, Andrew. "Papers Relating to the Acadian French." [Nova Scotia Historical Society] *Collections* 2 (1881).

Browning, Reed. *The War of the Austrian Succession.* New York: St. Martin's Press, 1993.

Bumsted, J. M. *The Peoples of Canada: A Pre-Confederation History.* New York: Oxford University Press, 1992.

Calloway, Colin G. *The Scratch of a Pen: 1763 and the Transformation of North America.* New York: Oxford University Press, 2006.

Calnek, W. A., ed. *History of the County of Annapolis, Including Port Royal and Acadia,* by A. W. Savary. Toronto: William Briggs, 1897.

Campbell, Gary. *The Road to Canada: The Grand Communications Route from Saint John to Quebec.* Fredericton: Goose Lane Editions and the New Brunswick Military History Project, 2005.

Canny, Nicholas. "The Origins of Empire." In Louis, *Oxford History of the British Empire,* vol. 2.

Chandler, David. *The Art of Warfare in the Age of Marlborough.* Staplehurst, England: Spellmount, 1990.

Clark, Andrew Hill. *Acadia: The Geography of Early Nova Scotia to 1760.* Madison: University of Wisconsin Press, 1968.

Conrad, Margaret, ed. *Intimate Relations: Family and Community in Planter Nova Scotia, 1759–1800.* Fredericton, N.B.: Acadiensis Press, 1995.

——, ed. *Making Adjustments: Change and Continuity in Planter Nova Scotia, 1759–1800.* Fredericton, N.B.: Acadiensis Press, 1991.

——, ed. *They Planted Well: New England Planters in Maritime Canada.* Fredericton, N.B.: Acadiensis Press, 1988.

Conrad, Margaret, and Barry Moody, ed. *Planter Links: Community and Culture in Colonial Nova Scotia.* Fredericton, N.B.: Acadiensis Press, 2001.

Countryman, Edward. "Indians, the Colonial Order, and the Social Significance of the American Revolution." *William and Mary Quarterly* 53 (1996): 342–62.

Curtin, Philip. *The Rise and Fall of the Plantation Complex: Essays in Atlantic History.* New York: Cambridge University Press, 1992.

Daigle, Jean, ed. *The Acadians of the Maritimes: Thematic Studies.* Moncton, N.B.: Centre d'Études Acadiennes, 1982.

——. "Nos amis les ennemis: Relations commerciales de l'Acadie avec le Massachusetts, 1670–1711." Ph.D. diss., University of Maine, 1975.

D'Arles, Henri. *La déportation des Acadiens.* Ed. Abbé Lionel Groulx. Soirées de l'action française. Montreal: Editions Albert Lévesque, 1932.

Daugherty, William. *Maritime Indian Treaties in Perspective.* Ottawa: Indian and Northern Affairs Canada, 1983.

Davis, Stephen A. *The Peoples of the Maritimes: Mi'kmaq.* Halifax: Nimbus, 1997.

Demos, John. *The Unredeemed Captive: A Family Story from Early America.* New York: Vintage Books, 1995.

DePlanne, Veronique, and Peter Vance, ed. *Colonial Fortifications in North America, 1541–1763.* Baltimore, Md.: Johns Hopkins University Press, forthcoming.

Desbrisay, Mather B. *History of the Country of Lunenburg.* Halifax: James Bowes and Sons, 1870.

Dickason, Olive P. "Amerindians between French and English in Nova Scotia, 1713–1763." *American Indian Culture and Research Journal* 10 (1986): 31–56.

——. "La 'Guerre navale': Des Micmacs contre les Britanniques, 1713–1760." In *Les Micmacs et la mer,* ed. Charles Martijin. Montreal: McGill-Queen's University Press, 1986.

——. "Louisbourg and the Indians: A Study in Imperial Relations, 1713–1760." *History and Archaeology* 6 (1976): 3–206.

Eaton, Arthur W. H. *The History of Kings County, Nova Scotia: Heart of the Acadian Land.* Salem, Mass.: Salem Press Company, 1910.

——. *Lt.-Col. Otho Hamilton of Oliveston.* Halifax: C. H. Ruggles and Co., 1899.

Eccles, William J. "Fur Trade and Imperialism." In Eccles, *Essays on New France.* Toronto: Oxford University Press, 1987.

——. "The Social, Economic, and Political Significance of the Military Establishment in New France." *Canadian Historical Review* 52 (1971): 1–21.

Edwards, Joseph Plimsoll. "The Militia of Nova Scotia, 1749–1867." [Nova Scotia Historical Society] *Collections* 17 (1913).

Ellis, John. *A Short History of Guerrilla Warfare.* New York: St. Martin's Press, 1976.

Faragher, John Mack. *A Great and Noble Scheme: The Tragic Story of the Expulsion of the French Acadians from Their American Homeland.* New York: W. W. Norton, 2005.

Fergusson, Charles Bruce. "The Boundaries of Nova Scotia and Its Counties." *Bulletin of the Public Archives of Nova Scotia* 22 (1966).

——. "Early Liverpool and Its Diarist." *Bulletin of the Public Archives of Nova Scotia* 16 (1961).

Finn, Gérard. "Jean-Louis LeLoutre vu par les historiens." Société Historique Acadienne (Moncton, N.B.). *Cahiers* 8 (1977): 108–47.

Foote, Alfred William. "The American Independent Companies of the British Army, 1664–1774." Ph.D. diss., University of California–Los Angeles, 1966.

Frégualt, Guy. "L'Empire britannique et la conquête du Canada (1700–1713)." Pp. 58–85 in Frégualt, *Le XVIIIè Siècle Canadien: Études.* Montreal: HMH, 1968.

——. *La guerre de la conquête.* Montreal: Fides, 1955.

Ghislain, Michaud. *Les gardiens des portages: L'Histoire des Malécites du Québec.* St.-Foy, Province of Quebec: Les Editions GID, 2003.

Godfrey, William G. *Pursuit of Profit and Preferment in Colonial North America: John Bradstreet's Quest.* Montreal: Wilfrid Laurier University Press, 1976.

Gould, Eliga H. *The Persistence of Empire: British Political Culture in the Age of the American Revolution.* Chapel Hill: University of North Carolina Press for the Institute of Early American History and Culture, 2000.

Greene, Jack P. "Transatlantic Colonization and the Redefinition of Empire in the Early Modern Era." In *Negotiated Empires: Centers and Peripheries in the Americas, 1500–1820,* ed. Christine Daniels and Michael V. Kennedy. New York: Routledge, 2002.

Grenier, John. *The First Way of War: American War Making on the Frontier, 1607–1814.* New York: Cambridge University Press, 2005.

Griffiths, Naomi E. S. *The Acadians: The Creation of a People.* Toronto: University of Toronto Press, 1973.

——. *The Contexts of Acadian History, 1686–1784.* Montreal: McGill-Queen's University Press, 1992.

——. *From Migrant to Acadian: A North American Border People, 1604–1755.* Montreal and Kingston: McGill-Queen's University Press, 2005.

——. "The Golden Age: Acadian Life, 1713–1748." *Histoire sociale/Social History* 17 (1984): 21–34.

Gwyn, Julian. *Frigates and Foremasts: The North American Squadron in Nova Scotia Waters, 1745–1815.* Vancouver: University of British Columbia Press, 2003.

Haefeli, Evan, and Kevin Sweeney. *Captors and Captives: The 1704 French and Indian Raid on Deerfield.* Amherst: University of Massachusetts Press, 2003.

Haffenden, P. S. *New England in the English Nation, 1689–1713.* Oxford, England: Clarendon Press, 1974.

Haliburton, Thomas Chandler. *History of Nova Scotia.* Halifax: Joseph Howe, 1829.

Herbin, John Frederick. *History of Grand Pré.* 4th ed. Saint John, N.B.: Barnes and Co., c. 1914.

Hinderaker, Eric, and Peter Mancall. *At the Edge of Empire: The Backcountry in British North America.* Baltimore, Md.: Johns Hopkins University Press, 2003.

Hofstra, Warren R. "'The Extension of His Majesties Dominions': The Virginia Backcountry and the Reconfiguration of Imperial Frontiers." *Journal of American History* 84 (1998): 1281–1312.

Hutton, Elizabeth. "Indian Affairs in Nova Scotia, 1760–1834." [Nova Scotia Historical Society] *Collections* 34 (1963): 33–54.

Jaffee, David. *People of the Wachusett: Greater New England in History and Memory, 1630–1860.* Ithaca, N.Y: Cornell University Press, 1999.

Kamen, Henry. *Empire: How Spain Became a World Power, 1492–1763.* New York: HarperCollins, 2003.

Leach, Douglas Edward. *Arms for Empire: A Military History of the British Colonies in North America, 1607–1703.* New York: Macmillan, 1973.

Leavitt, Robert M. *Maliseet and Micmac: First Nations of the Maritimes.* Fredericton, N.B.: New Ireland Press, 1995.

Lenman, Bruce. "Colonial Wars and Imperial Instability." In Louis, *Oxford History of the British Empire,* vol. 2.

Louis, William Roger, ed. *The Oxford History of the British Empire.* 5 vols. London: Oxford University Press, 1998–99.

Lowe, Richard G. "Massachusetts and the Acadians." *William and Mary Quarterly* 25 (1968): 212–29.

Lynn, John A. *The Wars of Louis XIV, 1664–1714.* Harlow, England: Longman, 1999.

MacDonald, James S. "Memoir Lieut.-Governor Michael Francklin, 1752–1782." [Nova Scotia Historical Society] *Collections* 16 (1912).

MacDonald, M. A. *Fortune and La Tour: The Civil War in Acadia.* Toronto: Methuen, 1983.

MacFarlane, R. O. "British Indian Policy in Nova Scotia to 1760." *Canadian Historical Review* 19 (1938): 154–67.

Main, Gloria. "Gender, Work, and Wages in Colonial New England." *William and Mary Quarterly* 51 (1994): 39–66.

Mancke, Elizabeth. "Empire and State." In *The British Atlantic World, 1500–1800,* ed. David Armitage and Michael J. Braddick. New York: Palgrave, 2002.

——. *The Fault Lines of Empire: Political Differentiation in Massachusetts and Nova Scotia, c. 1760–1830.* New York: Routledge, 2004.

——. "Negotiating and Empire." In *Negotiated Empires: Centers and Periph-*

eries in the Americas, 1500–1820, ed. Christine Daniels and Michael V. Kennedy. New York: Routledge, 2002.

——, and John G. Reid. "Elites, States, and the Imperial Contest for Acadia." In Reid, *"Conquest" of Acadia.*

Marble, Allan Everett. *Surgeons, Smallpox and the Poor: A History of Medicine and Social Conditions in Nova Scotia, 1749–1799.* Montréal & Kingston: McGill-Queen's University Press, 1993.

Marshall, P. J. "Introduction." In Louis, *Oxford History of the British Empire,* vol. 2.

——. *The Making and Unmaking of Empires: British, India, and America, c. 1750–1783.* New York: Oxford University Press, 2005.

Mather, Cotton. *Decennium Luctuosum.* Ed. Charles H. Lincoln. Narratives of the Indian Wars. New York: Charles Scribner's Sons, 1913.

McCusker, John J., and Russell R. Menard. *The Economy of British America, 1607–1789.* Chapel Hill: University of North Carolina Press for the Institute of Early American History and Culture, 1991.

McNeill, John Robert. *Atlantic Empires of France and Spain: Louisbourg and Havana, 1700–1763.* Chapel Hill: University of North Carolina Press, 1985.

Milner, W. C. "Records of Chignecto." [Nova Scotia Historical Society] *Collections* 15 (1911).

Miquelon, Dale. *New France, 1701–1744: "A Supplement to Europe."* Toronto: McClelland and Stewart, 1987.

Moody, Barry. "'A Just and Disinterested Man': The Nova Scotia Career of Paul Mascarene, 1710–1752." Ph.D. diss., Queen's University, 1976.

Moore, Christopher. *Louisbourg Portraits: Five Dramatic, True Tales of People Who Lived in an Eighteenth-Century Garrison Town.* Toronto: Macmillan of Canada, 1982.

Morgan, Kenneth O., ed. *The Oxford History of Britain.* Oxford: Oxford University Press, 1988.

Morrison, Kenneth. *The Embattled Northeast: The Elusive Ideal of Alliance in Abenaki-Euro-American Relations.* Berkeley: University of California Press, 1984.

Murdoch, Beamish. *History of Nova Scotia.* Halifax: James Barnes, 1865.

Nicholson, Colin. *The "Infamous Govener": Francis Bernard and the Origins of the American Revolution.* Boston: Northeastern University Press, 2001.

O'Shaughnessy, Andrew Jackson. *An Empire Divided: The American Revolution and the British Caribbean.* Philadelphia: University of Pennsylvania Press, 2000.

Paratte, Henri-Dominique. *The Acadians.* Halifax: Nimbus, 1991.

Patterson, Steven. "Colonial Wars and Aboriginal Peoples." In *The Atlantic Region to Confederation: A History,* ed. Phillip A. Buckner and John G. Reid. Toronto: University of Toronto Press, 1994.

——. "Indian-White Relations in Nova Scotia, 1749–61: A Study in Political Interaction." *Acadiensis* 23 (1993): 23–59.

——. "In Search of the Massachusetts–Nova Scotia Dynamic." *Acadiensis* 5 (1976): 138–42.

Penhallow, Samuel. *History of the Indian Wars.* 1726. Reprint, Williamstown, Mass.: Corner House Publishers, 1973.

Piers, Harry. "The Old Peninsular Blockhouses and Road to Halifax, 1751: Their History, Description and Location." [Nova Scotia Historical Society] *Collections* 22 (1933).

Plank, Geoffrey. "New England and the Conquest." In Reid, *"Conquest" of Acadia.*

——. "The Two Majors Cope: The Boundaries of Nationality in Mid-18th Century Nova Scotia." *Acadiensis* 25 (1996): 18–40.

——. *An Unsettled Conquest: The British Campaign against the Peoples of Acadia.* Philadelphia: University of Pennsylvania Press, 2001.

Pothier, Bernard. "Acadian Emigration to Île Royale after the Conquest of Acadia." *Histoire sociale/Social History* 3 (1970): 116–31.

Pritchard, James. *Anatomy of a Naval Disaster: The 1746 French Expedition to North America.* Montreal: McGill-Queen's University Press, 1995.

Rawlyk, George. *Nova Scotia's Massachusetts: A Study of Massachusetts–Nova Scotia Relations, 1630–1784.* Montreal: McGill-Queen's University Press, 1973.

Reid, John G., ed. *The "Conquest" of Acadia, 1710: Imperial, Colonial, and Aboriginal Constructions.* Toronto: University of Toronto Press, 2004.

——. "The 'Conquest' of Acadia: Narratives." In Reid, *"Conquest" of Acadia.*

——. "The Conquest of 'Nova Scotia': Cartographic Imperialism and the Echoes of a Scottish Past." In *Nation and Province in the First British Empire: Scotland and the Americas, 1600–1800,* ed. Ned C. Landsmen. Lewisburg, Penn.: Bucknell University Press, 2001.

——. "Imperialism, Diplomacies, and the Conquest of Acadia." In Reid, *"Conquest" of Acadia.*

——. "*Pax Britannica* or *Pax Indigena*? Planter Nova Scotia (1760–1782) and Competing Strategies of Pacification." *Canadian Historical Review* 85 (2004): 669–92.

——. *Six Crucial Decades: Times of Change in the History of the Maritimes.* Halifax: Nimbus Publishing, 1987.

Robison, Mark Power. "Maritime Frontiers: The Evolution of Empire in Nova Scotia, 1713–1758." Ph.D. diss., University of Colorado–Boulder, 2000.

Sauvageau, Robert. *Acadie: La guerre de cent ans de Français d'Amérique aux Maritimes et en Louisiane, 1670–1769.* Paris: Berger-Levrault, 1987.

Shy, John. "The American Colonies in War and Revolution." In Louis, *Oxford History of the British Empire,* vol. 2.

Smith, Adam. *An Inquiry into the Nature and Causes of the Wealth of Nations.* Ed. R. H. Campbell, A. S. Skinner, and W. B. Todd. Oxford, England: Clarendon Press, 1976.

Steele, Ian. "The Anointed, the Appointed, and the Elected." In Louis, *Oxford History of the British Empire,* vol. 2.

——. *Betrayals: Fort William Henry and the "Massacre."* New York: Oxford University Press, 1990.

——. *Warpaths: Invasions of North America.* New York: Oxford University Press, 1994.

Szechi, Daniel. *1715: The Great Jacobite Rebellion.* New Haven, Conn.: Yale University Press, 2006.

Trask, William Blake, ed. "Battle of Minas." *New England Historical and Genealogical Register* 9 (1855): 105–12.

Upton, Leslie F. S. "Indian Affairs in Colonial New Brunswick." *Acadiensis* 3 (1974): 3–26.

——. "Indians and Islanders: The Micmacs of Colonial Prince Edward Island." *Acadiensis* 6 (1976): 21–43.

——. *Micmacs and Colonists: Indian-White Relations in the Maritimes, 1713–1867.* Vancouver: University of British Columbia Press, 1979.

Vickers, Daniel. "Competency and Competition: Economic Culture in Early America." *William and Mary Quarterly* 47 (1990): 3–29.

——. *Farmers and Fishermen: Two Centuries of Work in Essex County, Massachusetts, 1630–1830.* Chapel Hill: University of North Carolina Press for the Institute of Early American History and Culture, 1994.

Voltaire, Francois Marie Arouet de. "Revocation of the Edict of Nantes." In *The World's Greatest Events: An Indexed History of the World from Earliest Times to the Present Day by Great Historians,* vol. 5. Ed. Esther Singleton. New York: P. F. Collier and Son, 1916.

Waller, G. M. *Samuel Vetch: Colonial Enterpriser.* Chapel Hill: University of North Carolina Press, 1960.

Webb, Stephen Saunders. *The Governors-General: The English Army and the Definition of the Empire, 1569–1681.* Chapel Hill: University of North Carolina Press for the Institute of Early American History and Culture, 1979.

Webster, John C. *Charles des Champs de Boishébert: A Canadian Soldier in Acadia.* Shediac, N.B.: privately printed, 1931.

——, ed. *Thomas Pichon, "The Spy of Beauséjour": An Account of His Career in Europe and America, with Many Original Documents Translated by Alice Webster.* Halifax: Public Archives of Nova Scotia, 1937.

White, Richard. *The Middle Ground: Indians, Empires, and Republics in the Great Lakes Region, 1650–1850.* New York: Cambridge University Press, 1991.

Wicken, William C. "Encounters with Tall Sails and Tall Tales: Mi'kmaq Society, 1500–1760." Ph.D. diss., McGill University, 1994.

——. "Mi'kmaq Decisions." In Reid, *"Conquest" of Acadia.*

Wood, Gordon. *The Creation of the American Republic, 1776–1783.* New York: W. W. Norton, 1969.

Index

References to illustrations appear in italic type.